BRIEF LIVES

BRIEF LIVES

with some Memoirs
by

ALAN WATKINS

with Illustrations
by
MARC

HAMISH HAMILTON

LONDON

First published in Great Britain 1982
by Hamish Hamilton Ltd
Garden House 57–59 Long Acre London WC2E 9JZ

Copyright © 1982 by Alan Watkins

British Library Cataloguing in Publication Data
Watkins, Alan
   Brief lives.
   1. Great Britain – Biography
   I. Title
   920'.041   CT774
   ISBN 0–241–10890–X

Filmset by Northumberland Press Ltd, Gateshead
Printed and bound in Great Britain by
Richard Clay (The Chaucer Press) Ltd, Bungay, Suffolk

To
David, Frances, Jane and Rachel

CONTENTS

Introduction   xi

KINGSLEY AMIS   1
LORD BEAVERBROOK   9
LORD BRADWELL   20
ANTHONY CROSLAND   29
RICHARD CROSSMAN   35
MICHAEL FOOT   44
SIR IAN GILMOUR   50
DENIS HEALEY   55
PHILIP HOPE-WALLACE   60
RICHARD INGRAMS   67
ROY JENKINS   72
PAUL JOHNSON   79
SIR JOHN JUNOR   85
SIR OSBERT LANCASTER   91
IAIN MACLEOD   97
HUGH MASSINGHAM   112
G. E. MOORE   124
MALCOLM MUGGERIDGE   128
ANTHONY POWELL   140
SIMON RAVEN   147
MAURICE RICHARDSON   153
WILLIAM ROBSON   157
NORMAN ST JOHN-STEVAS   162
DAVID STEEL   168
A. J. P. TAYLOR   175
D. J. WATKINS   183

AUBERON WAUGH	191
PEREGRINE WORSTHORNE	200
A Note on Sources	207
Index	215

ACKNOWLEDGMENTS

I am grateful to Mr Mark Boxer, for doing the drawings; Mr Jeffrey Care, Librarian of the *Observer*, for checking various names and dates; Mr Matthew Coady, for establishing Maurice Richardson's date of birth; Miss Monica Craig, for establishing from *Observer* records Hugh Massingham's dates of birth and death; Mr Giles Gordon, of Anthony Sheil Associates, for encouraging me and making numerous suggestions; Professor J. A. G. Griffith, Mr Simon Hoggart, Mr Terence Kilmartin, Mr David Leigh, Mr David Lipsey and Lord McGregor, for reading and commenting on various Lives; Mr Paul Johnson, for letting me see his copy of Kingsley Martin's memorandum to the board of The Statesman and Nation Publishing Company on the unsuitability of Richard Crossman to edit the *New Statesman*; Mr Bruce Page, for giving permission to reprint some material which first appeared in the *New Statesman*, pointing out that, after he became editor of the paper, copyright in articles reverted to their authors; and Mr Christopher Sinclair-Stevenson, of Hamish Hamilton, for suggesting the book in the first place.

My principal debts are, however, to Mr Anthony Howard, who read the ms. and saved me from several errors, and Mrs Allan Rieck, who typed the ms. impeccably, filed correspondence and other material, and pressed me to make progress. Without Mrs Rieck's help the book would have been more difficult to complete.

I am solely responsible for any mistakes.

ALAN WATKINS

12 Battishill Street
London N1

April 1982

INTRODUCTION

THIS BOOK is neither an imitation nor a pastiche of John Aubrey's *Brief Lives*, though I have been influenced, as others have, by some of Aubrey's devices, such as introducing anecdotes, or writing: 'It was his habit ...', 'He would often say ...' and so forth. I have been more influenced, I think, by Johnson's *Lives of the Poets*, which I mention with humility. In any case, there is a long tradition of writing brief lives of contemporary figures, or 'characters' or memoirs – or combinations of these in one piece. The tradition extends from the works of Clarendon and Walton through Churchill's *Great Contemporaries*, and A. G. Gardiner's assessments of the public figures of the early twentieth century, to the newspaper and magazine profiles of our day. What follows is, I hope, a contribution to this genre.

It started off as a kind of *Figures of our Time*. As I came to write it, however, I found that the subjects selected themselves according to three criteria: I should know or have known them personally, I should feel a certain affection for them, and they should have had some influence on my life. When these principles of selection became apparent to me, I applied them consciously. Naturally the degrees of knowledge, affection and influence vary.

For my first eighteen years, until 1951, I lived continuously with D. J. Watkins; when I was at Cambridge I lived with him and my mother in the vacations; afterwards I visited him regularly until his death.

The late 1940s provided several influences. I read Anthony Powell's novels of the 1930s, or most of them, and became an early addict of his. I read A. J. P. Taylor's reviews, which persuaded me that history could be interesting and that essay-writing need not be a futile exercise. I read Hugh Massingham's political column in the *Observer*, though I did not know his name then – he wrote as 'Our Political Correspondent' – and he planted an ambition in me. And I read Sir Osbert Lancaster's *Drayneflete*

xii   *Introduction*

Revealed, which first opened my eyes to architecture. I did not meet any of these till the mid-1960s.

In the first half of the 1950s Anthony Crosland was my principal guide to domestic politics, and Richard Crossman to foreign. I was thus a Labour revisionist at home, a Bevanite abroad – a position I have roughly maintained, with fluctuating degrees of discomfort, ever since. Crosland had not then published his big book but was at work on it. He was a frequent visitor to Cambridge, where he would explain his views, and talk informally afterwards. Crossman did the same. I therefore knew both of them quite early, but did not come to know them well until after 1964; in 1970–2 Crossman was my editor at the *New Statesman*. Michael Foot and Iain Macleod I also met at Cambridge, though, like Crossman and Crosland, they did not re-enter my life until the mid-1960s, Foot as a Labour politician, Macleod as my editor at the *Spectator*. Denis Healey and Roy Jenkins are in the same category as Crossman and Crosland, even though they did not have the same influence on me, then or later.

Several of my friends were at University College, Swansea, where there was, it appeared, a new English lecturer called Kingsley Amis who gave parties and was writing the novel that turned out to be *Lucky Jim*; Amis, likewise, I met later. Sir (then Mr) Ian Gilmour was transforming the *Spectator*. Malcolm Muggeridge, another Cambridge visitor, was emerging as a public figure, saying things of which we approved on Churchill and the Monarchy and of which we disapproved on the cold war; I came to know him in the 1970s. Norman St John-Stevas, recently at Cambridge, then at Oxford, appeared as a young man who might 'do anything' in life.

From 1955 to 1957 I did my national service as an education officer at Duxford, a fighter station some ten miles from Cambridge. My wife and I lived in a converted stable at the bottom of G. E. Moore's garden off the Chesterton Road in Cambridge. On leaving the RAF I became William Robson's research assistant at the London School of Economics.

But I determined to become a journalist. I had met a Beaverbrook editor (not Sir John Junor) at Cambridge. He had invited me to approach him if I wanted a job. However, he would want to see what I had written. As I had then, in 1959, written hardly anything, I cast round for a suitable vehicle for my talents, and lighted upon *Socialist Commentary*. I then tried to think of a subject, and decided on Contempt of Parliament in relation to the case of the editor of the *Sunday Express* (then Mr Junor) and the Committee of Privileges. This case was about the *Express*'s comments on

MPs' petrol allowances in the aftermath of Suez. My intention was to show this piece not to Junor but to the Beaverbrook editor I had originally met. Junor saw it first and offered me a job as a feature writer at £20 a week on the strength of it; mainly, no doubt, because he appeared as Mr Integrity, the Fighting Editor. Beaverbrook I met only briefly, as my memoir explains.

In 1964 I wrote to both Ian Gilmour and Iain Macleod about the possibility of becoming political correspondent of the *Spectator*, and got the job, which I did till 1967, when Paul Johnson (whom I had known slightly before then) asked me to become political correspondent of the *New Statesman*. I first met Auberon Waugh when he succeeded me on the *Spectator* and I dispensed sage or, at any rate, well-intentioned advice to him. Richard Ingrams started to invite me to *Private Eye* lunches at around this time. Lord Bradwell (Tom Driberg) seemed always to be in attendance. I had already met David Steel at his by-election in 1965, and continued to see him at Westminster. Simon Raven I met through common friends, though I had already started to read his novels. Philip Hope-Wallace, Maurice Richardson and Peregrine Worsthorne were Fleet Street friends whom I first met in the 1960s. Most of my subjects are politicians, journalists or those who walk the tightrope between politics and journalism.

There is also, I think, a unity of place. My entire working life has been spent in the quadrilateral enclosed by the Euston Road to the North, the Thames to the South, Goswell Road to the East, and Whitehall and the Charing Cross Road to the West. It comprehends Lincoln's Inn, the London School of Economics, the *Sunday Express*, the *Spectator* (both its past and its present offices), the *New Statesman*, the *Observer*, the House of Commons, El Vino's public house (as Beaverbrook used to call it) and the Garrick Club. This may be limiting but there it is and there we are and it cannot be helped.

The pieces that follow are fresh, or at least new, with four exceptions. The memoirs of Beaverbrook, Macleod and Moore, and the essay on Massingham, first appeared substantially in their present form in the *New Statesman*. The memoir of Macleod and the essay on Massingham were originally intended to be part of a similar book to this. There are details in the Note on Sources at the back.

KINGSLEY AMIS

16 April 1922 –

KINGSLEY AMIS was the outstanding English novelist of those who began their writing careers after 1945. He was born and brought up in Clapham, in a standard semi-detached house of the inter-war period – basically two up and two down, with a kitchen and a bathroom. His father, William Robert Amis, was a senior clerk in a mustard firm in the City. W. R. Amis's family came from Norwich, where they had a glass-selling business. He played cricket, tennis and the piano. Kingsley's mother, Rosa Amis, was also musical, having a good singing voice, but resented that her sister had been musically trained, whereas she had not.

This sister went mad. Amis remembered perceiving her then undiagnosed insanity when he was a small boy, and she would take already extinguished matches out of the living room and into the kitchen. But she recovered her reason on the death of her husband. She was asked to stay on in the lunatic asylum to which she had been committed, on account of her competence and helpfulness. She ended her days in charge of the kitchens of a London teaching hospital. This piece of family history was sometimes retailed by Amis.

His parents both came from Denmark Hill, where they had met in the Baptist chapel. His own upbringing, however, was more moral – or moralistic – than religious. Masturbation was a particular cause of conflict; and Amis showed early strength of character in refusing to believe the exaggerated accounts given by his parents of the deleterious consequences of the practice. The wireless set, important in a small house in the 1930s, was another cause of conflict. Amis early developed a taste for classical music, while his father vainly tried to interest him in Gilbert and Sullivan. His father said with some justice that his reflections on Amis senior's musical taste would be more convincing if he could play a musical instrument himself. The house contained some books, though not many, chiefly encyclopaedias and novels from circulating libraries. One of his parents' recreations was singing round the piano with friends and relations.

He was an only child. He was educated first at a local fee-paying school and then, also as a day boy, at the City of London School, which his father and uncles had also attended. His father was determined that he should go there. He failed the scholarship examination to the school when he was eleven but was accepted nonetheless as a fee-payer: he won a scholarship a year later when he was already at the school. He admired the tolerance of the City of London, compared to other boys' schools of the time, and was grateful for the education he received there.

He distinguished himself not only in English and Classics but also in Mathematics. In later life he would sometimes regret – perhaps only half-meaning it – that he had not been a scientist or a mathematician. Certainly such mathematical knowledge as he possessed served him well in the Army, in the Royal Corps of Signals; significantly, he was in the 1950s one of the few men of letters who did not heap scorn on the Oxford school of linguistic philosophy because it was 'trivial' or 'did not deal with the real issues'. He enjoyed posing as a philistine because he caused annoyance thereby, but no one could have been more of an intellectual, though his genius was not for the analysis of political concepts.

While he was in the sixth form the school was evacuated to Marlborough College in Wiltshire, where he spent five terms. He was surprised, both then and later, by the inhospitable and aloof attitude of the college's masters and boys; but he was allowed to join the chapel choir, and found that singing in it was – and was to be – one of the most satisfying experiences of his life. He tried for a scholarship at St Catharine's College, Cambridge, but was unsuccessful. He then tried for one available at Christ Church or St John's College, Oxford. The choice of college was narrow because Amis was determined to win a scholarship in English: if he had made Classics his subject, as he could have done, the choice of college would have been wider, and the likelihood of winning a scholarship greater. He put down Christ Church as his first choice but was awarded an exhibition at St John's instead. He went up to Oxford in April 1941 but spent only four terms there before joining the Army. In this earlier period at St John's he first met Philip Larkin, who became a life-long friend.

He joined the Corps of Signals partly because he thought he would like the work – as he did, up to a point – and partly because he did not want to get killed. In this too he was successful, though he had a by no means restful or comfortable war. He was in France after the allied invasion and spent weeks at a time sleeping in a tent. He ended up as a Captain.

He was lucky to be demobilised quickly, and returned to Oxford. He won a first and then embarked on a B.Litt. degree. He was appointed a lecturer in English at University College, Swansea, on the reasonable assumption by the college authorities that he would be duly awarded this degree. In fact he failed, which, Amis later said, was virtually unheard of. He would recall with amusement that he was a B.Litt. (Failed). By this time, however, things had gone too far at Swansea, and the offer stood. Amis, in later years, would become irritated when people asked him: 'What made you choose Swansea?' He would reply: 'Swansea chose me. It was a job, that's all.'

In 1948, while still at St John's, he had married Hilary (Hilly) Bardwell, a fair-haired, beautiful girl who was at the Oxford art school. They quickly had three children, Martin, Philip and Sally. Amis was specially close to his sons – he used to kiss Martin on meeting him, when he was in his fifties, and Martin in his thirties. Both his sons were a source of comfort and strength to him when his second marriage, to the novelist Elizabeth Jane Howard (whom he married in 1965 following an affair begun at the Cheltenham Literary Festival), ended in 1981.

Amis was happy at Swansea. Looking back, he thought it was the best period of his life. He liked to drink with his students, who included John and Mary Morgan, and Geoffrey and Mavis Nicholson (all subsequently journalists of one kind or another). They remained his friends in London from the mid-1960s onwards. It was at Swansea that Amis wrote *Lucky Jim*, *That Uncertain Feeling*, *I Like it Here* and, his favourite novel, *Take a Girl Like You*. The last was his favourite because, though published in 1960, it had been written in the late 1950s, and anticipated with some prescience, so Amis subsequently thought, the dilemma of the 1960s about whether nice girls should sleep with men. (Though there were some reviewers who considered that he was writing about a non-existent dilemma, or one that had been resolved in favour of sexual intercourse, Amis's novel was almost certainly a more accurate reflection of the preoccupations of the time.)

Lucky Jim, which was published in 1954, was a seminal work in that it said: 'No, life isn't like that. It's like this.' The hero of the pre-1939 novels by Anthony Powell and Evelyn Waugh – and of Cyril Connolly's one venture, *The Rock Pool* – was a former public schoolboy who had recently come down from Oxford. His work was unsatisfactory to him but there was money in the background. He was either a homosexual or an incompetent and unlucky heterosexual. He had picaresque adventures either with members of the upper classes or with inhabitants of higher Bohemia. These adventures occurred usually in London, though sometimes in the country or abroad. Amis altered the conventions of this kind of novel with permanent effect. Though there had been heroes like Jim Dixon before (in the novels of C. P. Snow, for instance), they had been treated differently, with apparent sympathy and seriousness but, in reality, with patronage. Amis changed this way of looking at things (exemplified by *Jude the Obscure*) for ever. He struck a mighty blow for democracy in the English novel.

It was at this time that Amis was included as one of the leading 'angry young men' – among the others were John Osborne, John Wain, Colin Wilson and, through his autobiography *Time and Place*, George Scott. (The phrase was originally the title of Leslie Paul's autobiography, *Angry Young Man*. Paul was an amateur churchman, was little-known and received hardly any credit for the invention of the phrase.) In fact neither Amis nor Jim Dixon was specially angry about anything. Indeed, Amis became much angrier as he grew older. The angry young men were linked in the weekly journals to 'the Movement', that group of Oxford poets whose leading members were Amis, Larkin, Wain and Elizabeth Jennings. One weekly in particular, the *Spectator*, was instrumental. The then literary editor, J. D. Scott, claimed subsequently in a memoir that (aided by Iain Hamilton) he had virtually invented the whole Movement in an article deliberately designed to arouse controversy and interest. However, there is no doubt that the poetic side of the Movement was deliberately reacting against the rhetoric of the 1940s. There is equally no doubt that Amis and Wain were writing different novels from those which had been published before 1939. 'Angry young men' was a foolish phrase but it nevertheless had some meaning.

By 1961 Amis had decided that he could keep himself and his family by writing alone and that he did not have to go on teaching. When he left Swansea in 1961, however, he went not to London but to Peterhouse, Cambridge, as a Fellow and teacher of English. He went to Peterhouse partly because one of his friends, George Gale, had been an undergraduate there, and there was a kind of Peterhouse network or connection in which Amis was involved. But his time at Cambridge was not entirely happy.

What really drove me out was paradoxically what made me most reluctant to leave: teaching. Nobody who has not experienced it can fully imagine the peculiar drain which this activity makes on one's energy, nor its unique rewards. Ten or twelve hours a week, old boy? the businessman or journalist (or educationist) asks incredulously: you don't call that a job of work do you? I do. Leaving out preparation – and I had plenty of that, it never having occurred to me before that the works of Racine or Strindberg were necessary parts of an English course – I found myself fit for nothing much more exacting than playing the gramophone after three supervisions a day.*

Then there was the high table company:

The moment when I finally decided it was not for me came when I was dining out at – never mind. Throughout the first course and most of the second, the talk at my end had turned exclusively upon the paintings, drawings, engravings and whatnot my neighbour had been buying. Noticing, presumably, that I had nothing whatever to contribute to this discussion, another guest asked me: 'And what is *your* particular, er, line of, er, country in this, er?' With truly operatic humility of tone and gesture, I said: 'I'm afraid I don't sort of go in for any of that kind of thing.' The other man said: 'H'm' – not a vocable in actual common use, but he used it. Then he said: 'I think that's a dreadful thing to say.' I went on keeping quiet for some time after that, wishing, for perhaps the hundredth time since arriving at Cambridge, that I were Jim Dixon.'†

From 1965 he lived with his second wife Jane first in Hertfordshire and then in a large, detached Georgian house in Flask Walk, Hampstead. When he and Jane separated he lived with his first wife Hilly and her new husband, Lord Kilmarnock, in Kentish Town. For one of Amis's peculiarities was that he could not bear to be alone, especially at night. He required someone to share not so much his bed as his abode. He was also incapable – or claimed he was incapable – of doing anything for himself of a practical nature. He further had an aversion, not uncommon, to travelling by underground.

He was of medium height, with a tendency to put on weight. But he had never eaten much – he remembered his mother trying to force food

---

* Kingsley Amis, 'No More Parades' in *What Became of Jane Austen?* (1970), Penguin edn (1981), p. 176 at p. 184.
† Ibid., p. 186.

on him – and as he grew older he ate even less. Though he wrote an informative book *On Drink*, he was more a beer-and-spirits (mainly the latter) than a wine man. He disliked both the country and abroad. He was a disillusioned heterosexual but never a ladies' man: he liked pubs, clubs (especially the Garrick, of which he was a pillar) and masculine talk.

Having written a Fabian pamphlet in which he said he could not envisage voting anything but Labour, he moved to the right politically from the mid-1960s onwards. But his attack on Lord Robbins's expansionist plans for higher education, with the sentence which summarised his opposition, 'More will mean★ worse,' was written in 1960. The change in his political position came about largely through his distaste for the Soviet Union in both its internal and its external aspects. He was fortified in his attitude by his friendships with Robert Conquest and Tibor Szamuely. The three used to meet once a week (later, once a month) for lunch at Bertorelli's Restaurant in Charlotte Street.

Shortly after his second marriage Amis told the journalist Henry Fairlie, one of his friends, that Fairlie would not be so welcome at Amis's house as he had been in the past because his then new wife insisted on certain standards of decorum which Fairlie did not fulfil. Fairlie regarded this as a bit of a joke but was hurt nonetheless. Certainly Amis made some moves in the direction of a changed mode of life at around this time. For instance, he began to take snuff, though after some years he relinquished the habit, and smoked small cigars instead.

His eyes were slightly protuberant and were apt for simulating astonishment or rage. He was an excellent mimic who did not, however, press his impersonations on his friends. He dressed neatly but informally, in a jacket (often of corduroy), twill trousers, a checked shirt and a woven woollen tie. He liked to wear quite thick woollen socks. He rarely wore a suit. He was more a natural host than a natural guest, happiest at home with friends and a glass of whisky. His recreations were reading thrillers and listening to music, both classical music and modern jazz. His dislike of writers canonised by the Cambridge English School, such as Jane Austen, Henry James and D. H. Lawrence, and his elevation of other writers, such as Henry Newbolt, Rudyard Kipling and A. Conan Doyle, had about it an element of only doing it to annoy, but was nevertheless an honest expression of his literary judgment.

★ Not 'means'. See Kingsley Amis, 'Lone Voices' in *What Became of Jane Austen?*, p. 155 at p. 159.

He was frightened of loneliness but – though death makes several appearances in his novels and poems – denied that he was frightened of death: he was, he said, frightened of the process of dying, a different matter. He was a conscientious writer who, on a good day, would write – or, rather, type – 1,000 words of a novel. He was usually an amusing and sometimes a sad man. To which tribute he would have replied: 'Thanks very bloody much. Bloody marvellous.'

LORD BEAVERBROOK

25 May 1879 – 9 June 1964

WILLIAM MAXWELL AITKEN, the first Lord Beaverbrook (his son, Max, disclaimed the peerage but could not disclaim the baronetcy), was a financier. He was also successively an intriguing politician, a successful newspaper proprietor, an accomplished journalist, an energetic Minister and an original historian: but a financier is what he was to start with, and what he remained. He never lost his interest in money and markets, and he made his own money in Canada partly as a fixer or go-between working on a percentage basis, and partly as a cornerer of commodity markets.

He was the third son of the Reverend William Aitken, Minister at Newcastle, New Brunswick, and Jean Noble, of Vaughan, Canada. In 1906 he married Gladys Drury, the daughter of a Canadian Colonel who rose to General. They had one daughter and two sons, one of whom died. Gladys herself died in 1927. Thereafter Beaverbrook formed numerous liaisons, notably with Jean Norton. In 1963 he married Lady Dunn (born Marcia Anastasia Christoforides, and called Christa). She was the widow of his old friend, Sir James Dunn, and Beaverbrook and Lady Dunn had lived together for some years.

He went to school at the Board School, Newcastle. Having made his fortune in Canada, he came to England. From 1910 to 1916 he was Unionist MP for Ashton-under-Lyne. He founded the *Sunday Express* and acquired, and re-established, the *Daily Express* and the *Evening Standard*. From 1915 to 1917 he was a representative of the Canadian Government in France. He was knighted in 1911 and made a Baronet in 1916 and a Baron in 1917. In 1916 he helped to make David Lloyd George Prime Minister – the importance of his help is still disputed by historians – but considered himself inadequately rewarded by Lloyd George, though he was subsequently made Chancellor of the Duchy of Lancaster and Minister of Information. His fullest personal loyalty went to Andrew Bonar Law, who, as Prime Minister in 1922–3, did not reward him at all. In the Second World War he was successively Minister for Aircraft Production, Minister of State, Minister of Supply and Lord Privy Seal; and he remained on friendly terms with Churchill.

His chief characteristics were his love of mischief, his inability to organise his life (or, rather, his possessions) entirely to his satisfaction, his reluctance ever to make himself wholly clear to his subordinates, his energy and his fear of death – or, more precisely, of going to hell.

As to his love of mischief, A. J. P. Taylor denies in his *Beaverbrook* that, during the Conservative crisis over the succession to Harold Macmillan in 1963, Beaverbrook sang 'We'll sow the seeds of discord' to the tune of 'Polly put the kettle on'. The story was originally mine, and I was right, but I foolishly got the tune wrong. It was 'The more we are together', which, as a moment's humming will demonstrate, allows the words to scan:

> We'll sow the seeds of discord
> Of discord
> Of discord
> We'll sow the seeds of discord
> How happy we shall be.

Beaverbrook had so many houses that what he wanted was rarely to hand. Thus, if he wished to consult, say, the Authorised Version he found he had only the Revised Version; and some luckless minion would then be dispatched to acquire the volume that was needed in the back streets of New York, Nice or wherever it happened to be. His reluctance to make himself clear – his ability to cause endless confusion over the simplest aspects of the administration not so much of newspapers as of life itself – may have been deliberate. He may have thought that by constantly muddying the waters he was emphasising his own primacy and causing confusion in others, so keeping them keen and alert.

His fear of hell led Malcolm Muggeridge to think that Beaverbrook was only too conscious of his own wickedness, but this conclusion by no means followed, for, as a lapsed Calvinist, Beaverbrook may merely have feared that he had not been numbered among the elect. Of the people dealt with elsewhere in this book, Muggeridge and Anthony Crosland (for example) considered him evil, whereas A. J. P. Taylor and Michael Foot thought him, not exactly saintly, but a good and kind man. They said they loved him, and one cannot argue with love, any more than one can argue over whether something is or is not funny: but both views, Muggeridge-

Crosland and Taylor-Foot, still strike me as exaggerated and somewhat sentimental. He was not like this at all. I know because for five years, from 1959 until 1964, I worked for one of his papers, the *Sunday Express*: first as a general feature-writer, then as the New York correspondent, finally, for a year, as the author of the 'Cross-bencher' column. Unlike some journalists I did not go out of my way to seek his company. He certainly did not go out of his to seek mine. There was little reason why he should. Of my existence he was only vaguely and intermittently aware. Ian Aitken (who was not a relation but knew him better than I) tells me that he went under the impression that my name was Watkinson. Though, as will appear, we met several times, he never called me by this or indeed any other name. Our connection, at the beginning anyway, was indirect.

One day in February the editor, John Junor, called me into his office.

'Have you ever heard of Anthony Praga?' he asked.

I confessed I had not heard of him. The editor explained who he was. In the 1930s, so it appeared, Praga had written a series of articles for the *Express* in which the plots of well-known, unread, lengthy novels were summarised.

'Like short stories,' the editor said.

The series had been successful. Beaverbrook, at any rate, had been pleased with it. Some thirty years later he wanted to revive the idea. The editor read to me part of his dictated memorandum. He wished for a start to have summarised, in short story form, *East Lynne*, *Lorna Doone*, *The Scarlet Letter* and *Three Weeks* by Elinor Glyn. He was particularly keen on Elinor Glyn, maybe on account of her relationship with Lord Curzon or perhaps for some other reason. However, he foresaw trouble owing to her advanced views.

'Elinor Glyn,' he wrote, 'may present difficulties but we should be able to overcome them with tactful treatment.'

The assignment, I confess, did not greatly appeal to me. The prospect of reading *Lorna Doone* was particularly distasteful. This was a book I had been at pains to avoid. It had been on a school reading list and I had failed to progress beyond the first chapter. To read it now, in Fleet Street, at the request of Lord Beaverbrook, would be to suffer some kind of defeat in life.

'What about Bob Pitman?' I asked.

The late Robert Pitman was then the literary editor of the paper.

'Bob is much too busy with other things,' the editor said, which seemed a comprehensive enough reply. 'You are the only other person on the staff with enough literary ability to do this job.'

The flattering effect of this opinion was slightly spoiled by what came next.

'I may say,' the editor went on, 'that this series will appear in the *Sunday Express* over my dead body, but as the idea comes from Beaverbrook we have to go through the motions at first.'

It was one of the editor's several virtues that he was a by no means obedient follower of his proprietor's frequently incomprehensible instructions. One of Pitman's functions was to decode the strange, garbled messages which would issue from Cherkley, Montego Bay or the South of France.

'Bob has a genius for seeing what's in the old man's mind,' the editor would say.

When the intructions were deciphered he would sometimes procrastinate or deliberately misunderstand them. However, he was rarely as frank about his ultimate intentions as he was on this occasion. I cannot say I was wholly discouraged by the promise of non-publication. I had no wish to acquire a reputation, however slender, as a compressor of the works of Elinor Glyn.

'He wants the first piece to be on *East Lynne*,' the editor said. 'Just to see how it goes.'

I bought a Collins Classics edition of Mrs Henry Wood's work and, hour after hour, sat reading it at my desk. Occasionally the editor would pass by on his errands of encouragement or reproof to his staff.

'You're a slow reader, I see,' he would say, and laugh as if he had made a joke.

Eventually I produced a piece of about 1,500 words which was dispatched to Beaverbrook.

'He thought it was all right,' the editor said some days later. 'Now he wants you to have a go at Elinor Glyn.'

Happily I never did have a go at Elinor Glyn. I pretended to forget the task, the editor made no more references to the matter and Beaverbrook, as far as I am aware, showed no further interest. Elinor Glyn, like *Lorna Doone*, remains a gap in my reading.

Beaverbrook next impinged on my work when a Labour MP, J. P. W. Mallalieu, appeared to be in trouble with his constituency party over a divorce case in which he was involved. (Eventually, I believe, there was no trouble.) On this general issue, as on a few others – bishops, the royal family, the powers of the House of Lords, access to Ascot – Beaverbrook's views were broadly radical though he was not entirely consistent. This time, however, he did not require an 'opinion piece' or a polemic but an historical article about the effects of divorce or similar irregularities on the careers of politicians. Over the dictaphone came a list of suitable cases for inclusion. Inevitably that of Parnell appeared on it. He had been brought down, Beaverbrook stated, because at a meeting of the Irish MPs he had said: 'I am still the master of the party'; to which Tim Healy had interjected: 'Who is to be the mistress of the party?' Collapse of Parnell: or so I was given to understand.

Perhaps rashly, I decided to verify the story in Tim Healy's own published reminiscences. He was clear that the interruption had come not from him but from some other, unnamed Irishman. Nor was the remark in the form of a neat question: rather the phrase 'the mistress of the party' had been heard above the general noise of the meeting. I consulted various other political memoirs of the nineteenth century. They all told the same story. This was decidedly worrying. I faced the choice of either taking Beaverbrook's perhaps first-hand version or preferring the accumulated evidence of others. I chose the latter. The editor was alarmed.

'Do you realise,' he said, 'that Beaverbrook is a great historian?'

I produced Healy's reminiscences together with other works. The editor was slightly mollified but still unconvinced. We compromised on retaining the question 'Who is to be the mistress of the party?', attributing it not to Healy but to an unnamed Irish MP. Beaverbrook accepted this version.

'He says he must have been mistaken about Healy,' the editor said.

Some months afterwards I was sent to New York as the paper's correspondent there.

'Scrub the nicotine off your fingers, don't light up unless he gives you permission and don't argue with him unless you're very sure of your facts,' the editor advised me. 'If you make a bad impression on Beaverbrook it could have a fatal effect on your career. After all, it's his newspaper.'

For one of the curious features of life on the *Express* was that it was only in New York that an employee was likely to come across Beaverbrook. In London senior journalists had grown grey in his service without once setting eyes on him. In New York, on the other hand, the most junior reporter might find himself suddenly called upon to accompany his proprietor on his constitutional in Central Park, which was less dangerous in those days. Indeed on one of these expeditions a predecessor of mine, Arthur Brittenden, had succeeded in losing his – and Beaverbrook's – way. For hours, so the story went, the two of them had wandered about, lost. Subsequently an instruction had gone out to the effect that every member of the New York office must acquaint himself with the geography of Central Park. The conversation on these tours consisted chiefly of questions from Beaverbrook about the value of skyscrapers or other buildings which caught his eye.

'How much would ya say that was worth?' he would ask; and, as his companion was usually ignorant of, and uninterested in, New York property values, the only possible response was a desperate guess.

Oddly, these answers – quite literally, as I have explained, made up – would not anger or even amuse Beaverbrook but make him appear worried, particularly if the sums were on the high side.

'Ten million dollars? Ya really think so? Now why d'ya say that?'

'Well, it's in a good position.'

'It's in a good position. But ten million dollars. Ya can't be right.'

Every day he would telephone the office, generally between seven and eight in the evening. Perhaps he did this to satisfy himself that the staff had not all departed. On the whole, however, I do not think that this was the reason.

'What's the news?' he would inquire in jaunty and hopeful tones.

Alas, as most members of the New York office spent their time rewriting agency copy or reproducing stories from American newspapers, transmitting the results to London at great expense, there rarely was any news.

'Oh I see,' Beaverbrook would say, disappointed, and replace the receiver.

He made his presence felt in less obtrusive ways. In a corner of the office was a cupboard which contained stationery. It also contained a supply – about a dozen tins – of Campbell's tomato soup. I asked a secretary why they were there.

'That soup belongs to Lord Beaverbrook,' she said. 'It's the only kind of soup he likes, and one day he couldn't get any, so we have to keep a supply. You leave it alone.'

From time to time the secretary or one of her colleagues would take a foolscap envelope from the cupboard and then maltreat it, screwing it up, scoring it with pencil and even skating on it across the floor. The envelope, it turned out, was to contain copy to be sent to Beaverbrook at the Waldorf Towers. He considered it wasteful not to re-use envelopes. The secretaries quite reasonably considered it irksome and uneconomic of both effort and storage space to hoard used envelopes. They therefore processed new ones to look like old. Everyone was satisfied.

Eventually a summons to lunch arrived. It was communicated by the butler, Raymond, a reddish-haired man of uncertain age with protruding eyes, a surprisingly strong handshake and a camp conversational style.

'Oh, the old bugger. He's in such a *temper* these days. I pity you all, I really do. Some of the things, you wouldn't believe.'

Peter Hopkirk and I presented ourselves at Beaverbrook's suite in the Waldorf Towers. Ian Aitken was already there. Beaverbrook questioned Hopkirk and me about the stories we had lately sent. He appeared satisfied though unenthusiastic.

Then followed a waddya-think-of session. Though the subject-matter of these conversation pieces might vary, the form was unchanging. First Beaverbrook would ask, 'Waddya think of . . .' – it might be Kennedy, Khrushchev or Harold Macmillan. Whatever the answer might be, he would go on to ask: 'Now why d'ya say that?' Whether the reply to this question was satisfactory or not, he would conclude with, 'Oh, I see.'

A Washington correspondent, one 'Lobby' Ludlow, once got drunk and announced: 'We're going to play the game differently this evening, Lord Beaverbrook. We're going to ask *you* the questions.'

He was afterwards dismissed.

'He is a bad man,' Beaverbrook was reliably reported to have remarked. 'If he spoke to me in that manner, what would he say if he met the President?'

On this occasion there was no encouragement to behave in such a dangerous fashion. At any rate there was no opportunity to get drunk, because no drink was provided. Nor did matters improve at lunch itself. We ate boiled chicken, boiled rice and a mixture of frozen carrots and peas. We drank water. However, the only woman present, Lady Dunn (as she then was), consumed steak and a large baked potato. For most of the time Beaverbrook talked about Bonar Law. He summoned Raymond to cool his coffee, which he did by pouring it repeatedly from one cup to another until the required temperature was achieved.

Afterwards, in the sitting-room, we were talking in a desultory way when a large man appeared in the doorway and advanced towards Beaverbrook with hand outstretched.

'Lord Beaverbrook ...' he said.

'Go away,' Beaverbrook said. 'I can't see ya today. I am much too busy to make any arrangements now. Ya must make an appointment. There are no vacancies on my newspapers.'

He spoke these words gently, almost timorously. Then he raised his voice and shouted: 'Raymond, that man is here again.' To Ian Aitken he whispered in tones of appeal: 'Ian, get rid of him. Tell him to go away.'

Aitken was fully equal to the situation. He rose and took the man by the arm, leading him into the tiny entrance hall of the suite.

When he returned, having handed the intruder over to the charge of Raymond, Beaverbrook said: 'He is an Australian. He has been pestering me for a job. I have told him that no jobs are available but he will not listen.'

'He must be a good reporter,' Aitken said, 'to get in here at all, past all those people.'

'Takes more than cheek to make a good reporter,' Beaverbrook said.

Some weeks afterwards I was working late in the office one Saturday when a telephone call came from Beaverbrook's grand-daughter, Lady Jean Campbell, in Montego Bay. She asked me to listen carefully to her instructions. Lord Beaverbrook wished to have dispatched to him quantities of honey, coffee and cider vinegar, all of specified brands with which I was unfamiliar. In fact I did not have the slightest idea of where to obtain these commodities at eight o'clock on a Saturday in the middle of New York. I went to several delicatessens and did the best I could.

However, I rebelled against packing a parcel: partly as a gesture of protest, partly because I have an intense dislike of, am highly incompetent at, packing parcels. Instead I left the assortment of groceries on the desk of the then chief of the *Daily Express* bureau, Henry Lowrie, together with a note saying they were to be sent to Lord Beaverbrook clearly marked 'unsolicited gift' – a point on which Lady Jean had placed great emphasis. The goods were duly sent off but they were the wrong goods. I had made a mess of things, obtaining 'White Rose' instead of 'Red Rose' coffee – or it may have been the other way about – and committing various other more or less fundamental errors in regard to the honey and the cider vinegar. Beaverbrook blamed Henry Lowrie.

'The New York office,' he wrote in a letter of reproof, 'is going to rack and ruin.'

One might have expected him to take a close interest in the 'Crossbencher' column. In fact, in his later years anyway, he rarely intervened. Returned to London, I was puzzled to receive, via the editor, a dictated memorandum in the following terms: 'There is a man in the West Country called Bessemer or something like that I believe he is a Liberal I have a good opinion of him I commend him to your attention you might mention him in your political notes.' (He usually referred to the 'Cross-bencher' column as 'your political notes'. His memoranda were rarely punctuated as those responsible for taking them down were frightened of putting the full stops and commas in the wrong places, thereby altering the meaning, if any.)

An examination of the list of Liberal candidates produced the name of Peter Bessell, who was standing for Bodmin. A colleague said he thought Bessell was in the habit of writing to Beaverbrook about the Common Market and other matters. Inquiries showed this to be so. Indeed, if anything exceeded Lord Beaverbrook's high opinion of Mr Bessell, it was Mr Bessell's high opinion of Lord Beaverbrook. However, I could think of nothing sufficiently flattering or interesting to say about him. Besides, I did not see why the column should, for no very good reason, devote space to obscure parliamentary candidates. The editor agreed with me. We decided that for the moment we should ignore Peter Bessell.

About six weeks later the editor sent for me. He bore a concerned expression. He read out part of one of those dictated messages.

'Some time ago,' it went, 'I offered you a piece of advice about your political notes I see that you have not taken this advice perhaps you could give me the reason.'

'Look,' the editor said, 'no one's asking you to attack anybody. You're being asked to praise. There's no question of principle remotely involved. Just write a short paragraph saying something nice about this chap. It would make all our lives a lot easier.'

And so I wrote the paragraph. I said that Bessell had inaugurated the Liberal revival at Torquay in 1955 – which was, as it happened, true – and that he would win Bodmin for the Liberals at the general election. This also turned out to be true. It must have been one of the few correct predictions I made.

The next intervention occurred when the editors of the *Sunday* and the *Daily Express* were both away at the same time. Beaverbrook moved into his flat in Arlington House and began to interfere.

'I haven't enjoyed myself so much in years,' he said.

On the Friday afternoon his new secretary, Colin Vines – a put-upon individual who wrote an extremely funny book, *A Little Nut-Brown Man*, about his master – asked me to send the 'Cross-bencher' copy to Arlington House. I was to follow later.

'Tired old notes,' Beaverbrook said when I arrived. 'Ya political notes were tired,' he added as if to leave no room for misunderstanding on the point.

I did not dissent.

'Tired old stuff on Home and Wilson. Home is not worth bothering with. He has not made good. He is a failure.'

Again I did not quarrel with this judgment.

'What I suggest to you,' Beaverbrook went on, 'is a note on the financial position of the Liberal Party. That will be something fresh. Have ya got a pencil?'

I said I had a pencil.

'Take down these notes. Have ya heard of Lord Sherwood?'

Lord Sherwood, I subsequently discovered when working on a book about the Liberals, was an obscure benefactor of the party. At this earlier time, however, his name was unfamiliar to me. I admitted as much to Beaverbrook.

'Ya never heard of Hugh Sherwood?'

The gap in my knowledge seemed to present him with endless possibilities for wonder and amusement.

'Ya call yaself a political writer and ya never heard of Hugh Sherwood? Well, ya better learn about Hugh Sherwood, that is my advice if ya wish to be a political writer.'

Beaverbrook dictated some material of chiefly historical interest on the Liberal Party's funds, or lack of them. He then asked how I passed my working day. In the course of my reply I said – not entirely truthfully, I must confess – that I spent a good deal of time making assiduous inquiries on the telephone. This, it soon became evident, was the wrong thing to say.

'Vines,' he suddenly yelled. 'Drat that Vines, where is he?'

Colin Vines appeared.

'Vines, I wish to send an urgent message to the staffs of my newspapers about the use of the telephone.'

Vines stood at the ready. 'Mr Brittenden,' the message went (for during this period of activity Arthur Brittenden was editing the paper temporarily), 'a member of your staff tells me that he spends a good deal of his time on the telephone I do not recommend this practice have nothing to do with the telephone that is my advice rip out the cord and throw it away two feet after the subject of your inquiry that is the way to beat the agencies and get exclusive news.'

The use of the telephone at the *Express* did not, however, noticeably decline as a result of this message.

Beaverbrook's last instruction to me concerned Anthony Nutting. I never discovered what Nutting's crime had been. Certainly his behaviour at the time of Suez (the official house-reason) did not seem fully to explain the ferocity with which he was pursued. Anyway, Beaverbrook discovered that Nutting was the Conservative candidate for Oldham East. This was well-known – had been well-known for many months – but it came as news to Beaverbrook. He therefore demanded a paragraph attacking Nutting. I refused to write it both because the information was scarcely fresh and because the attack was supposed to mention some divorce proceedings in which Nutting had been involved. So the matter uneasily rested.

And then Beaverbrook died. *Cadit quaestio*: or so one might have thought. But no. In the same week the editor called me in and suggested that 'as a last tribute to Beaverbrook' I should carry out his ultimate known instruction and attack Anthony Nutting. In the circumstances this seemed to me unnecessary and irrational, not to say bizarre. I said as much, perhaps more. However, the attack duly appeared, written by Douglas Clark. Shortly afterwards I moved to the *Spectator*.

LORD BRADWELL

22 May 1905 – 12 August 1976

LORD BRADWELL was a Labour life peer for only a year before he died. He was better known as Tom Driberg, and will be so referred to for the rest of this essay. He was a journalist, an aesthete, a politician, a High Churchman and a promiscuous homosexual. During and perhaps before the war he worked for MI5. Many people (some of whom liked him personally) also suspected him of being a Russian agent, but this was never established satisfactorily one way or the other.

Thomas Edward Neil Driberg was the youngest son of John James Street Driberg, a former civil servant and inspector of prisons in India, who had retired to a large house at Crowborough in Sussex. Tom Driberg acquired an early detestation of the pine-, gorse- and heather-clad countryside around him and of the 'bourgeois' and 'philistine' values which he took it to represent. J. J. S. Driberg was twenty-five years older than his wife, who was herself thirty-five when Tom was born. She came from Scotland. The name 'Driberg' was thought to be Dutch. Though Tom would say, when he referred to the matter at all, that he came from the 'stockbroker belt', the family was conducted on Victorian lines, with family prayers shortly before eight in the morning.

He had two brothers who were young men when he was a child. One, Jim, was a first-class doctor who subsequently had troubles with women and money and turned to drink: he died in middle age, and Tom grumbled about having to look after him in his declining years. The other brother, Jack, was even more outstanding, though as an anthropologist. As a colonial administrator in North-East Africa he refused to burn down a village as a punitive measure. He concocted an account of the burning, was discovered in his invention and was dismissed. He then lectured at Cambridge and wrote several books. He too died in middle age.

Jack, the elder, was the subject of one of Driberg's earlier sexual experiments. Crawling about on the floor, he observed a small gap in the crutch of Jack's flannel trousers – Driberg was precise that they were flannel. He

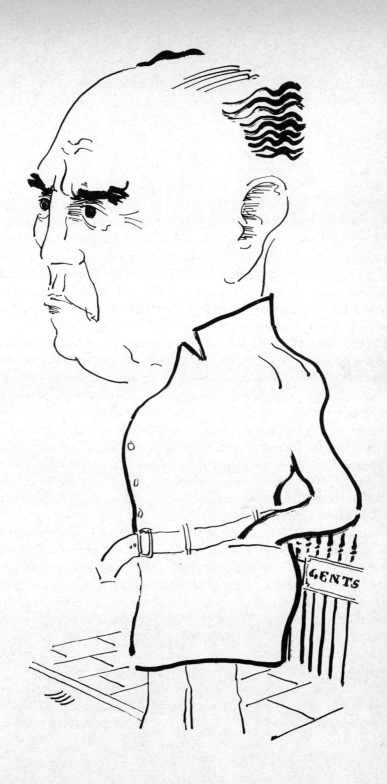

gently inserted his finger in the gap, which Jack did not seem to notice, and experienced 'the first authentic sexual thrill of my life'. At the age of five he was sent to a kindergarten run by two elderly sisters. Every day he was escorted there by the Dribergs' gardener, who was called Hemsley. One day he stopped and said: 'Hemsley, will you please take down your trousers?' This, at any rate, was Driberg's recollection, though he did not remember the reply, if any, which Hemsley made. But he was certain that Hemsley refused to take down his trousers. This was one of Driberg's earliest sexual rebuffs.

Homosexuality was, in his words, one of the 'ruling passions' of his life. The others were High Anglicanism and left-wing politics of a never very clearly defined fellow-travelling nature. It is convenient to deal with this most important aspect of him in one piece, so to speak, analytically rather than chronologically. His sexual proclivities were never ambivalent, but he was himself ambivalent about them. On the one hand, he was prone to self-pity, to declare that he had 'made a mess of' his life, and to blame his parents, in particular his mother (who survived his father for some years, and seems to have treated him with gentleness and consideration) for saying to him, as a child, that he ought to have been a little girl. On the other hand, however, he showed no desire either to be 'cured' – for 'curing' was, in general, mentioned as a possible 'treatment' by otherwise intelligent people until quite recently – or to acquire a permanent partner of his own sex.

He had no taste for buggery, though occasionally he would indulge in it if his partner of the moment seemed to expect or desire it. His preferred activity was *fellatio*, with him playing the oral role. As a schoolboy at Lancing he would combine visits to churches with forays into public lavatories: with lavatories he had, as he wrote, a lifelong 'love-hate relationship'. Indeed, he could rise to genuine eloquence on the lavatories, now mainly destroyed, of pre-1939 London (though there is a dark green, cast iron survivor in an alley between Lincoln's Inn and Chancery Lane):

> Why municipal vandals should have thought it necessary to destroy so many of them I do not know: I suppose it is one expression of anti-homosexual prejudice. Yet no homo, cottage-cruising, ever prevented a hetero from merely urinating;* while to do one's rounds of the cottages – the alley by the Astoria, the dog-leg lane opposite the Garrick

---

* This is arguable. A. W.

Club, the one near the Ivy, the one off Wardour Street, the narrow passage by the Coliseum, ending up always in Of Alley, off Villiers Street – provided homos, not all of whom are given to rougher sports, with healthy exercise.

His preference was for those he described as 'young proletarians'. He enjoyed much luck, not least in avoiding physical injury or death itself. In this last respect he was more fortunate than the writer, James Pope-Hennessy, or another ex-chairman of the Labour Party like Driberg, George Brinham of the Woodworkers' Union. He was equally lucky in avoiding either public disgrace or conviction, for Driberg's activities were punishable until the change in the law. Some of them remained so afterwards. Though he had no taste for little boys as such, he was certainly no observer of a twenty-one-year age limit; and some of his approaches were (as the law continued to define them) indecent irrespective of the age of the object of his desire. But he had several close shaves.

On 12 November 1935 he was arraigned at the Old Bailey on a charge of indecent assault, on two unemployed Scottish miners he had picked up and taken back to his flat in South Kensington, for the purpose, as he claimed at the trial and subsequently, of 'journalistic research': he was then writing the 'William Hickey' column in the *Daily Express* (as he did from 1928 to 1942). The three found themselves in bed together, even though there was room in the (admittedly small) flat for them to arrange themselves separately, if less than luxuriously, for the night. One of them complained to the police about improper advances by Driberg. He was acquitted mainly because of the exalted social positions of the character witnesses he produced: Colonel the Honourable Wilfred Egerton of 38 Albermarle Street and Lord Sysonby of St James's Palace. Certainly this was the reason Driberg himself later gave.

Lord Beaverbrook used his best endeavours, almost entirely successful, to keep the case out of the papers. He also paid for Driberg's defence. When, in 1956, Driberg published a critical, but by no means hostile or uninformed, biography of Beaverbrook, the latter accused him of being ungrateful. 'Tom Driberg is a bad man,' Beaverbrook would say long afterwards; what he had principally in mind was Driberg's treatment of him in the book.

Then again, in the war Driberg was briefly in Edinburgh, where he picked up a Norwegian sailor and was about to perform *fellatio* with him in an unused air-raid shelter when a policeman arrived to interrupt proceedings. The sailor made, or was allowed to make, his escape. Driberg disclosed his identity, pleaded for clemency, said he had been foolish, promised not to repeat his error. The policeman was moved. Anyway he let Driberg off, and subsequently entered into a friendship with him, though this relationship fell short of any sexual connection.

It is necessary to make this last qualification because Driberg, by his own account, possessed an extraordinary gift for turning an acquaintanceship with a man or boy who took his fancy into a (usually temporary) homosexual relationship. He did this with a pathetic young man who was posing as 'Hickey'. He even did it with a bereaved husband whom he visited going about his journalistic tasks on the *Express*.

He maintained his enthusiasm into old age. He would appear in the Colony Room, better known as Muriel's, in Dean Street, with a succession of young men – usually in their early twenties, though it was difficult to tell – whom he would invariably introduce individually to the assembled company as 'one of my constituents'. He would then provide the young man of the afternoon with a handful of loose change, and direct him to the fruit machine in the corner to divert himself, while Driberg gossiped with his cronies.

Driberg would also attend the fortnightly *Private Eye* luncheon at the Coach and Horses public house, not far from Muriel's. He was a regular attender in the 1960s, but stopped coming well before his death in 1976. Oddly enough, Richard Ingrams, the editor, did not make him feel unwelcome on these occasions despite his well-advertised aversion to homosexuals. Not that Driberg contributed much in the way of gossip or information. His principal activity was to point out or engage in argument about solecisms, whether syntactical, ecclesiastical or social, as in: 'My dear Richard, I am astonished that you don't appear to know the correct way to refer to the younger daughter of a Marquess.' The real reason Driberg was such an assiduous attender at these luncheons was that he had conceived a passion for Patrick Marnham, likewise a regular attender. Marnham, who was heterosexual, did not respond favourably to his advances.

When he was over seventy Driberg was dining with a journalist acquaintance. At half past ten or so this acquaintance announced that he would shortly have to return home, as his son, aged fifteen, was alone in his flat. 'So you have a son?' Driberg said. 'Of fifteen? Do, please, bring him to see me.' (Driberg was then living in a flat in the Barbican.) 'I have all kinds of books and pictures that might interest him.' Driberg's acquaintance politely declined this invitation, explaining that his son was busy with examinations, and was chiefly interested in cricket.

A. J. P. Taylor once advanced the view that much of Driberg's purported sexual activity was made up, 'fantasy' as it is called. This is doubtful. Taylor himself said that Driberg nearly ruined the former's twenty-first birthday dinner in Oxford by making advances to the waiter. The waiter complained to Taylor and threatened to depart if Driberg persisted in his conduct. To emphasise his displeasure, he said he was a married man of over forty. 'What had his being married to do with it?' Driberg replied to Taylor.

At Lancing Driberg developed his other interests also: in Church ceremonial and architecture and in aesthetics generally. His school friends included Evelyn Waugh and Roger Fulford. Though resolutely unathletic, he was happier than he had been at his preparatory school. He was much influenced, in voice and manner, by the sixth form master, J. F. Roxburgh, also a homosexual, though of a less bold variety than Driberg. He was expelled for homosexuality but was allowed to remain at Lancing to take a scholarship to Christ Church, being segregated from the other boys in the intervening period. Driberg later claimed that the school authorities had been harsh not so much in expelling as in segregating him.

At Oxford he did little or no academic work but wrote poetry: Edith Sitwell, who took him up, said he was the most promising young poet of his generation. She it was who inaugurated his career as a journalist rather than as a poet. Driberg, shortly after coming down from Oxford, was working as a waiter in a small Soho café and living with another waiter – more by necessity than choice – in a small room above the establishment. He later said that, though he was neither affluent nor comfortable, this was the happiest period of his life so far. But Edith Sitwell was shocked. She introduced him to her acquaintance Beverley Baxter, then editor of the *Daily Express*. Driberg was taken on to the staff in 1928 and prospered.

He was a ceremonious young man. He once rebuked Osbert Lancaster for neglecting to stand up when the editor (by this time Arthur Christiansen) entered the room. He was the most famous of the 'Hickey' columnists. Beaverbrook's idea was that the traditional social column – 'I hear that the Honourable Somebody Something is holidaying in Nice' – was boring and that 'Hickey' should be about people who were not, in his phrase, social butterflies. The altered subject-matter was to be accompanied by an altered style. Beaverbrook instructed Driberg to study and emulate *Time* magazine. Driberg later claimed that he plagiarised several *Time* telescope-words, such as 'cinemagnate'. A study of 'Hickey' for this period – which can most conveniently be carried out by reading the selection *Colonnade* (1949) – shows that, though Driberg occasionally went in for telescope-words, the most marked imitative features of his style were a liking for 'isn'ts' and so forth, and a tendency to omit 'ands' and 'buts': 'He doesn't care for London, lives in Suffolk, collects china cats.'

The pieces of which he was proudest were about ceremonies of various sorts – the coronation, the enthronement of the Pope. Driberg had loved ceremony since childhood. He also possessed an irritatingly didactic side. He liked to explain, instruct, put people right: but he did it less from a concern for truth than from a wish to demonstrate his own knowledge and the ignorance of his companion.

He could be specially irritating about wine and food. He possessed high standards, but he applied them in a foolish and undiscriminating way. When, later in his life, he was working as a columnist on *Reynolds News*, he took to lunching on Saturdays with the editor, William Richardson, at a nearby restaurant. The management asked Richardson to 'stop bringing Mr Driberg' to the restaurant as he 'upset the waiters' by his constant complaints about the wine, the food, the service, everything – though it may be that he upset them also by making sexual advances. At a Labour Party conference he once rebuked the manager of the Imperial Hotel, Blackpool, for having sauce bottles on the tables. He could be tiresomely dogmatic about drinking tea rather than dry white wine with Chinese food, and milk rather than beer with curry. (The last injunction derived from 'The Great Beast', Aleister Crowley, who had been a friend of his.)

For the greater part of his period on the *Express* – until the early days of the war – he was a member of the Communist Party. He was expelled for undisclosed reasons.* One advantage of his expulsion, he said later, was that when he stood as an Independent for Maldon in 1942 he could conscientiously claim that he was a member of no political party. In 1943 he was dismissed by the *Express*, not for his political activities generally –

---

*An article in the *Sunday Times Magazine* of 18 October 1981 stated that Driberg was expelled on account of his employment by MI5. This seems likely enough. However, the article also stated that Driberg had been 'infiltrated' into the Communist Party shortly before the war by the head of Driberg's section, who was in love with him. But Driberg had been an open Communist since Oxford.

the paper had written a sympathetic leader on his successful candidature – but for revealing in a political speech information which had been given to him confidentially by the paper's industrial correspondent, Trevor Evans.

On this occasion he did not consider himself unjustly treated. Beaverbrook said he had opposed the sacking; Christiansen asked him to return. Driberg declined and accepted an invitation to write a column in *Reynolds News*, which, after the war, was probably more than anything else responsible for his election to the National Executive Committee. In this column he insisted on spelling words in his own way ('tho", 'connexion', 'judgement') contrary to the normal style of the paper: this was during a period when papers had house styles, before the present decline in printing standards.

His connection with Maldon was real enough. Shortly before the war he had bought an Adam House at Bradwell-juxta-Mare for £4,000. It was church property, and he was given preference because he was an active churchman. When he was elected for Maldon, Evelyn Waugh noted in his diary (26 May 1942): 'The newspapers have behaved very curiously over this by-election, giving no news of what any of the candidates are saying. In recording the result they simply describe [Driberg] as a journalist and a churchwarden, which gives a very imperfect picture of that sinister character.' Shortly before the election Beaverbrook had advised him to buy a hat: 'The British electors will not vote for a man who doesn't wear a hat.' Driberg disregarded this advice.

The most mysterious episode in his life was his marriage to Mrs Ena May Binfield on 13 June 1951. She was a kindly, partly-Jewish widow from Yorkshire, some years older than he (shortly before the marriage she became a Christian). The wedding took place in his favourite London church, St Mary's, Bourne Street, near Sloane Square. It was no hole-in-corner affair. The church was packed with political and other notables, including Aneurin Bevan, who said that his nonconformist conscience was shocked by the ceremonial; the best man was John Freeman; the reception was held on the Terrace of the House of Commons. Evelyn Waugh was unable to attend owing to his absence abroad, but wrote to Driberg: 'I will think of you intently on the day and pray that the church is not struck by lightning.' (This sentence in this same connection is, oddly enough, attributed to Aneurin Bevan and Winston Churchill also.) Freeman said later that Driberg took this course because he was becoming lonely and wanted someone to look after him, but the couple soon went their separate ways, and the marriage ended in divorce.

He took the Labour Whip in January 1945 and sat for Maldon until he retired in 1955. However, he returned to politics as Member for Barking from 1959 to 1974. He was a member of the Labour Party's National Executive Committee from 1949 to 1972 and chairman of the party in 1957–8. Even before he held this last post, whose nature often misleads foreign observers, Driberg was assumed by several Russian politicians to be leader of the Labour Party. This was on account partly of his grave, episcopal manner, and partly of his ability to get on well with Russians.

Driberg was fairly frank about his activities: he would go out to lunch with diplomats from the Soviet Embassy and tell them what he knew about the state of politics. It was, he used to say, desirable that foreign countries should be fully and accurately informed; he would, he claimed, have performed the same service for the Americans. He was a friend of Guy Burgess, wrote a book about him (for which he received £60,000 in serialisation fees) and, finally, on a visit to Moscow, found him a young lover in an underground lavatory, Burgess being more diffident in his approaches than Driberg.

He was a resourceful journalist and a good though occasionally affected writer, whose general correctness did not always compensate for a certain lack of vigour. His best book was *Beaverbrook* (1956), which was by no means superseded by A. J. P. Taylor's subsequent biography. He was basically a tall, thin, dark man. Though he later became overweight, he looked imposing rather than fat. He was hopeless with money and always in debt. He died shortly after dining at his favourite restaurant, the Gay Hussar in Soho. People used to say: 'Poor Tom is really very sweet when you get to know him.'

ANTHONY CROSLAND

29 August 1918 – 19 February 1977

CHARLES ANTHONY RAVEN CROSLAND was born in 1918. His father was a senior civil servant, his mother a university lecturer and French scholar. Both his parents were members of the Exclusive Brethren Sect. He was educated as a weekly boarder at Highgate School (where, owing to his parents' religious beliefs, he did not join the army cadet corps) and, having won a classical scholarship, at Trinity College, Oxford. His university education was interrupted by the 1939-45 war, in which he served first in the Royal Welch Fusiliers and then in the Parachute Regiment. After the war he returned to Oxford, took a first in Philosophy, Politics and Economics, became President of the Union and Chairman of the University Labour Club, and was made a Fellow of Trinity.

He was encouraged to become active in Labour politics nationally by Hugh Dalton. From 1950 until 1955 he was Member for South Gloucestershire and, from 1959 until his death in 1977, Member for Grimsby. He held numerous government posts in the Wilson Administration of 1964-70 and in the Wilson and Callaghan Administrations from 1974 until his death, when he was Foreign Secretary. Immediately before that he had been Secretary for the Environment. He would probably have gone on to become Chancellor of the Exchequer, a post James Callaghan had half-promised him. He might (though this is more disputable) have become Leader of the Labour Party and Prime Minister. His reputation, however, rested not on his abilities as a politician or his more considerable skills as an administrator but on his influence as a socialist writer. This influence derived from his book *The Future of Socialism* (1956). It derived also from his personal characteristics.

Crosland was a tall man, of something over six feet. His hair remained dark to the end. His eyes were dark blue. When he was amused they would narrow, and the skin on the outer edges would crinkle, giving him a more boyish appearance. Some people thought that this appearance, in these moments of amusement, was simulated: that he tried too hard to make his

eyes narrow, and so forth. Though one cannot be sure, this thought was probably unjust, for Crosland possessed a lively sense of humour.

Some of it could be rather childish. It depended on getting people's names slightly wrong. 'How is Corinna Adams these days?' he would inquire, referring to a then writer on the *New Statesman*, Corinna Adam. The *New Statesman* itself he could hardly bear to call it by its proper name at all. He would pretend to confuse it with the *Spectator* or the *Tatler*. He was also adept at assuming a pompous tone for humorous purposes. 'I don't mind whether the fire's lit or not,' he would say, 'but could we please take a *view* one way or the other.'

He could also be very rude indeed. Tony Benn once publicly announced that he was concerned to lose the stigma of the intellectual. Crosland replied that, in order to lose a stigma, it was first necessary to acquire one. For some reason – maybe sexual, but it is profitless to speculate – he could be very rude to young and attractive women who intended no harm but were merely trying to make serious conversation to the best of their ability. His own tactics consisted in asking one or more of the following questions: Who exactly are you? What do you know about this? What precisely do you mean by that? What is your evidence? Admittedly these were questions which he addressed also to people better able to look after themselves: but women certainly brought out an aggressive side to his nature.

Once he was lying on the floor at a party, not because he was incapacitated but because he thought he would be more comfortable in that position. (At parties he would usually insist on sitting in an arm-chair. He would also arrive wearing carpet slippers, even though the rest of his attire might be fairly formal. He would further have demanded previously of his host or hostess to be told who, who precisely, would be attending the gathering. If the party, or whatever other social function it might be, was to take place on a Saturday, he would in addition have asked whether he would be able to see *Match of the Day* on television.) On this occasion a woman appeared within his field of vision. 'Hello, ugly-face,' he said. 'What do you want?'

Crosland, however, disliked large parties, even though they might be informal; he also disliked formal social gatherings. He refused to wear full evening dress and compromised on a dinner-jacket. Once, being about to escort a member of the Royal Family to Covent Garden in his ministerial capacity, he sought permission from the Palace authorities to wear his dinner-jacket. Permission was granted after some comings and goings.

He was well aware of his capacity to hurt verbally, and made some attempt to contain it. Though it was broadly true to say that he treated everyone alike, there were exceptions. He was considerate to those who he thought were doing dull or menial jobs: 'would you be *so* kind ... if you can possibly manage it ... if it isn't too much trouble ...' and so forth. Unfortunately, owing perhaps to his drawling tones, these careful attempts at courtesy tended to produce the opposite effect to that intended: the person of whom the request was being made would clearly think that his or her leg was being pulled, or that a rebuke was being administered.

Again, in political, as distinct from social, circumstances Crosland could be quite timid. Once, when he was in charge of the Department of the Environment, he agreed to give a verbatim interview on the problems of London's housing. Not unreasonably, he insisted on seeing a copy of the interview before it appeared in the paper concerned, even though this condition had not been agreed beforehand. Crosland, however, went well beyond removing repetitions, correcting minor errors or clarifying his meaning. He showed the interview to his senior civil servants, which might have been formally required by the rules, but was certainly asking for trouble. The civil servants tried to insist on over forty different alterations: on the substitution, for example, of 'unlicensed occupation' for 'squatting', the word Crosland had actually used. The journalist refused to make these numerous alterations required by the civil servants; and the interview, of a fairly conventional nature in any case, duly appeared, and caused no harm to anyone.

He was easily hurt. He was hurt by the charge, made frequently during his later political career, that he was 'lazy'. He had always worked hard, he said – had been brought up by his parents to work hard. He felt guilty, he claimed, if he spent a day without doing anything. These days were infrequent. He liked to take long holidays, of three or four weeks, by himself, in France or Italy. He would have with him several improving works of history or literature. In London he would often work till two in the morning when he would begin what he called his 'light reading', of the political weeklies and *Private Eye*, to which he was attached, though he pretended not to be. He possessed a serious interest in art and literature, and read virtually the entire works of Joseph Conrad shortly before he died. He preferred working in an arm-chair to working at a desk. The whole of *The Future of Socialism* was written in this former way.

Contrary to much of what was written about him immediately after his death, he was also physically active. He enjoyed walking, swimming and playing tennis, and admitted to seeing one family more frequently than he might otherwise have done because they had a private tennis court. He used to smoke cigarettes but switched to small cigars. He drank a good deal, though not excessively by the standards of many politicians and journalists. He liked gin in the middle of the day and whisky in the evening. He enjoyed wine too, though he made a fuss about not fussing. 'Let's just have the carafe wine,' he would say, 'and leave the vintages to Roy Jenkins.'

He was always fond of Jenkins, though there were strains towards the end, caused partly by Crosland's half-heartedness (as Jenkins saw it) over the Common Market, partly by his opposition to any new social-democratic grouping and partly to his feeling that, compared to himself, Jenkins was receiving altogether too much favourable publicity.

It was natural and maybe inevitable that a man of Crosland's characteristics should be thought indolent. There was a sense in which he was perhaps so. This was as a party politician. After Labour had lost the 1970 election he contemplated 'going into industry', though he was determined he would not go near the City: but no suitable offers arrived. He also played with the idea of a part-time academic post, though he did not wish to return to Trinity, Oxford: again, nothing appropriate turned up. He accordingly resolved to become, as he put it, a full-time politician. To this end he made numerous speeches in the country in an endeavour to be elected to the National Executive Committee. He failed to be elected but was not humiliated in the voting.

Yet his heart was not in the business: both through personal shyness and through an intense scrupulosity over the use of words, he could never quite bring himself to make the correct, the acceptable, noises at the right moments. This was not true of his performances in the House of Commons. There (contrary to the still-received opinion about him) he could be an outstanding debater, dialectically defeating Peter Walker in several encounters. But in the Labour Party nationally he was never wholly accepted.

This saddened him – more so than the charge of indolence – because he loved the party. *The Future of Socialism* was, in essence, the case for Socialism as Equality. Crosland's carefully argued view was that public ownership, at any rate on the old, Morrisonian pattern, was largely irrelevant to equality. This view infuriated the Left. A more serious flaw in the book was its assumption of automatic and relatively painless economic growth. An equally serious flaw was his declared determination to treat Britain as a 'closed' economic system, which debarred him from dealing at length with the problems of sterling and the exchange rate. Crosland could see these faults as clearly as anyone: but it was for others to correct them if they could: his theoretical work was done.

In a way, Crosland retreated into an easy neo-populism, scorning the pre-occupations, chiefly about libertarian questions, of, as he put it, S.W.1 and E.C.4, and contrasting them with the concerns of 'my constituents in Grimsby'. But partly this was teasing, and partly a genuine expression of his feelings for the people of Grimsby. In particular, Crosland was worried about 'participation' as a device that would in practice give increased power or influence to the active and intelligent members of the middle class. He was worried likewise about the Welfare State as a form of organisation that could be and was used to provide benefits to people who did not really need them.

His first wife was Hilary Sarson. His second wife was the American journalist Susan Barnes. It was often said: 'Susan has mellowed Tony' to which some people replied: 'What can he have been like before he married Susan?' His solitary annual holidays apart, he was uxorious, and unhappy if he spent more than three or four nights away from his wife. He also had his jealous side, and virtually prohibited Susan from social engagements with old men friends, though, if they were sufficiently interesting, they were welcome at his Holland Park house. Shortly before his death he and Susan bought a house at Adderbury in Oxfordshire. It was there that he suffered a cerebral haemorrhage. He lay for a week unconscious in the Radcliffe Infirmary, Oxford. Susan lay by his side for this whole time. There was a memorial service in Westminster Abbey, and his ashes were scattered into the sea near Grimsby by Susan. He was much loved, and much misunderstood.

RICHARD CROSSMAN

15 December 1907 – 4 April 1974

THE LATE Francis Hope's mother once had a dream about Richard Crossman. She was seated in a dentist's chair and he, attired in a white coat, was about to attend to her teeth.

'Don't be so silly, Dick,' she said. 'You know you're not a dentist.'

'I know I'm not, you fool,' Crossman replied, 'but I can work it out quite easily from first principles.'

Hugh Gaitskell, who was staying in the same house, and to whom this dream was related at breakfast, said that it perfectly expressed the reason he would not give Crossman any post in a Government formed by him.

Richard Howard Stafford Crossman was born on 15 December 1907, the son of Charles Stafford Crossman, a barrister, the Attorney-General's 'devil' at the Chancery bar who, in accordance with precedent, was duly made a judge of that division of the High Court. Mr Justice Crossman was a descendant of John Danvers, presumably of the Danvers family dealt with by John Aubrey. When, on his third marriage, to Anne McDougall, Richard Crossman acquired Prescote Manor, Cropredy, near Banbury, he noticed the Danvers family crest over a fireplace. This discovery provided him with much innocent pleasure.

Mr Justice Crossman had been 'founder's kin' at Winchester: through the Danvers connection he was descended from William of Wykeham. Owing to the reforms of the nineteenth century, this distinction was of no use to Richard Crossman in obtaining a scholarship to Winchester. When he was seven, his father started to teach him Latin with a view to this award. He came thirteenth in the list. The Winchester scholarship dominated his childhood; there was a lot of talk also from his father about being 'founder's kin'. Crossman used to say that, because of his strong constitution, he suffered no subsequent ill-effects from this early cramming. But he was determined that his own two children (who arrived late in his life) should not undergo the same experience; nor did they.

The Christian name 'Howard' came from his mother. She was one of the Howards of Ilford, who had long established themselves as pharmaceutical chemists in the district. There was some Huguenot blood on his mother's side. There was no truth in the story, repeated in his *Times* obituary, that Crossman was of German extraction. The story seems to have gained credence partly from his guttural 'r', partly from his bullying manner, partly from his enthusiasm, at Oxford and later, for German culture (though some of the things he said about Germans could well have been matter for the Race Relations Board) and partly from Auberon Waugh's habit of calling him, in print, Grossbaum or Crossbum.

His parents were professing Christians, his father conventional, undoubting and lawyerly, his mother devoted and Anglo-Catholic. When his first marriage, to a beautiful German-Jewess (referred to by Crossman afterwards as 'my German tart'), was on the point of collapse, caused partly by the first Mrs Crossman's addiction to drugs, Crossman deposited her at his parents' house and speedily removed himself, saying: 'You claim to be the big Christians. You can jolly well look after her.' This was Crossman's own account.

The house was at Epping. There were family prayers at 7.55 (Crossman was precise about the time) and Mr Justice Crossman insisted on dressing for dinner. There were six children, three girls and three boys, all educated at independent schools: one brother went into the City, another was killed in the RAF in 1940. The household was sustained by a nannie, an under-nurse, a cook, three maids, a gardener and a boy. The Crossmans also possessed a tennis court. On this Clement Attlee and his wife, neighbours on the outskirts of North-East London, would be invited to disport themselves.

Attlee and Crossman early acquired an antipathy towards each other. Crossman disliked Attlee's (as Crossman thought) drab and conventional appearance, manner and intelligence, all of which reminded him of his father, whom he despised, as he later despised all lawyers – with the possible exception of Geoffrey Bing, whom Anne Crossman, however, refused to have in the house, on account not so much of his illiberal actions in Ghana as of his disgusting eating habits. Attlee, for his part, disliked Crossman's maltreatment of his parents: his evident contempt for his worthy, industrious, scholarly but timid father and his intellectual bullying of his pious, intelligent but academically unaccomplished and dialectically inept mother.

Crossman later regretted his treatment of his mother. About his father he was uncontrite. To Crossman, Mr Justice Crossman represented, even after his death, everything he most hated in English society and the British State. The only concession Crossman was prepared to make was to say that, if he had been older, he would have treated his father more civilly; in view of Crossman's robust methods in argument, at best a speculative claim. The conflict would have been there all the same.

Partly on account of these past experiences in the Crossman household, Attlee refused to give him a post in the 1945 Government, saying: 'Plenty of brains. Character's the trouble.' On another occasion Crossman, following a visit to Israel, had an interview with Attlee to give an account of developments in that country and urge a change in the Labour Government's policy towards it. Crossman having completed his speech, Attlee paused and said: 'Saw your mother in Bond Street not long ago. Looked well. Good day.'

At Winchester Crossman read the classics and (among others) D. H. Lawrence, played in the football team, was a general success, and knew Douglas Jardine and Douglas Jay. Though he never showed the slightest knowledge or appreciation of cricket, he was prouder of the former acquaintance.

At New College, Oxford, he read Classical Greats, in which he obtained a first, wrote poetry and displayed homosexual tendencies, forming a friendship with W. H. Auden. Auden it was who convinced Crossman of the superiority of things German over things French. This had less to do with the tolerant, or what was thought to be the tolerant, attitude towards homosexuality in Berlin in the 1920s than with a reaction to the Bloomsbury group, which Crossman and his friends considered lamentably provincial and 'bourgeois'. Crossman acquired an attachment not only to Auden but also to a young man he used later to describe as 'a beautiful scrum-half', a description of his physical attributes rather than of his prowess on the rugby field. This rugby player found a teaching post at Sedbergh, and Crossman was about to pursue him there as master in charge of the sixth form – the position had been offered and accepted – when another offer turned up, of being a Fellow of New College.

Crossman taught philosophy, mainly political and ancient. This period, 1931–7, produced three books, *Socrates*, *Government and the Governed* (actually published in 1939) and *Plato Today*. The latter was a spirited attack on Plato's idea of 'the Guardians' which anticipated the later criticisms of Plato by, notably, Karl Popper. Indeed, Crossman's attitude to Plato was the foundation of his whole structure of politics. He believed, first, that ordinary citizens were deluded by their governors – that democracy was in many respects a sham – and, second, that government would become not only more dramatic but more efficient if ordinary citizens played a greater part in it. He maintained the belief that emperors had no clothes. He weakened in the belief that to point this out would necessarily improve matters. In his diary for 31 December 1967 he wrote:

> Ever since I was a young don I've believed in the WEA, in training the mass of the people for responsibility for self-government and I've been convinced that if we could use education for that purpose we would be able to substitute genuine social democracy for oligarchy. Now, after this experience of a social democratic government [i.e., since the election of 1964], I have seriously begun to doubt. Of course I've known for a long time that the belief in the rationality of a man is a *credo quia impossibile*. But this experience has really shaken that ultimate faith in the political educability of man or, more deeply even, in the possibility of a government where decisions are taken by ordinary people.*

At this time he not only taught for the Workers Educational Association but served on the Oxford City Council, becoming leader of the Labour Group. He also travelled in Germany and witnessed the beginnings of Hitler's regime. This period came to an end when he fell in love with the wife of another Fellow of New College. (As the second Mrs Crossman, she herself was to die suddenly in 1952.) H. A. L. Fisher, Warden of the college, said he would do everything he could to obtain Crossman a post at another (probably provincial) university: but he also advised Crossman to go into politics young if he wanted to go into politics at all, for he, Fisher, had made the mistake of entering them too old and too near the top.

Crossman's first non-academic job was as Berlin correspondent of the *Spectator*. In 1938 he joined the editorial staff of the *New Statesman* under Kingsley Martin. Crossman later said that the happiest, most liberating experience of his life was his realisation that he could write English. It came comparatively late, when he was over thirty. He had always enjoyed high academic success: but his tutors, both at Winchester and at Oxford, had told him that his 'style was bad'. He was miserable about this both because he wanted to write well in any case and because he had early realised that

---

* Richard Crossman, *The Diaries of a Cabinet Minister*, 3 vols (1975–7), vol. II, p. 627.

he did not possess a truly original or creative mind. He saw himself as a populariser, as, in Lady (Jennie) Lee's words, 'a compulsive communicator'. His powers as a journalist were probably at their height between 1945, when he returned to the *Statesman* on a part-time basis (having been in psychological warfare, he was elected MP for Coventry East) and 1958, when he published *The Charm of Politics*, a collection of pieces, chiefly book reviews – one of the few enterprises of this kind that bear re-reading.

Martin, however, was determined that Crossman should not succeed him as editor. He left a memorandum addressed to his fellow directors of The Statesman and Nation Publishing Company explaining why he considered Crossman a poor, indeed an impossible, choice. Oddly enough, this severe document setting out Crossman's defects of character, as Martin perceived them, was not seen by the directors of the paper when, in 1969, Crossman was secretly selected to succeed Paul Johnson after the general election. (There was nothing disreputable about this secrecy: it was necessary because of Crossman's position as a Minister.) Johnson's view was that, if the *Statesman* board had seen Martin's minatory memorandum, Crossman would not have become editor in 1970. This might or might not have turned out to be the case: it is impossible to say.

At all events, Martin's opinion was that Crossman was the finest leader-writer he had known with the exception of H. N. Brailsford (whose 'controlled passion' he lacked), a magnificent book-reviewer, an excellent contributor of 'diary' notes (though his notes were interesting only when on politics) and, in short, a most useful man to have around the place, if kept under strict supervision. However, Crossman was unpredictable and disloyal both to his colleagues and to the paper as such. He had told Martin he could keep his mouth shut if specifically asked to do so: otherwise he regarded himself as free to speak. This, in Martin's view, was not good enough: a man should know when to stay silent. In the mid-1950s it became clear to Crossman that he would not succeed Martin as editor, so he took himself off to the *Daily Mirror* to write a twice-weekly column.

In 1966 the *Statesman*'s circulation under Johnson reached its highest figure of 93,000. Thereafter it began to fall, not catastrophically, but steadily and worryingly. In 1970, immediately after Crossman became editor, circulation rose, but afterwards it fell even more steeply. As editor he remained a Labour MP. He had promised the *Statesman* board – certainly unfairly to the voters of Coventry East, who had, after all, just re-elected him – that he would soon resign his seat. He tended to re-fight battles of the 1964–70 Administrations in the pages of the paper, importing for this purpose MPs and former Ministers whose journalistic abilities were not evident at first sight. Crossman justified this course on the ground that he was 'making Labour policy' (one of his favourite phrases and, occasionally, activities). Editorial conferences at the paper proliferated. He attempted to exclude several members of the editorial staff from a grand 'policy-making' weekly conference attended by such luminaries as Mrs Barbara Castle, Lord Balogh, Lord (then Harold) Lever and Tony Benn: but the staff successfully secured re-admission.

His greatest success in this period came not over policy but over personalities. He was preoccupied by the need to re-build the relationship between the Labour Party and the trade unions which had been damaged by Mrs Castle's aborted proposals of 1969. He was probably more responsible than anyone for bringing together Harold Wilson and Jack Jones, an old acquaintance from Midlands Labour days.

In 1972 he was dismissed by the board. His memory was not what it had been, quite apart from other considerations, such as his tendency to upset members of the staff with his rough verbal ways. He once asked his political correspondent to 'cover' a Labour Party document – to make a brief mention of it, so that he would not have to devote to it a whole paragraph of his diary, which he wrote as 'Crux'. The political correspondent did as he was asked, only to find that 'Crux' had also animadverted on the document. An observer hazarded that this was psychological warfare by Crossman, who was trying to create that mental confusion which interrogators and suchlike are supposed to create.

This was almost certainly unfair. In a sense, no one could have been more straightforward than Crossman. Most of the scrapes in which he found himself, most of the offence that he caused throughout his life, came about not through duplicity or guile but through his habit of blurting out whatever happened to be in his head. And he loved to cause offence, to go to the very limit of what was socially acceptable, and often beyond it. He was once dining with Douglas and Peggy Jay. Their son Peter was doing his national service with the Navy in Cyprus. Crossman said that right was on the Cypriots' side and that they would win in any case: for Crossman hated intellectually what he called the moralistic, legalistic, canting, essentially nonconformist (in the religious sense) approach to foreign affairs. This was fair enough as far as it went, but Crossman proceeded to express the hope that Peter Jay ('that beautiful son of yours', in Crossman's version of the story) would be killed. Mrs Jay ordered him to leave the house. On another occasion he was discussing Northern Ireland with the journalist Peter Jenkins.

'What the Northern Irish need,' Crossman said, 'is a nice, short, clean war.'

'If you believe that,' Jenkins said, 'you are a very wicked man.'

Yet Crossman was not a very wicked man. He liked to appear wicked partly to shock the bourgeoisie, partly because he believed that illusions were dangerous. This belief led him not only to despise the moralistic approach to foreign affairs but also, in domestic politics, to cast doubt on that bundle of attitudes and practices which goes under the general name of the 'rule of law'. Lawyers were a conspiracy of the upper middle classes, courts a sham. He could not understand how an Attorney-General, say, could make a political decision which was not also a party political decision. He went further, saying that an Attorney who did not make party political decisions was not doing his job properly. Certainly when he was Minister of Housing and Local Government in 1964–6, and accordingly responsible for confirming the recommendations of the Boundary Commissioners, he never moved without first consulting the apparatchiks at Transport House about the probable effect of the recommended changes upon the electoral fortunes of the Labour Party. He said that any sensible politician would have behaved likewise and that the Conservatives did the same.

He was tall and heavily built, physically inept and unable either to drive a car or even to light a gas fire. Towards the end of his life his lack of dexterity was aggravated by arthritis, which made writing difficult: from 1970, certainly, most of his work was dictated to a secretary. He found it hard to sleep and awoke at six but possessed abundant energy. He used to smoke forty old-fashioned Players cigarettes a day but virtually relinquished the habit in his fifties when he was wrongly suspected of having lung cancer. Shortly afterwards he underwent a major operation for an ulcerated stomach. The doctors gave him the choice either of having a new, artificial stomach or of living the rest of his life on an illiberal diet. He chose the former and claimed that, owing to his new stomach, he never suffered hangovers. He enjoyed his food and imbibed generous quantities of gin and wine but did not drink whisky or brandy. He never smoked cigars. Towards the end of his life he would occasionally cadge cigarettes, provided they were tipped.

An agnostic, he decided during an illness in the war to conduct an experiment on the existence of God. In the presence of his second wife, Zita, he opened the Bible at random and, without looking, selected a verse with a pin. Crossman said that the verse was utterly meaningless. From this he concluded that God did not exist.

Of his achievements, he was proudest of his *Diaries*. He lived to write the Introduction to the first volume but did not see its publication. His first intention had been to write a contemporary version of Bagehot's *The English Constitution*, using his diaries as sources. He did not abandon this aim: had he lived, he would have tried to accomplish it. But mainly owing to the publication of Harold Nicolson's, 'Chips' Channon's and, in a new edition, Pepys's Diaries – above all, Pepys – he adopted the view that in triviality lay truth. It was erroneous to believe, as Sir Harold Wilson claimed to believe, that if he had lived Crossman would have published the diaries in a briefer and maybe kindlier form.

As a politician, Crossman possessed the gift of surviving set-backs and reverses with unimpaired cheerfulness. Morning sittings of the House were a failure, soon abandoned; reforms of the House of Lords were jettisoned; national superannuation remained unenacted. One half of Crossman talked solemnly about 'policy' and its implementation: the other half simply enjoyed the activity of simultaneously being a politician and an observer of other politicians.

He took great delight in Prescote Manor and his two children. His first wife had borne children by another man. So had his second wife. There were no Crossman products of either union. He concluded that he was, as he put it, 'impotent' – he did not seem to grasp the distinction between sterility and impotence. He explained this, as he thought, disability to his third wife, Anne, before their marriage. Two children, a boy and then a girl, soon arrived. Crossman used to read Victorian novels to them.

He was exuberant but possessed no true sense of humour, except on a childish level. He desired Anthony Crosland's friendship, which Crosland declined to give on the ground that Crossman was a bully. It is profitless to pretend he was not a bully, but there was no malice in him. He could never understand the way in which others bore grudges against him. He could not grasp that one rough session in Crossman's dialectical gymnasium left bruises and strains which, in the sensitive, could last a lifetime. He died of cancer of the liver, though without great pain, in 1974.

Knowing he had a fatal disease, he nevertheless appeared with Sir John Foster in a series of television programmes on the election of February 1974. Like Hazlitt, he said: 'I have had a happy life.'

MICHAEL FOOT

23 July 1913 –

MICHAEL MACKINTOSH FOOT was a journalist, author and politician. In 1980 he became Leader of the Labour Party after defeating Denis Healey in the second ballot. His accession surprised many people, but, though Foot had entered the contest late, and with apparent reluctance, he had for the previous decade held offices at or near the top of the party. In 1970 he was elected to the Parliamentary Committee (the Shadow Cabinet) of the Parliamentary Labour Party, and served successively as Opposition spokesman on Fuel and Power, on House of Commons Affairs and on Europe. In 1974 he entered Harold Wilson's Cabinet as Secretary for Employment; between 1976 and 1979 he was Lord President of the Council and Leader of the House. In 1976 he came second to James Callaghan in the election for the leadership but became deputy leader; he had previously contested the deputy leadership in 1970, 1971 and 1972. From 1972 onwards he was a member of the party's National Executive Committee (as he had previously been from 1948 to 1950). All this does not show what the lawyers call 'a consistent course of conduct', directed in Foot's case towards the leadership of his party but that, in party terms, Foot in 1980 did not suddenly arrive from nowhere.

There was something else that was curious in the accounts of Foot (often by otherwise well-informed commentators) towards the end of his life. For some reason, people thought he was Welsh, or partly Welsh. This error may have derived from his friendship with Aneurin Bevan, or from the fact that he sat as Bevan's successor – the succession, in fact, caused some trouble and ill-feeling in the local constituency party – as Member for Ebbw Vale, or from his distinctive style of oratory, which depended, for its effect, on placing the emphasis on the wrong or unexpected word. In private he could be scornful or dismissive of the Welsh, deploring their national characteristics (if they are characteristics) of indolence, procrastination and nepotism.

In fact he was partly Scottish: the 'Mackintosh' in his name came from his mother. His father was the Rt Hon. Isaac Foot, Liberal MP for Bodmin. Foot was brought up in Plymouth, whose Devonport division he represented between 1945 and 1955 (he was defeated there in 1955 and 1959). However, though he was quite happy to be described as a Plymouth man or a West Countryman, he regarded himself as a Cornishman; family holidays tended to be spent in Cornwall; the Foot family looked West. Isaac Foot was a prosperous solicitor, a bibliophile (a reader rather than a collector, though his collection of books spread to virtually every room in the house), a Methodist lay preacher, a teetotaller and a lover of music, who would make special journeys to London for concerts. He had seven children, who included John, later Lord Foot; Dingle, later Sir Dingle; and Hugh, later Lord Caradon.

Michael was educated at Leighton Park School, Reading, a Quaker school, and at Wadham College, Oxford, where he obtained a second in Philosophy, Politics and Economics and, as a Liberal, was President of the Union. He always retained an affection for Wadham and was proud of his Honorary Fellowship there. After leaving Oxford he worked for a time as a clerk in Liverpool. He came to London and spent a year as a dogsbody on the *New Statesman*, only to be sacked by Kingsley Martin, the editor. He learned something of layout and typography from Allen Hutt of the *Daily Worker*. He then joined *Tribune*, at that time closer to the *New Statesman* in style and layout than it subsequently became. *Tribune* introduced him to Bevan; Bevan introduced him to Lord Beaverbrook. Foot was, as he admitted, a natural hero-worshipper; by his middle twenties he had met the two heroes of his life, Bevan and Beaverbrook, though his father was a semi-hero to him as well.

Foot and Beaverbrook loved each other, though it was more difficult to explain Foot's need for a substitute-father than Beaverbrook's need for a substitute-son. Beaverbrook loved his real son Max too, but seemed to feel guilty because he did not love him more – or because he did not get on with him more easily. Beaverbrook admired Max's dashing qualities, his athleticism, his attractiveness to women, his bravery as a fighter-pilot. But he could not really talk to Max about politics and newspapers. He could talk to Foot about these things. Foot responded because Beaverbrook had around him an aura of excitement.

Another bond, not to be discounted, was that both suffered from asthma. Beaverbrook tended to advance the careers of fellow-sufferers: another example was Robert Pitman of the *Sunday Express*. Indeed, for much of his life Foot suffered quite badly from asthma and its associated skin complaints. Though he was always a nervous man, in his middle years he was tense, looking older than he was, and virtually chain-smoking untipped Players cigarettes. He was cured, or his condition was greatly alleviated, by a car-crash that happened when he was returning to London from Ebbw Vale. He woke up in hospital to the strains of a Methodist hymn remembered from his youth, and thought that he had gone to heaven. In fact the sound came from a band playing in the street below. After the accident Foot gave up smoking cigarettes. He also became rosier and more relaxed; his style of speaking in the Commons changed. Previously he had been inclined to address the House as if it were a *Tribune* rally. 'Michael shouts,' his brother Dingle had said dismissively. In the 1960s Foot began to make more jokes: jokes fill the House, whereas oratory does not, or not always.

Beaverbrook invited his fellow-sufferer to join the *Evening Standard*. The editor was Frank Owen, who had been Liberal MP for Hereford at only twenty-four. Owen had that quality of zest which Foot always admired. It was a *motif* of his writing: he liked making heroes of figures, contemporary or historical, who 'shocked the timid Establishment'. This *galère* comprised, in addition to Bevan, Beaverbrook and Owen, Charles James Fox, Benjamin Disraeli, William Hazlitt and, perhaps even more oddly, Jonathan Swift. (Foot seemed to regard Swift less as a Tory than as a founder-member of the Tribune Group.)

When Owen was called up, Foot replaced him as editor of the *Standard*. Shortly before this, they had co-operated with Peter Howard, then the political columnist of the *Sunday Express*, in writing the extended pamphlet *Guilty Men*, an attack on the politicians who had supported or implemented the policy of appeasement. This project was thought up on the roof of the *Evening Standard*, where Foot and Owen would meet for a chat before opening time in the Two Brewers public house. It created a myth about pre-war British foreign policy which survived both the War and the years immediately following it, and almost certainly contributed to the Labour Party's victory in 1945.

Afterwards Foot would hark back to these war years both in conversation and in his speeches and writings. The attraction of this period was that, as he used to say, Britain came within inches of being turned into a Socialist country. Evelyn Waugh said that both during the conflict and afterwards Britain was a police State, with conscription and forced labour in the mines:

for Waugh, Britain was indeed a Socialist country in this period. Yet Foot's commitment to freedom of speech and writing, and to parliamentary government, was unquestioned. Indeed, Barbara Castle wrote of him that he was really a soft liberal at heart, liable to come up with awkward arguments about the freedom of the individual. The truth was that he was both a liberal and a romantic: the embattled Britain of the early 1940s appealed to his romantic side.

He resigned from the editorship of the *Evening Standard* because he knew that he and Beaverbrook would never agree politically. There followed a period of estrangement, which may have been partly caused by Foot's falling in love with one of Beaverbrook's mistresses, a Jewish-Yugoslav ballet-dancer called Lily Ernst. The friendship was resumed in 1948, when Foot spoke at a dinner for Beaverbrook's seventieth birthday at the Savoy Hotel, quoting Milton on Beelzebub, much to Beaverbrook's gratification. In 1944 Foot went to the *Daily Herald* to write a political column which he maintained until 1964. This was less a political column as developed by Hugh Massingham, Henry Fairlie and others than a weekly polemic, which was understandable enough, for by this time Foot was actively engaged in Labour politics on the Left, what later became known as the Bevanite, side. Thereafter his career fell roughly into three phases: the phase of rebellion against the leadership of the Labour Party in the 1940s and '50s; the phase of 'responsible' opposition in 1963–70, for he was, until the end, prepared to give Harold Wilson the benefit of the doubt; and the phase of ambition of the 1970s and '80s.

In his later years he suffered from trouble with his eyes, and wore a sidepiece on his spectacles. He had never liked reading from a prepared text: when he was a Minister he would in effect say: 'I am sorry, but I now have to read something very boring prepared for me by my civil servants.' When he became Leader of the Labour Party this disinclination, and partial inability, to read from a text led him, from time to time, into imprecision. For though he was a powerful speaker, he tended to be both vague and repetitive. When, in the summer of 1981, he delivered a Grand Remonstrance to Tony Benn, challenging the latter to stand against him for the leadership, people were surprised not so much by its content as by Foot's having taken the trouble to write it all out, to the length of 2,500 words. Like Richard Crossman (a friend of his later years) and Bevan himself, Foot regarded writing and speaking as different activities. He prepared speeches in his head while going on his morning walk with his dog on Hampstead Heath.

He would often walk longer distances. Altogether he was a stronger man than he was commonly supposed to be, both taller and more wiry than his representation by the cartoonists. When he was well into his sixties he would turn out for *Tribune* in the annual cricket match against the *New Statesman*. He was a promising batsman but negligent in the field.

He attributed his sexual liberation as a young man to reading Bertrand Russell. He was attractive to both men and women, in the sense that, having met him, most people liked him and wanted to be in his company. Yet the appearance he gave on television, at any rate in his middle years, when he appeared regularly on the programmes *In the News* and *Free Speech*, was of a bitter and biased man. Later, as leader of the Labour Party, he appeared more benign. But always there was this discrepancy, more pronounced than with most politicians, between the public and the private face. Inside the Labour Party, however, his public face was liked also. People who had never met him referred to him as 'Michael'. His close friends tended to call him 'Mike'.

He was a sociable though shy man, but disliked clubs. 'The whole of Soho is my club,' he used to say, 'just as it was Hazlitt's.' He had a particular fondness for the Gay Hussar restaurant in Greek Street. In conversation he was never aggressive but could be awkward, not knowing quite what to say next. At these moments of awkwardness he would avail himself of phrases such as 'So. What's next?' and slap his leg in a decisive manner. He was without snobbery, but preferred the company of journalists or bookish people to that of more workaday members of his party.

He had a conservative side, deploring, for different reasons, specialist committees of the House of Commons and also attacks on government secrecy by his friends Crossman and Barbara Castle. He deplored specialist committees because he thought they depreciated the Chamber itself. He deplored assaults on Cabinet secrecy, and was none too enthusiastic about the calls for open government and freedom of information, because he thought government business would be more difficult to transact as a result. He had a highly developed sense of honour, of doing, or trying to do, the right thing.

He had a feline side. He said of Anthony Crosland that he had 'a bogus Oxford accent'. He never forgave Cecil King for being responsible for ending his column in the *Daily Herald* after the paper had been taken over by the *Mirror* Group. He tried to persuade journalists to write attacks on King, though on other, and maybe justified, grounds. Towards Hugh Gaitskell he was always uncharitable. There was some reason for this: once, when Foot was on holiday with his wife, Jill Craigie, in Portofino, he happened to be in the same local bar as Hugh and Dora Gaitskell. Gaitskell ignored him; Maurice Bowra, who was with the Gaitskells, detached himself from them to say a few apologetic words to Foot.

He was also kind-hearted. He was once staying with Lord Beaverbrook in the South of France when a complaint to Beaverbrook came through from George Brown (as he then was). The *Sunday Express* had discovered that Brown was being retained as an 'adviser' by the *Daily Mirror*. This was a matter of some political, not to say journalistic, interest. A *Sunday Express* reporter had telephoned Brown, saying: 'We've got the story, George, and we're going to publish* so it's better for you to give us your side of things.' Brown's version of this, in his complaint to Beaverbrook, was: 'If you don't tell us the truth it'll be the worse for you.' Beaverbrook, contrary to his reputation, had a tendency to timidity when confronted by a complaint from a senior politician. He contemplated dismissing the reporter concerned, saying: 'The young man should not have spoken to Mr Brown like that.' Foot interceded on the reporter's behalf, arguing that there were at least two sides to every story, that Beaverbrook had not heard the reporter's version and that he was probably only trying to do his job. The reporter stayed.

Foot's marriage to Jill, a former film producer, later a journalist and author, was happy, though they had no children. He liked women and was an old-fashioned feminist. He was romantic not only in his literary tastes but about the working-class, and wore the badge of the National Union of Mineworkers in his lapel. His favourite holiday resort was Venice.

---

* In fact Beaverbrook instructed that the story be kept out of the *Sunday Express*. A very short, un-bylined news-item appeared in Monday's *Daily Express* instead.

SIR IAN GILMOUR

8 July 1926 –

IAN HEDWORTH JOHN LITTLE GILMOUR was a Conservative politician and an independent journalist who, as editor and proprietor, re-created the *Spectator* between 1954 and 1959. He wrote one of the best books of modern times on the British constitution, *The Body Politic*, and a somewhat less convincing study of Conservative political theory, *Inside Right*.

He was the elder son of Lieutenant-Colonel Sir John Little Gilmour, the second Baronet, and Victoria Laura Cadogan, the daughter of Lord Chelsea. He was descended directly from the earlier Baronets of Craigmillar whose fortunes had been founded by the Scots lawyer Sir John Gilmour, who had advised the Marquess of Montrose. Ian Gilmour succeeded his father in 1977. In 1951 he married Lady Caroline Montagu-Douglas-Scott, the younger daughter of the eighth Duke of Buccleuch; they had four sons and one daughter. He was a rich man whose money came from Meux's brewery.

He was educated at Eton and Balliol College, Oxford, was in the Grenadier Guards from 1944 to 1947 and was called to the Bar by the Inner Temple in 1952, practising briefly in Quintin Hogg's (Lord Hailsham's) chambers. In 1954 he bought the *Spectator* and was its editor until 1959, its proprietor until 1967. Between 1962 and 1974 he was Conservative MP for Norfolk Central; from 1974, owing to redistribution of the Norfolk seat, for Chesham and Amersham. He was Parliamentary Under-Secretary for the Army from 1970 to 1971, Minister of State for Defence Procurement from 1971 to 1972, Minister of State for Defence from 1972 to 1974 and Secretary for Defence in 1974. From 1979 to 1981 he was Lord Privy Seal and, under Lord Carrington's Foreign Secretaryship, the Government's principal spokesman in the House of Commons on foreign affairs. In 1981 he was dismissed for insubordination.

Gilmour was unknown outside his immediate circle until he bought the *Spectator*. It used to be edited by Wilson Harris and conveyed an atmosphere that was elderly, smug and prim. Its chief contributor was Harold

Nicolson, who wrote a column, 'Marginal Comment', much commended for its correct style. Gilmour changed this tone, though not the correctness of style. (The first changes had been made by Walter Taplin, who was briefly editor under the old regime.) Iain Hamilton was first Gilmour's acting and later his deputy editor. In 1959 Brian Inglis became editor. The first, roughly pre-1959 period, introduced to the paper such writers as Anthony Hartley, Henry Fairlie, Bernard Levin, Peter Fleming, John Betjeman, Randolph Churchill, Michael Oakeshott, George Gale, Conor Cruise O'Brien, Richard Rovere, Christopher Hollis, Kingsley Amis, Denis Brogan, Hugh Trevor-Roper and Robert Blake. Inglis brought in such writers as Katharine Whitehorn and Alan Brien.

Gilmour espoused the Arab cause when it was not so popular in progressive circles as it since became. He continued to espouse it in the House of Commons, where his chief ally was Dennis Walters. His pro-Arabism does not seem to have been held for or against him by Mrs Margaret Thatcher when she made him (chiefly on Lord Carrington's recommendation) spokesman on foreign affairs in the Commons. It is possible that she did not even consider the matter.

There is an analogy here with her short-lived appointment of Gilmour in 1975 as Shadow Home Secretary. For he possessed markedly libertarian views on virtually everything in the social area. He and Ronald Bell (a pairing that may surprise some readers) were the only Conservatives to vote for all the libertarian or humanitarian changes – over hanging, homosexuality, abortion and divorce – of the 1964–70 Parliaments.

Indeed, in many respects Gilmour's *Spectator* of the 1950s anticipated the Britain of the 1960s. Under Brian Inglis it attained its highest circulation of almost 50,000, though it must be said, without depreciating either Gilmour's or Inglis's achievement, that these were good times for the political weeklies generally: in 1966, under Paul Johnson's newly-begun editorship, the *New Statesman* reached its highest circulation of 93,000.

Gilmour was a conscientious proprietor. He was particularly energetic at the staff's Christmas party, which was held at the paper's offices in Gower Street. Everybody attended, from switchboard operator to editor. Gilmour, a highly strung man at the best of times, clearly found the jollity which was expected – or which he thought was expected – of him on these occasions something of a trial. He would fortify himself with a half-bottle or so of Teachers whisky during the course of the afternoon. At the party itself he would then noisily but efficiently organise games – bingo or, as he called it, housey-housey, and a particularly appalling game of lying on the floor blindfolded and hitting, or trying to hit, one's opponent with a rolled-up newspaper, calling the while, 'Are you there, Moriarty?' Few if any of those present wished to play these games. Gilmour had presumably learned them in the Army, and considered them appropriate to the *Spectator*'s staff party.

The *Spectator*'s summer party was different. Gilmour established the tradition, maintained to this day, that the *Spectator* gives the best parties in London. The paper had pleasant, Georgian premises (the present offices in Doughty Street are even pleasanter). He did not confine his guests to the famous, the eminent, the successful and those who, for one reason or another, might do the paper a bit of good but invited also interesting, even disreputable people. Above all, he was not mean with his drink. He once observed a waitress serving drinks by means of a measuring cap. Gilmour politely asked her to desist, on the ground that he did not pour drinks in this way for his guests at The Ferry House, Isleworth. The result of Gilmour's intervention was that several people got drunker than they would otherwise have done.

He was easily bored, and became a Conservative MP in 1962 not so much because he wished to exercise political power as because he wanted a change in his life. He had been at something of a loose end ever since relinquishing the editorship of the *Spectator* in 1959. He began work on his excellent study *The Body Politic* partly to occupy his time, partly to leave some solid memorial – for, though never in the least snobbish about or dismissive of journalism as an activity, he tended to emphasise its limitations compared to both politics and book-writing. Partly, also, he began this work to justify himself more generally. He had a desire to prove himself of intellectual worth. He did not flaunt his wealth and seemed uneasy about it.

As an MP he continued as proprietor of the paper. He intervened less but grew more nervous about articles or items which outsiders might attribute, wrongly, to him. Iain Hamilton, more naturally sympathetic to the Conservative Party than Brian Inglis had been, returned to the paper for a second spell as editor.

In 1963 Iain Macleod, with Enoch Powell, refused to join Sir Alec Douglas-Home's Government. Gilmour, an admirer of Macleod, saw the opportunity to do both his political colleague and his paper a good turn by appointing Macleod editor. It is possible that Gilmour had wished to replace Hamilton in any case. Unfortunately the proposal, about which Macleod had rashly talked to some of his Westminster friends, appeared in the *Evening Standard* before Hamilton was due to meet Gilmour to discuss it. Gilmour offered him the deputy editorship under Macleod but Hamilton declined. Attitudes were struck by contributors, angry letters written and lawyers called in, but the fuss soon died, and Hamilton and Gilmour ended on good terms.

Gilmour was unjustly attacked over this episode, which came about through bad luck – or, precisely, through Macleod's indiscretion. It is arguable that he was more open to just criticism for his disposal of the paper in 1967 to Harry Creighton, who had found fortune with his Scottish Machine Tool Corporation. Gilmour was a friend of the Conservative MP, later Minister, Peter Walker. With another Conservative MP, Charles Morrison, they shared an office-cum-flat in Gayfere Street, Westminster. Gilmour placed the sale of the paper in the hands of the then wonder-working concern, Slater, Walker, having formed the view that it would be better for all concerned if he kept out of the way. George Hutchinson, who had been managing director of the *Spectator* since 1964 and was close to Gilmour, assembled a rival consortium that included himself, Nigel Lawson (the editor after Macleod's return to full-time politics in 1965) and David Wills of the tobacco family. But, according to Gilmour, there was never any firm offer: 'the money wasn't there.'

In 1975 Gilmour wanted Edward Heath to be replaced as Conservative leader, but by William Whitelaw rather than by Mrs Margaret Thatcher. However, Mrs Thatcher early took to him. Some politicians attributed her admiration and affection to her supposed liking for toffs; others said she was dazzled by his intellect. Even Gilmour's friends, such as Norman St John-Stevas, thought she overestimated him as a political thinker. One explanation advanced was that she did not read what he wrote or, if she did, failed to understand it. For after 1979 he was fundamentally opposed to the Government's domestic policies. It was not that he thought they had failed to 'work', though he thought that too. He did not like them in the first place. In January 1981 he was saved from dismissal by the intervention of Lord Carrington. In the autumn he was dismissed, and went on to the back benches.

Gilmour was a very tall, very thin man with a handsome face that was long and rectangular. When he laughed he would throw his head back and display most of his teeth. He had a pale, lined complexion. He did not smoke but ate and drank normally, though there were times when his tendency to stomach-trouble made him cautious or abstemious.

He was once a member of the Garrick Club, but resigned as a gesture of solidarity with Malcolm Muggeridge, who had himself resigned following a club row over Muggeridge's observations in America on the Queen. His principal club became White's. He once said to his luncheon companion, not a member of White's: 'This club is full of shits.'

'Why, in that case, are you a member of it?'

'In any institution of which you are a member, there are bound to be more people you don't wish to meet than people you do.'

Despite his easygoing and generous ways, he was tense. He was not a ready man in speech, and was in this respect unsuited to the life of politics. Notwithstanding his liberal opinions, he did not take kindly to contradiction. If challenged on some such statement as 'Scottish devolution is not a problem that will go away,' he would tend to become cross. He insisted that he was a Conservative and not a Whig, a Liberal or a Social Democrat. He had a house in Tuscany, and he and his wife Lady Caroline were friends of Roy Jenkins. On the whole, Gilmour was a force for good.

DENIS HEALEY

30 August 1917 –

DENIS WINSTON HEALEY was a Labour politician, an amateur photographer, a cultivated man – an aesthete – and something of a bully. He was Secretary of State for Defence from 1964 to 1970, Chancellor of the Exchequer from 1974 to 1979 and Deputy Leader of the Labour Party from 1980. He twice unsuccessfully contested the leadership of the party, in 1976 and 1980.

Until he was five he lived in a wooden bungalow on a First World War housing estate facing Shooters Hill in South-East London. His father was then employed as an engineer at Woolwich Arsenal. He moved to Yorkshire when his father was appointed Principal of Keighley Technical College, and lived on a hill on the edge of Ilkley Moor. He won a county scholarship to Bradford Grammar School, nine miles away. To begin with he travelled to school by train. The bigger boys would ill-use the smaller ones by hitting them with the leather window straps. Healey acquired a scar on a knuckle of his right hand by punching one of the bigger boys' heads through the glass of the carriage door. Nevertheless, he was a pacifist at school and resigned from the Officers' Training Corps on that account.

In 1936 he won a classical scholarship to Balliol College, Oxford. In the period between school and university he spent five weeks bicycling through the Low Countries and Germany to see Max Reinhardt's production of *Faust* at Salzburg. By this time he was a Communist. He joined the Communist Party in 1937 and remained a member until the outbreak of war when, before sitting his examinations, he volunteered for the Royal Artillery. After waiting three months to be called up he was sent back to Oxford to complete his degree. He obtained a first in Classical Greats. As Chairman of the University Labour Club (to which he had transferred his allegiance), he organised a series of lectures on Greek Drama and Society. He helped set up the New Oxford Art Society, putting on one of the first surrealist exhibitions in Britain and inviting Anthony Blunt from Cambridge to lecture on Poussin. And he introduced Iris Murdoch, a

lifelong friend, to Samuel Beckett's first novel, *Murphy*. In 1940 he was offered a research fellowship by Merton College – his chief interest was then the philosophy of art – but was unable to take it up because of the war.

Returned to the Army, he ruptured himself on a field training course and after an operation was sent to a depot in Woolwich to await posting. He was dispatched from Woolwich to replace a drunken bombardier as a 'railway checker' at Swindon station. He there acquired a distrust of statistics. He was expected to count the number of servicemen and -women getting off every train, getting on every train and – for some reason – getting off and on again. He would make up the figures. Assailed by conscience, he asked the ticket collector at the barrier to give him the number of those getting off every train. After three weeks, he discovered that the ticket collector made up the figures too. He was duly commissioned in the Royal Engineers in Movement Control.

He then volunteered for Combined Operations, and served with the Americans in the North African landing at Arzeu, with the British Beach Group for the landing in Sicily, and as Military Landing Officer for the landings in South Italy and Anzio. He first met Anthony Crosland in Sicily. In Naples he made a lifelong friend of his colonel, Jack Donaldson, subsequently Lord Donaldson and Minister for the Arts in James Callaghan's Government. With Donaldson, he set up a music society for the British Army in Naples, and sought out the first violin of the San Carlo Opera so that the latter could assemble a quartet. He ended as a Major and was mentioned in dispatches.

In 1945 Healey was adopted in his absence as the Labour candidate for the safe Conservative seat of Pudsey and Otley. His brigadier sent him to deliver some documents at the War Office just before the pre-election Labour conference at Blackpool. He spoke in uniform, and created something of a stir with a leftist speech. Harold Laski, Philip Noel-Baker and Hugh Dalton (a patron of Healey's, as he was of Crosland's) each urged him separately to apply for the post of International Secretary at Transport House.

The army wanted him to join a small team of officers with academic backgrounds to write the official history of the Italian campaign. This would have involved living in Austria. Healey wanted to return to England to rejoin his fiancée Edna Edmunds, a girl from a working-class background in Gloucestershire whom he had known since their Oxford days.

He could have taken up the Merton Fellowship, but had formed the view about himself that he thought well only under stress and would be likely to go to seed if he spent his life in a university. Accordingly he married Edna and became International Secretary.

In this post he was close to both Clement Attlee and Ernest Bevin, and agreed with most of the latter's views on foreign policy. But he hesitated long before deciding to become a Labour MP. Despite his robust manner, which was to become accentuated – almost a parody of itself – in his later years, he was a vulnerable man, who feared that politics was a 'dirty business'. Having sat for South-East Leeds from 1952, and for East Leeds from 1955, he came to the conclusion that politics was no different from most other trades or professions.

But he was always a somewhat lonely politician. He explained this by saying that 'my sense of the damage done to the Labour Party by the personal cliques which surrounded so many of the Ministers in the Attlee Government is one reason I have always steered clear of cliques myself.' Indeed he seemed more at ease in the company of foreign than of British politicians. He appeared more relaxed at the Königswinter Anglo-German conference than in the House of Commons or at the Labour Party's own conference. When out of office, he would try to visit the United States once a year, financing himself by lecturing at universities and foreign affair clubs. Outside the United States, most of his overseas political friends came from Germany. He first met Willy Brandt just after the war when the latter returned from exile in Norway to Berlin. And he wrote a weekly column (in English) for the Norwegian Labour paper *Arbeiderbladet*, Brandt writing a similar column from Berlin. Healey's contributions ceased in 1964, when he became Secretary of State for Defence.

No politician since Anthony Eden schooled himself more consciously than Healey for eventual occupation of the Foreign Office. He saw himself as having a mission to educate the Labour Party in the realities of national and international power. He believed that the control of force was the most serious of all political problems. He was unlucky that he was not given his opportunity earlier. But he did not always show political decisiveness in the Departments he occupied. At Defence the abandonment of the 'East of Suez' policy, which had been nurtured both by him and by the Prime Minister, Sir Harold Wilson, seemed to be forced upon him by economic circumstances. At the Treasury, his policy was changed in 1976 by the demands of the International Monetary Fund.

Neither period of office added to his popularity in the Labour Party, for Labour Ministers of Defence are never highly regarded in their own party, and Labour Chancellors rarely so. From 1979 the adverse criticism came more from his old admirers on the right of the party. They complained that he refused to speak his mind forcefully or indeed at all. And they made another complaint. What, they would ask, does Denis Healey really stand for, when you come down to it? The answer was that he stood for something that can be called Labourism. He believed in the Labour Party. Though he was himself one of the most intellectual of men, he was prone to dismiss theoretical speculation as airy-fairy nonsense.

Despite his apoplectic complexion, he enjoyed excellent health: both parents were long-lived. He had a huge capacity both for work and for food and drink. He did not smoke. One of his favourite questions was: 'Do you have sexual fantasies when you smoke cigars?' At restaurants he liked to try his French, Italian or, less frequently, German on the waiter or proprietor. As a linguist, he was the superior of the great majority of British politicians. He relaxed by taking photographs, reading detective stories, playing the piano or listening to gramophone records. He would often nip into Victoria Station to view the bargain records on the bookstall there.

If James Callaghan had resigned as leader of the Labour Party immediately after losing the general election of 1979, Healey would probably have succeeded him. Callaghan did not try deliberately to block his chances – to do what Attlee did to Morrison – but simply procrastinated, as Healey himself did for two years afterwards. He had one of the most powerful minds in British politics yet was a surprisingly inept party politician. But he never believed that politics was the whole of life.

PHILIP HOPE-WALLACE

6 November 1911 – 3 September 1979

PHILIP ADRIAN HOPE-WALLACE was a great critical journalist who wrote chiefly for the *Manchester Guardian*, later the *Guardian* (a transformation he did not much care for). His father, Charles Hope-Wallace, was a Charity Commissioner with musical and artistic interests. His mother, Mabel Chaplin, had the same interests. For a time Philip Hope-Wallace, through the Hope connection, was heir to the Marquess of Linlithgow, but some accident of birth or death supervened. His mother was partly Jewish. The Jewish strain was important to him. It accounted, so he used to say, for his melancholic streak, which became more pronounced towards the end of his life. It also partly accounted for his talent. He did not claim this openly, but clearly felt it, for when some artistic performer or professional acquaintance was being discussed, he would often say: 'Extraordinarily gifted. Must be Jewish blood there, I suspect.'

He was brought up with his sister Jacqueline (later a distinguished civil servant) in Wimbledon in a large house as one of the old professional English upper middle class – a category in which he firmly 'placed' himself. One of his numerous conversational tricks was to create the impression that he was older than he actually was. Accordingly one felt that he was describing a prosperous household of before 1914, even of the nineteenth century, whereas in fact he was describing his life as a child in the 1920s.

Nostalgia for Wimbledon worked powerfully in him, but while in his written reminiscences he would tend to emphasise the more agreeable aspects of life at that period – the endless summer afternoons, the ladies playing tennis, or 'the tennis' as it was then called, the children's parties with conjurors, and tangerine ices fetched specially from Harrods – in his conversation he would be franker. People smelt, he would say, they all smelt, because they did not bathe often enough, and because the dry cleaning of clothes had not then become common. Gentlemen would change their shirts once a day and their underclothes once a week. The food was appalling because its cooking was entrusted to ignorant servants. Wine was drunk only at Christmas and on other special occasions. Above all, there was the cold.

Indeed, cold – or the problem of keeping warm – exercised Hope-Wallace throughout his life, at home in Wimbledon, at school at Charterhouse, in France, in Germany and, later, when he shared a house in St John's Wood, with his sister and their friend Dame Veronica Wedgwood. He possessed many gifts, but making himself comfortable was not among them. 'Oh dear,' he would lament to his friends when he was in his sixties, 'I had such an awful night. The rain came in again, and I had to fetch a bucket.' Asked why he did not get the roof mended, he would look uncomprehending, muttering something about 'difficulties' and 'expense'. It was the same with suggestions that he might instal central heating. 'It would mean tearing the whole house apart, and I'm too old for that sort of thing, too old. I feel somehow' – this would have been in the 1970s – 'that my life is coming to an end, so it's not really worth the fuss and bother, never mind the expense.'

His memories of childhood and adolescence were dominated not only by cold but also by ill-health. At Charterhouse he had mumps, which left a mark on him. A tall, thin, awkward schoolboy, he was sent first to a heart sanitorium in Germany and then to lodge with a Protestant pastor's family in Rouen. These turned out to be the most important intellectual experiences of his life. Unlike the majority of British journalists, he was not insular in his culture. He knew his Shakespeare, his Dickens and his Bible, particularly the Old Testament (he took a special delight in the more disastrous scriptural episodes, of people being hewn in pieces, turned into pillars of salt or eaten by she-bears); but next to Shakespeare he loved Racine; and he was one of the few critics who had read the whole of Goethe. At Rouen he went to the opera as often as he could and to the Christmas mass in the Roman Catholic cathedral, where, he would later recall, he heard some of the finest French tenors.

At Balliol he read modern languages, which, combined with his earlier continental experiences, left a permanent mark on his style. He always wrote good English. In the circumstances of his trade – dictating from notes at night in a telephone kiosk – he wrote marvellous English. But, even after more leisured composition, he did not write classical English. An absence of verbs. He was, without pedantry or tiresomeness, fascinated by words, their meaning or derivation, but he was bored by grammar and syntax: a gentleman, he seemed to suggest, would know that kind of thing instinctively, without any need for further tedious dispute. This aversion of his to discussion of syntax or grammar was part of a wider aversion, which was to discussion of most abstract questions.

He loved spectacle and performance: Gielgud's Hamlet, Nilsson's Brunnhilde: these were what excited and moved him. And he possessed that rarest of journalistic gifts, the gift of communicating enthusiasm not just from his favourite seat in El Vino's but in print. (This seat, in the back room, was marked on his sixtieth birthday by a small brass plaque in the wall, put up by the management. 'Looks like a coffin plate,' he said. Moreover, his name had been incorrectly inscribed as 'Phillip'. But he was pleased nonetheless, as he was by the other marks of recognition that came his way, such as his CBE in 1977 and the Gerald Barry Award made by Granada Television's *What the Papers Say* programme in 1976.)

Both his wish to communicate enthusiasm and his punctiliousness with words made him angry with the misuse of 'criticism' to imply censure. Whenever possible, he liked to praise: 'Mme Callas never fails to hypnotise her audience. She takes the stage as Rachel must have taken it. Visually she is magnificent. Musically she exerts so much will-power and bends art to her fashioning in such an imperious manner that even if she were to whistle the music ... she would still make us hang upon her every phrase.' Talking of the same singer, he said: 'She sings like a cat and looks like Anthony Lejeune★ – but what an artist!'

In print he could be sharp when the performance seemed to demand some correction on his part. Thus on Pavarotti in 1976: 'He seemed to have put on a lot of personality, if nothing else on this occasion .... A long way to go until he gets into the Gigli or Schipa class.' Or: 'I do like power evenly distributed and capable of real control. In this matter the Greek soprano Elena Suliotis has me worried: her chest notes come out like a paper seller announcing the outbreak of war.'

Sometimes sheer high spirits prevailed: 'Like a trusted old firm of haberdashers *Samson and Delilah* (one can almost see the name on the shopfront) produces yards of high quality stuff.'

These examples belong to the period between 1946 and his death, when he was a professional critic. On coming down from Balliol he returned to France to work as an announcer or 'uncle' for the International Broadcasting Company (Radio Normandie). His stay was brief. He was dis-

---

★ An author and journalist.

missed for grousing about the company into a microphone which he mistakenly thought was not functioning, with the result that his complaints were broadcast.

He then found a job in the public relations department of the Gas, Light and Coke Company:

> I despised the job and when I got the push wasn't a bit surprised. Actually the push was towards Fleet Street.
> 'What's a man like you doing here anyway?'
> 'Only job I could get.'
> 'What do you want to do?'
> 'Write about the theatre.'
> 'Nothing like trying.'
> And this greatest of my benefactors picked up the phone and spoke to a famous newspaper. After a while he put his hand over the mouthpiece and said: 'Do you speak any German?'
> I nodded. I could. It was true.
> 'Well, they want a German play covered tonight: it's been sent over by these new Nazi people in Berlin. The editor is keen but their Mr Charles Morgan says: "Over his dead body".'
> With a heart going like a sledge-hammer I went and collected that pair of first-night tickets, first of many.*

The 'famous newspaper' to which he referred was *The Times*. Charles Morgan, once highly regarded as a novelist, now perhaps unjustly depreciated, was then the paper's dramatic critic. Hope-Wallace had numerous kindnesses from him. For a short period Hope-Wallace continued to work for the Gas Company while writing occasional notices for *The Times*. He then joined the paper full-time. In 1939 he was rejected for active service on medical grounds, and spent the war as an Air Ministry press officer, 'censoring parish magazines', as he put it. His memories of war-time London were less about Dylan Thomas and J. Maclaren-Ross (though he had met them) than about Myra Hess, CEMA and the difficulty of getting hold of copies of *War and Peace*. In 1945 he started to write for the weekly *Time and Tide*, then owned and partly edited by Lady Rhondda. ('*Time and Tide* waits for no man,' he would say, apologetically, for it was not up to his customary standard.)

* *New Statesman*, 2 March 1973.

In 1946 he joined the *Manchester Guardian*, writing from its London office. The next twenty years or so were probably the happiest and most productive of his life. He was not, however, specially attached to the *Guardian*. At any rate he enjoyed grumbling about it. He liked to recall his father's advice: 'Never work for a Liberal, my dear boy. They always give you the sack just before Christmas.' Hope-Wallace was neither sacked nor in danger of being sacked – though he was deprived of his dramatic, as distinct from opera, criticism, not altogether to his regret, for he was out of sympathy with much of the English theatre since the mid-1950s. But he complained about how little he was paid, some £4,500 a year towards the end of his life. The *Guardian*, he used to say, echoing – maybe anticipating – Malcom Muggeridge, destroyed those who worked for it.

At the same time he had a pained affection for the paper. Once he intercepted a female sub-editor ('Why must they always employ young women from New Zealand?') sending down to the printers his review of 'Doris Godunov'. On another occasion he finished dictating a notice: 'The programme had begun with an admirable performance of Elgar's overture "In the South". End (i.e., *finis*).' This appeared as 'Elgar's overture "In Southend"'. Then there was his notice of *La Traviata*: 'The music hall direction was in the capable hands of . . .' And there was his account of *The Merchant of Venice* with Olivier as Skylark. But his own favourite, though not from the *Guardian*, concerned his description of a Tosca as being 'like a tigress robbed of her whelps'. The editor, a feminist (possibly Lady Rhondda), changed 'tigress' to 'tiger'. The printer, on his own initiative, changed 'whelps' into 'whelks'. So Tosca appeared 'like a tiger robbed of his whelks'.

His taste was independent of fashion. As an undergraduate he was asked who the two greatest composers were. He replied Handel and Verdi, whereas the 'correct' answer was Mozart and Schubert. Indeed, Verdi and Handel in music, Dickens in literature, were his test-figures where other people were concerned. Those who found, or claimed they found, them second-rate were, he would say, themselves second-rate. He championed Gounod, Massenet and Donizetti long before they became part of the English repertoire. And he was unembarrassed by his enthusiasms. He was once discussing the prologue to *Pagliacci* on the wireless. 'When I cease being moved by that music', he said, 'I shall know I am dead.' It was the same with places. He preferred Brussels to Vienna, loved French provincial towns, especially in the autumn, and disliked Edinburgh.

His wit depended largely on timing and inflection, and is difficult to recapture in print: 'One of the worst things you can say about anyone is that he was a good broadcaster' – though he sometimes attributed this to Harold Nicolson, himself, like Hope-Wallace, a notable broadcaster. He used to recall that the actress Gladys Cooper had a sister, Doris, also on the stage. When she appeared the audience would whisper: 'That's Doris, she's Gladys Cooper's sister.' The sibyllants produced the effect of hissing. 'Poor girl,' he would say. 'Couldn't stand it any longer, had to leave the stage permanently.' He once sat in front of two Edinburgh ladies at a Festival performance of *Swan Lake*. 'It's very pretty,' one said to the other, 'but don't you think it's a little bit *exaggerated*?' (Most story-tellers, attempting to be Scottish ladies, would have said 'a wee bit'. Hope-Wallace had too good an ear for that.)

He was a big man, well over six feet, heavy, with a splendid Roman head. He drank a great deal. A friend once came across him in a lavatory at Broadcasting House finishing off a quarter-bottle of Gordon's gin. Though a good broadcaster, he was a nervous one. 'When you reach my age,' he said, 'you will be doing the same.' His habit was to get up early – he was a poor sleeper – and, if it was light, go for a walk in Regent's Park. He would later go to a pub just north of Holborn which opened at half-past ten. He would then walk down to El Vino's wine bar in Fleet Street, which opened at half-past eleven, where he would drink red burgundy or champagne and talk to his friends until about two. He would eat a substantial but by no means epicurean lunch in Fleet Street, and spend the rest of the afternoon, from half past three or so until five, drinking at one of the afternoon clubs, such as the Wig and Pen Club, Scribes or the City Golf Club (which was by St Bride's church, and had no connection with golf). At five El Vino's re-opened; he would stay there until it was time to go to the opera.

He did not smoke, except very occasionally; smoking, he said, made him nervous and on edge. He took no interest in clothes and, whatever the weather, wore a woollen cardigan and a scarf, and carried an umbrella. He also carried a large bundle of newspapers and periodicals.

He was a homosexual who neither flaunted nor apologised for his tastes, but seemed to be saddened by, or stoical about, them. Towards the end of his life he formed a liaison with a House of Commons policeman, but it broke down, and Hope-Wallace developed a rash which persisted for some months. After that he found a younger friend who gave him comfort, though not of the physical variety.

It was with this young man that, against the strong advice of several of his other friends, he enrolled at a health farm. He there fell and broke his hip. There was an operation which was successful orthopaedically but which caused an infection of the liver that turned out to be fatal. The *Guardian* organised a memorial service at St Paul's, Covent Garden. Paul Johnson, in his address (the other was given by Dame Veronica Wedgwood), truly said that Hope-Wallace, without censoriousness, imposed a standard on those in his company – that people behaved better when they were with him.

RICHARD INGRAMS

19 August 1937 –

RICHARD REID INGRAMS was not the first editor of *Private Eye* – that was Christopher Booker – but he edited it from 1963 and was largely responsible for its success. He was the son of Leonard St Clair Ingrams, whom he described as 'a kind of freelance merchant banker,' and Victoria Reid. He had three brothers, two of whom died; one in a car crash and the other in the Andes, while the youngest, a former director of Barings in Riyadh, became a sort of *éminence grise* in Saudi Arabia. Both his parents were members of the Anglo-German Fellowship before the war, but Ingrams denied that they were sympathetic to Hitler or Nazism. During the war he was taken by his mother to Scotland, where he was brought up in his grandmother's house (she was a cousin of the Roman Catholic writer Maurice Baring). His father, a Protestant, and his mother, a Roman Catholic, had agreed that their sons' education should be apportioned equally as far as religion was concerned. Accordingly Ingrams was to be a Protestant.

He was sent to Shrewsbury, where his grandfather had taught. Having arrived there in 1950, he won the top scholarship in the following year: in the same examination Booker was third and Paul Foot fifth. He was usually around the top of his form, sang in the choir, played the cello, became a prefect and edited the school magazine. But, though he obtained a place at Oxford, he failed to win a scholarship. Nor did he get a commission in his pre-university period of national service, which he did as a sergeant in the Education Corps. He went up to University College, Oxford (where Paul Foot also was) to read Classical Greats, but did not take to the philosophical side of the course in particular, devoted most of his time to acting and obtained a third.

At this time his ambition was to be an actor rather than a journalist. Indeed, his first job was in an acting company called 'Tomorrow's Audience' which toured schools, presenting dramatic anthologies. When this enterprise came to an end he joined *Private Eye*, which had already been

inaugurated by Booker and another Shrewsbury contemporary, William Rushton. Booker went off to Scotland for a holiday lasting months rather than weeks, and returned to find a note from Ingrams and Rushton informing him that his services were no longer required. Later he re-established relations with Ingrams and composed some masterly parodies in the *Eye*. (The paper's other notable parodists were Ingrams himself, Barry Fantoni and John Wells.) Rushton increasingly devoted himself to his other – chiefly performing – interests, and Ingrams was left effectively in charge. He was candid later about his having forced Booker out of the editorship: he said he had done so partly because of the length of Booker's holiday and partly because he was 'impossible to work with'.

He was a tall, strongly-built man with good features but a pitted complexion on account of acne. His usual expression was of boyish puzzlement. He often appeared to be trying to keep a straight face. His conversational style was deadpan, perhaps to some extent modelled on that of one of his journalistic heroes, Claud Cockburn: 'Went to see this chap – delightful fellow – thick carpets – beautiful secretaries – telephones in all sorts of colours – clearly an undischarged bankrupt.' He usually wore a corduroy jacket and a pullover which only the hottest weather would persuade him to discard. He used to be a serious drinker, but became ill one weekend in 1967 and was told he would have to give up drink entirely, which he did. He also gave up smoking, having once been a heavy smoker of old-fashioned Players cigarettes.

He lived in a converted cottage, Forge House, at Aldworth in Berkshire with his two children (one of whom was called Fred) and his wife Mary. She was Irish, was fond of horses and quite liked being referred to as 'Lady Gnome', Lord Gnome being the press magnate in whose name Ingrams addressed *Private Eye*'s readers. His recreations were topography and playing cricket, the piano and the organ in his local church. In his *Who's Who* entry he gave his recreation as 'editing *Private Eye*'. When taxed by a friendly critic with affectation, even pseudery, in so doing, he replied that, while getting a piece right on the piano was quite difficult, journalism was really a bit of a laugh.

He was quite happy editing *Private Eye* and put in for the editorship of the *New Statesman* in 1972, as he put in for other editorships over the years, not exactly as a joke but rather to make the point that advertised vacancies were a fraud, because the internal, staff candidate always got the job – as Anthony Howard became editor of the *Statesman*, Peter Preston of the

Guardian and Donald Trelford of the *Observer*. But Malcolm Muggeridge maintained that Ingrams had been serious. Ingrams denied this.

Both he and his paper were sometimes accused of anti-semitism. He denied this charge, though he admitted he was anti-Zionist: he thought the creation of Israel had been a mistake. But he said that *Private Eye* liked to 'go after City stories' (many of them written by Michael Gillard) and, as Ingrams would put it, 'the people at the centre of these stories tend to be Jews'. He would add that he disliked Sir James Goldsmith 'not because he is a Jew but because he is a German'.

His feud with Sir James lasted for years, and reached its apogee when Sir James tried to have him imprisoned for criminal libel after *Private Eye* had wrongly stated that Sir James and his friends had obstructed police inquiries into the disappearance of Lord Lucan. Ingrams had reconciled himself to going to prison, but Sir James was persuaded to desist by Charles Wintour, the former editor of the *Evening Standard* (as Sir Charles Mostyn-Wintour, an occasional butt of the *Eye*). Sir James was at this period keen to acquire the *Daily Express*, and Wintour pointed out to him that his credentials for newspaper proprietorship would appear more impressive if he were not trying to send an editor to prison.

He also disliked homosexuals. His attitude was that they should neither proselytise nor pretend that their way of life was to be emulated or envied. He was against harassing them under the existing law or restoring the former law, but he believed it was their duty to resist their inclinations to the best of their ability. This harsh attitude partly accounted for his friendship with Sir John Junor, the editor of the *Sunday Express*, whose views were similar. What, Ingrams was once asked, would he do if one of his nearest and dearest turned out to be a homosexual? 'I should try to dissuade him,' he said.

However, he was somewhat disapproving of sexual activity generally. One of his friends once said: 'I sometimes feel Richard thinks it's wrong even for married people to do it.' *Private Eye*'s phrase was 'Ugandan (sometimes East African) relations (sometimes activities)'. It derived from a party of the early 1970s when a woman journalist emerged from a bedroom after spending some time there with a black, one-legged diplomat who was a refugee from Idi Amin. Asked what she had been doing, she replied: 'Talking about Uganda.' Ingrams claimed he ran his Ugandan stories only when they served a purpose or made a point. However, Clive James once wondered in print how a man who wrote *God's Apology* –

Ingrams's book on the friendship of Malcolm Muggeridge, Hugh Kingsmill and Hesketh Pearson – could also send children 'crying from school' because of what the *Eye* had said about their parents. Ingrams replied that it was not he who made the children cry, but their parents.

Among his favourite writers were William Cobbett, Hilaire Belloc, G. K. Chesterton and J. B. Morton ('Beachcomber'). The greatest contemporary influence on him, Cockburn apart, was Malcolm Muggeridge, whom he would often visit at Robertsbridge. He himself was a good and clear writer, though occasionally careless in his journalism. However, his regard for the language, and his eye for the false and overblown, often misled him. He failed to see that artistic activities other than literature had necessarily to be described by simile or metaphor. Likewise he was impatient of abstraction. He could not see that some subjects were inherently difficult and had to be discussed in abstract language.

He sometimes admitted he was wrong. 'Pseuds' Corner' once carried an extract from Colin Welch's obituary of George Hutchinson, attributing the contribution to Geoffrey Wheatcroft, a friend of Ingrams and an all-purpose *Eye* figure. Wheatcroft had made no such contribution. Moreover, he was a friend of both Welch and the deceased Hutchinson. Wheatcroft made his displeasure known to Ingrams, who duly inserted a straight apology in the paper. Unfortunately most people thought he was playing some arcane joke.

He did not believe in checking stories too closely or often at all. He said that the truth was frequently met with a flat denial and that he possessed an instinct for recognising the truth. This was a large claim but it was often justified. He did have this instinct, as he had one for recognising good and bad people. However, his universe left no room for in-between people. And he could be gulled. Thus the journalist Christopher Hitchens once claimed as a joke that he was a member of White's Club. The *Eye* duly 'revealed' that Hitchens could be observed in White's, ostentatiously perusing *Tribune* and the *New Statesman*. Like several of his friends and colleagues – Auberon Waugh, Richard West – he persisted in believing something even when contrary evidence was produced. Once he had got hold of a belief or an attitude, once an idea was planted in his head, it was very difficult to persuade him to let it go, which was at once a strength and a weakness in him.

ROY JENKINS

11 November 1920 –

ROY HARRIS JENKINS was a political biographer and literary reviewer of much ability and the second most successful Minister since 1945 (the first having been Lord Butler). As Minister of Aviation from 1964 to 1965, as Home Secretary from 1965 to 1967 and, perhaps above all, as Chancellor of the Exchequer from 1967 to 1970 he was the only Labour Minister who gave the impression of being, as he in fact was, fully in command of his Department. His second period at the Home Office, from 1974 to 1976, was less distinguished, because he would have liked (as he deserved) to be Foreign Secretary. He was Deputy Leader of the Labour Party from 1970 to 1972, but resigned over the party's support for the referendum on British membership of the Common Market. In 1976 he left Labour politics to become President of the Commission of the European Communities.

He was, in effect, forced out of British politics temporarily by Sir Harold Wilson's successor, James Callaghan. On becoming Prime Minister, the latter informed Jenkins that he had no intention of making him Foreign Secretary in the foreseeable future, but that he would be the 'front runner' (this was Callaghan's phrase) in any dispositions he might make at the Treasury, then occupied by Denis Healey. Jenkins rejected these possibilities both because he had done the Chancellor's job before, and did not wish to do it again, and also because the half-offer of the Treasury did not, in Jenkins's words, 'make sense'. The reversion was thought to belong to Anthony Crosland, then the newly appointed Foreign Secretary, who did not, as matters turned out, live long enough to take up the option. Callaghan told him that, as far as he could see, Jenkins had no future in British politics. He advised him, in his own best interests, to take the Brussels job. (It is only fair to add that this is Jenkins's version of what happened. Another version is that he had wanted to go to Brussels for a long time – and that the job had been firmly arranged by this stage.)

Shortly before this he had fought Callaghan for the leadership of the party (and, as Labour was in power, the Premiership). He was third in the election with 56 votes, the second being Michael Foot; he then withdrew from the contest, to the disappointment of many of his supporters. Three years later, still at Brussels, he gave the Richard Dimbleby memorial lecture on BBC television and in it called for the realignment of British politics. The next year he repeated his call at a luncheon of the parliamentary press gallery. Having returned from Brussels, he formed the new Social Democratic Party with David Owen, William Rodgers and Mrs Shirley Williams. In July 1981 he fought the Warrington by-election as the SDP candidate with Liberal support, and surprised most commentators and all opinion polls by running a close second to Labour and obtaining 42 per cent of the vote. Warrington was rightly hailed as a personal triumph for him. In March 1982 he had an even greater triumph when he won the Hillhead by-election.

He was the only child of Arthur Jenkins and Hattie Harris who, to her regret, was unable to have any more children. Arthur was a miner, an official of the miners' union, Labour Member for Pontypool from 1936 to 1946 and parliamentary private secretary to Clement Attlee. He was in the great (now largely lost) tradition of Welsh self-improvement. His house was full of books, he spoke French and he sometimes took his son with him to union or other Labour conferences in Europe.

When Arthur was sent to prison for three months at the time of the General Strike for alleged incitement to riot, Roy was told by his mother that his father was on union business in Germany. He was not told the true story until he was sixteen. Several later writers on Roy Jenkins, largely English and of the middle class, claimed to detect in this episode firm evidence of Hattie Jenkins's social ambition for her son and of her lack of sympathy with the *mores* of the working class. But most Welsh mothers would have behaved in the same way. In any case, she had been instructed to act as she did by Arthur, who did not wish his son to grow up with hatreds or prejudices.

Hattie was the daughter of a steel works section manager. She became a magistrate and a county councillor. The Jenkinses early removed from their terraced house in Abersychan to a larger, detached house, Greenlands. They had a car and a living-in maid. Though there is no reason to dispute the recollections of contemporaries that Hattie was 'a bit stuck-up' and 'liked to play Lady Bountiful' (the last a typical South Welsh accusation), too much was made, in assessments of Jenkins, both of the detached house and of the maid. Before 1939, domestic service was almost as common an occupation in South Wales as elsewhere. And a detached house would have seemed natural and desirable for a man in Arthur's position. In any event, many ordinary miners themselves lived in detached houses, built in the late nineteenth or early twentieth century – though this pattern was perhaps more common in the South-West than in the South-East, where the Jenkinses lived.

Roy attended Abersychan County (later Grammar) School, where he played as a wing at rugby, showed promise as a leg-break bowler at cricket and appeared more refined than his contemporaries. At seventeen he went for a year to University College, Cardiff, travelling by bus every day between Cardiff and his home.

He then won a place at, rather than a scholarship to, Balliol College, Oxford. The fees were paid by his father. He read Philosophy, Politics and Economics. One of his tutors was Thomas (later Lord) Balogh. Some years afterwards Balogh said: 'All Welshmen are lazy.'

His companion replied: 'Yes, we all know about Nye, Tommy.' (Balogh was by this time one of Aneurin Bevan's entourage.)

Balogh: 'I am not talking about Nye. I am talking about Roy Jenkins.'

As it turned out, Jenkins obtained a first, was Chairman of the University Democratic Socialist Club, and became Secretary and Librarian of the Union, being defeated for the Presidency by James (later Mr Justice) Comyn. But the charge of laziness was to pursue him unfairly throughout his life. At Oxford he knew Healey and Edward Heath, who were at the same college.

He met his wife Jennifer at a Fabian Summer School. She was at Girton College, Cambridge, and was the daughter of Sir Parker Morris, Town Clerk of Westminster, and the inventor of the onerous 'Parker Morris Standards' for dwellings. They married in 1945, and began married life in a flat over a café in Marsham Street, Westminster. Jennifer was a formidably energetic woman, active in good works of the modern kind: the Consumers Association, the Design Council, the Historic Buildings Council. They had three children, two boys and a girl. After Marsham Street, their London home was first at Ladbroke Square and then at Kensington Park Gardens. They also bought an old vicarage at East Hendred, Berkshire, where Jenkins played tennis and indulged his passion for croquet.

He took his degree in 1941, before joining the Army. He was a Captain in the Royal Artillery, and was for a time seconded to the cipher decoding group at Bletchley. At one period, for six months or so, he was posted to a camp where he had little to do. However, the camp possessed a collection of nineteenth-century political biographies. He read these and so acquired his knowledge of what was to become his special subject.

In the 1945 election he unsuccessfully contested Solihull. His father was still Member for Pontypool but died in 1946. Jenkins failed to obtain the Pontypool nomination coming second to Lord (as he later became) Granville-West. Some people attributed his lack of interest in Welsh affairs and general air of not being Welsh to this rejection by his native constituency. But contemporaries at Oxford said that he did not sound Welsh even at this earlier period in his life. One of them remembered him saying that he came from the 'border country', which was true, if only in a sense. Like most Welshmen, he never mastered the standard English pronunciation of 'situation', which came out as *sidooazhun*, or of similar words such as 'devaluation'. (Over his unWelshness, some observers drew a contrast with Bevan. But though Bevan retained his Monmouthshire accent and liked to emphasise his membership of the working class, he neither interested himself in Welsh affairs – which he regarded as a distraction from the serious business of politics – nor spoke Welsh. Moreover, his tastes were as patrician as Jenkins's own.) The main charge made against Jenkins by Labour politicians was not that he was affected, though some said he was, but rather that he was foolish not to exploit his background and parentage to serve his interests in the Labour Party. 'If my father had been a Welsh miner you wouldn't have heard the end of it.'

From 1946 to 1948 he was on the staff of the Industrial and Commercial Finance Corporation. In 1948 he became Labour Member for Southwark Central. The seat was redistributed and in 1950 he was elected for Birmingham Stechford, which he represented for the next twenty-six years. He got on well with his constituency party, though he did not much care for Birmingham. He once said to a fellow-Labour MP for the city, as the train left for London: 'Don't you always feel an enormous sense of relief when you leave this place?' On the back benches he was encouraged by Hugh Gaitskell, though there was later a coolness between them on account of Gaitskell's finally hostile attitude towards British membership of the Common Market. Nor was he notably to the Right in these early days: though he was never a Bevanite (as, for example, Woodrow Wyatt and Desmond Donnelly were), one of his earliest productions was a

Tribune pamphlet entitled *Fair Shares for the Rich*, setting out the case for a capital levy.

On the whole, however, he gave questions of political and economic theory a widish berth, preferring to write history and biography. He produced three notable books in this period: *Mr Balfour's Poodle* (1954), an account of the 1910 Liberal Government's crisis over the Lords; *Sir Charles Dilke: a Victorian Tragedy* (1958), which managed tastefully to combine serious political history with a fairly full description of Dilke's sexual activities; and *Asquith* (1964), which filled a gap until the publication of Stephen Koss's more recent work, but was perhaps unduly partial to its subject.

He saw a good deal of Lady Violet Bonham Carter, Asquith's daughter, when he was writing this last book. (He was already a friend of Lady Violet's son, Mark Bonham Carter, and his wife.) Lady Violet used to address him not as 'Roy', 'Mr Jenkins' or whatever but as 'Mr Roy Jenkins', as in 'Mr Roy Jenkins, I believe I left my book in the other room. Would you be so kind as to fetch it for me?'

He was always a clear and correct writer, often a witty one but rarely an exciting one. However, he possessed a gift for narrative which many full-time historians lacked. The mark of his style was a certain judicious coolness, as in:

> None of [the pre-1916 Liberal leaders apart from Gladstone and Asquith] possessed that combination of long life and persistent ambition which, allied with adequate political talents, is the best recipe for leaving a big imprint on events. Hartington, later 8th Duke of Devonshire, was too easy-going and too little of a party man. He was not without strong views or strong passions, but he rarely exercised them about the most controversial issues of the day. 'The Duke of Devonshire is like myself,' Lord Goschen said on one occasion, 'a moderate man, a *violently* moderate man.' And although politics may be a battle for the centre, a leader needs a little support from the wings before he can start waging it.★

As a back-bencher his outstanding achievement was his sponsorship of the Obscene Publications Act, 1959, which introduced the defence of

---

★'From Gladstone to Asquith' (G. M. Young Memorial Lecture, March 1964), published *History Today*, July 1964, reprinted Roy Jenkins, *Essays and Speeches*, ed Anthony Lester (1967), p. 11.

literary merit into prosecutions for obscene libel. Jenkins was frank that this was a compromise and that he would have preferred a more libertarian approach.

As Home Secretary he was an architect of what was dubbed the permissive society and what he defended as the civilised society: he found parliamentary time for back-benchers' reforms on the law on abortion, on homosexuality and on divorce. He was also criticised for introducing, in the wake of several embarrassing escapes from prisons and a consequential report from Lord Mountbatten, an oppressive regime for certain prisoners. However, he did not go as far as Lord Mountbatten, who had recommended watch-towers, barbed wire, guards with guns, and large dogs.

Mrs Margaret Thatcher considered him the best Chancellor since 1945. Several Labour politicians thought he lost them the 1970 election because he refused to engineer the pre-election boom traditional in the 1950s and 1960s. The Treasury's obsession of the 1960s was not with the rate of inflation but with the balance of payments and its effect on the value of sterling. Jenkins, though an advocate of a more rational international monetary system, shared this obsession. He was helped in his objective of getting Britain in balance by his discovery – which followed some work by a foreign professor – that the Treasury had been doing its sums wrong and that Britain had actually been in balance all, or for a good part of, the time. He revealed this truth in a largely unreported speech in the country. Hardly anyone took any notice, presumably because of the complexity of the subject.

Contrary to his reputation as a *boulevardier*, *flâneur* or man of the *salons*, he was a formidable parliamentary performer. Iain Macleod hated him because as Chancellor he almost always had the better of Macleod in debate. When George Blake, the spy, escaped from his monstrous forty-two years sentence, the Conservative Opposition put down a motion of censure, and Lord Hailsham (then Quintin Hogg for the second time round) made a tremendous show of indignation in moving it. After Jenkins had finished replying, it seemed that the Conservatives had themselves organised Blake's escape to serve their own partisan ends. As a debater, he was a great taker on and off of his glasses, emphasiser of words, swiveller towards his own back benches and demonstrator of outrage.

He was highly competitive. If asked, say, to name three Belgian writers, he would mind if someone else managed to perform the feat before he did. He was equally serious about his favourite ball games, tennis and, even more so, croquet. Otherwise he was physically somewhat inept. Bonham Carter used to say that he could not put some coal on the fire without spilling it. His wife said that he could not peel an apple. In this respect he resembled Richard Crossman.

When writing he aimed to compose 1,200 words a day. He wrote in longhand, with little revision. He was once asked why he did not use a typewriter. 'I find it hurts my fingers,' he replied. In his later years he took up the fashionable activity of jogging, but did not enjoy it much. He smoked expensive but not ostentatiously large Havana cigars, which he bought in drums or bundles of fifty. He was expensively but negligently dressed: his shirt collars turned up, though his shoes were always clean. He was a member of Brooks's Club but used it only if he had a firm appointment. This was typical of his way of life. He liked to have as many things as possible planned in advance. He was precise but not pedantic.

He was famous for his fondness for claret but liked burgundy too. His devotion was more to red wine generally, which (often justifiably) he would eat with fish. He liked simple but good food – roast lamb, fishcakes, shepherd's pie. He had a glass of whisky at six. Sir Harold Wilson used to criticise him for leaving the Treasury at seven, but Jenkins remained unmoved. He said he worked a full day and saw no reason why he should take work home. Though he enjoyed life, he was a shy man. He took a long time to become used to somebody.

He was loyal to his friends. He saw to it that his press adviser, John Harris, was made a life peer as Lord Harris of Greenwich. (Some, though not all, of Jenkins's success with the newspapers was due to Lord Harris's activities.) Though he could be tiresome, he was an outstanding public servant who received insufficient credit on that score.

PAUL JOHNSON

2 November 1928 –

PAUL BEDE JOHNSON was a good popular historian and the outstanding polemical journalist of his day. In the mid-1970s he changed his political allegiance from the Left of the Labour Party (or the Left as represented by such figures as Anerurin Bevan, Mrs Barbara Castle and the earlier Harold Wilson) to the Right of the Conservative Party (as represented by Mrs Margaret Thatcher). He was the son of William Aloysius Johnson, the proprietor of an art school at Lytham St Anne's in Lancashire, where he was brought up.* He was educated at Stonyhurst and at Magdalen College, Oxford, where he obtained a second in History. He did his national service in the Army, served in Gibraltar and, unusually for a conscript, attained the rank of Captain.

From 1952 to 1955 he was an assistant editor of *Réalités* in Paris. In 1955 he joined the editorial staff of the *New Statesman* under Kingsley Martin, who was succeeded as editor by John Freeman. In this period he was also a reporter, chiefly from abroad, for the television programme *This Week*. In 1965 he succeeded Freeman, though, for the first six months, as acting editor. Shortly after he took over, the *Statesman* attained its highest circulation. In 1970 he resigned to make way for Richard Crossman. At this stage he had published four books, including a novel. Thereafter his output increased, both of books and of articles.

He learnt most about journalistic writing from Aylmer Vallance, Martin's unsung assistant on the *Statesman*. As editor he lamented that he did not possess Vallance's gift for instruction. But he was a good editor, one of the best in the paper's history. Beneath his irascible manner – he was red-haired, and Jonathan Miller once said that he looked 'like an explosion in a pubic hair factory' – he was nonetheless a kind man. He never intruded himself on the staff at the *Statesman*, but had a personal concern for anyone in trouble. Unlike his successor, Crossman, he was not

---

* Paul Johnson did not talk much about his parents or his early life.

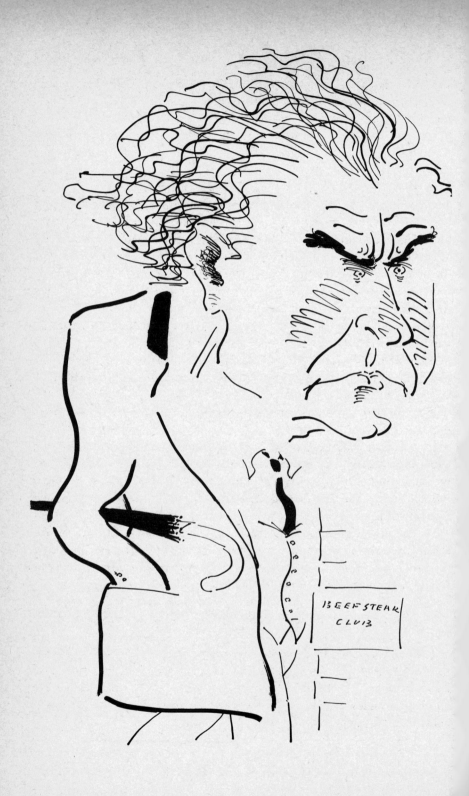

an egotist, not, at any rate, in the editorial sense. He did not see his function as that of (in one of Crossman's favourite phrases) 'imposing my personality on the paper'. He was also loyal to his staff, in that he took the journalists' side in any dispute with the authorities. If any apology or correction had to be made, it was made: but he never recriminated afterwards.

In 1967, however, the paper's circulation began to drop. Johnson attributed this to a loss of faith not only in Sir Harold Wilson's Government but also, more generally, in that self-confident, managerial approach to politics which the *Statesman* had respresented over the years through the Webbs, Shaw, Keynes, Tawney, Laski and Crossman. Johnson had neither the ability nor the wish to change the paper's basic approach. It would remain rational and somewhat superior. He agonised more over whether to continue to give broad support to the Wilson Administration in 1966–70. He decided to do so, though he admitted later than he might have made a mistake. He became particularly exercised to support the Wilson-Castle proposals for trade union reform embodied in *In Place of Strife*, though several members of the staff took a different view, which they were allowed to express in the paper.

'Harold, Barbara and I,' Johnson once said, 'are going to see this through together.'

He was not altogether sorry to leave the editorship, and said shortly after departing that five years was the term he had planned. Certainly he worried constantly, in particular about possible libel actions, he overworked and he had to take two periods away from the office for rest and recuperation.

He had his eccentric side. Indeed, it was difficult to decide whether the eccentricity was assumed, or was part of the real Johnson, or had, even though assumed, nevertheless become part of the man. For example, he would occasionally appear with a walking-stick.

'Why,' he would be asked, 'do you have that stick, Paul?'

'To protect me from the Arabs, of course' (for he was a notable friend of Israel).

It would later turn out that he had ricked his back. He was once, with this stick of his, in El Vino's. This establishment was owned and managed by Christopher Mitchell and his brother David, then a Conservative MP and later a junior Minister. Johnson began to bang his stick on the floor and to glare alarmingly.

'This is an extraordinary place,' he said, as if he were paying his first visit, whereas in fact he had drunk there scores of times. 'D'you know, I'm told that one of the waiters here is a Tory MP.'

He liked simulating outrage. It was his companionable practice to invite friends and colleagues to Sunday lunch at his eighteenth-century brick house at Iver in Buckinghamshire, where his wife Marigold would accomplish prodigies of good and efficient cooking, often feeding ten adults and even more children. On one such occasion the main course consisted of roast beef, yorkshire pudding, roast potatoes, brussels sprouts and courgettes. Johnson began to glare at the dish of courgettes.

'What are those things, Marigold?'

'You know perfectly well what they are, Paul. They're courgettes.'

'Filthy, foreign, Elizabeth David muck. Take them away.'

'But other people may like them. You needn't have any if you don't want to.'

The courgettes stayed where they were, though Johnson continued to excoriate 'foreign muck' under his breath.

He was a great one for generalisations. Once *The Times*, when it was edited by William Rees-Mogg, a West Countryman and, like Johnson himself, a Roman Catholic, produced a leading article that gave some comfort to the South African Government.

'It is a well-known fact,' Johnson said, 'that all West Country Catholics are racially prejudiced. Especially,' he added, 'if they are of Welsh extraction.'

At another time a French referendum was unfavourable to de Gaulle, whose Government, Johnson affected to believe, was not a legitimate or proper Government at all. ('They simply assumed power.')

'It is well-known,' Johnson said, 'that the female population of Alsace-Lorraine are violently opposed to Lesbianism.'

'What's that got to do with it, Paul?'

'Why, I thought everybody knew that Madame de Gaulle was a notorious Lesbian.'

At a Conservative Conference in Brighton during the early 1970s he said: 'Do you know what's wrong with Anthony Barber?'

'No, you tell me what's wrong with him.'

'He simply isn't a gentleman.'

As with his other eccentricities, it was hard to say whether his snobbery was affected or not. Though highly accomplished both as an historian and as a reviewer of historical works, he perhaps showed too great an interest in Lords and Ladies, to say nothing of the Royal Family. A colleague was once discoursing on the Queen's affairs.

'Tell me, Sir,' Johnson inquired, 'are you personally acquainted with the Monarch?'

Moreover, most of his attacks on the Conservatives, in the days before 1975 when he did attack the Conservatives, were on their *parvenu*, lower middle-class or suburban characteristics. Even Lord Carrington (whose family, the Smiths, had, it appeared, entered the peerage after dabbling in trade in the eighteenth century) was as much a target for his strictures as the, according to his standards, more obvious figure of Edward Heath.

He broke with Labour on libertarian grounds, in particular his opposition to the power of the trade unions as exemplified, above all, by the closed shop. Yet, paradoxically, he had never been a notable libertarian. At the *New Statesman* he fitted in well enough because he was a bit like Beatrice Webb. He was snobbish, he believed in an *élite*, he thought he knew what was good for people and he had no faith in the working classes. In 1967, on a Wednesday night – press night – Celtic were playing Inter Milan in the European Cup and the *Statesman*'s printing works in High Wycombe came to a virtual halt.

'Those people ought to be shot,' he said.

He considered William Pitt the Younger a great constructive statesman, and Charles James Fox a dissolute wrecker. He was really a Tory paternalist who, for a time, fitted into the Fabian tradition. Though he did not truckle to any politician, he felt the need to have both a party and a leader. To begin with, this need was filled by the Labour Party, Aneurin Bevan and, up to a point, Sir Harold Wilson. Though Johnson's conversion to Conservatism preceded James Callaghan's accession by a year or so, he put the blame for the state of the Labour Party on Callaghan and Michael Foot: he tended to make excuses for Sir Harold, Mrs Castle and Tony Benn. Likewise, he blamed Mrs Margaret Thatcher's colleagues, advisers and civil servants for her failures. He put his trust in princes and was inevitably disappointed.

He had considerable inner resources. His recreations were painting and mountaineering. He was an excellent committee-man (on the Board of The Statesman and Nation Publishing Company, for instance): good-humoured, sensible, quick to take a point and anxious to compromise if at all possible. These characteristics were in apparent contrast both with his occasional behaviour to family and friends and also with his writing, which, though always elegant and correct, seemed to be propelled forward by a terrible anger, resentment and, sometimes, hatred.

He and Marigold had four children. He used to smoke old-fashioned untipped Virginia cigarettes but gave them up, he was more a spirits than a wine man and he was left-handed. He was a member of the Beefsteak Club. He was a gifted journalist who added much to the gaiety of nations, but one was never sure about whether or when he was going to explode.

SIR JOHN JUNOR

15 January 1919 –

JOHN DONALD BROWN JUNOR was a Scottish journalist. He was the editor of the *Sunday Express* from 1954 and also, towards the end of his editorship, a columnist in the same paper, who replaced old John Gordon when the latter died. He was the son of Alexander Junor, once of the Black Isle, Ross and Cromarty, later a steel works manager in Glasgow, where Junor was born. There was the extraordinary story, current at one time in Fleet Street, that he was the illegitimate son of the war-time Liberal leader, Sir Archibald Sinclair: but no evidence was produced for this tale, and it is difficult to see how it came about in the first place.

Junor was educated at Glasgow University, where he read English. During the war he served in the Fleet Air Arm. He was the unsuccessful Liberal candidate for Kincardine and Aberdeen West in 1945, for Edinburgh East in 1948 and for Dundee West in 1951. He fought the last seat with Conservative support and came within 3,306 votes of John Strachey, the Labour candidate. Thereafter, though obsessed by politics, he relinquished political ambition, partly because he fell out with the Liberal Party over the Suez operation, and partly because journalism with Lord Beaverbrook's newspapers offered a more attractive career. This giving up of active politics was, however, a slow process: throughout the 1950s there were rumours that Junor might pop up as a candidate (Conservative or Liberal, who could say?) in some seat or other.

He was a notable 'Cross-bencher' columnist in the *Sunday Express*. His principal sources were Lord Hailsham, Lord Butler and, later, Sir Harold Wilson. Before becoming editor of that paper he was assistant editor of the *Daily Express* and deputy editor of the *Evening Standard*. Both before and after the death of Lord Beaverbrook in 1964, suggestions were made to him that he might return to the *Daily Express*, this time as editor. Several experienced journalists believed that he might have saved the *Daily Express* if he had followed this course. But Junor, though – perhaps because – he ruled the *Sunday Express* despotically, was reluctant to thrust himself forward in the Beaverbrook organisation as a whole. He had his area of personal sovereignty, which he meant to retain. Besides, he used to say, being editor of the *Daily Express* was a taxing existence. With the Sunday paper he could do a day's work and return comparatively untroubled to his farmhouse near Dorking. With the *Daily Express* he would be expected to be doing the job for twenty-four hours a day.

This is not to say that Junor was indolent. On the contrary: he worked from ten till six, four days a week, with two hours off for lunch, and from ten till midnight on Saturdays. He was equally exigent with his staff. Indeed, he was about the only editor in Fleet Street to insist on rigorous time-keeping by quite senior members of his editorial staff, unless they could produce some plausible excuse to explain their absence, such as that they were going about their tasks in the House of Commons. Some observers explained Junor's severity in regard to office hours by reference to Sir (then the Hon.) Max Aitken's practice of telephoning – in Fleet Street argot, 'buzzing' – him at one minute past ten each morning. According to this explanation, Junor saw no reason why his subordinates should not be in the office at ten also.

But this severity was apparent at the other end of the working day as well. The late Tim Carew, a former professional soldier and a holder of the Military Cross, who had been hired by the *Sunday Express* to produce shot-and-shell (or, as a variation, sinking ships) serials, took to leaving the office at half-past five with an underemployed younger colleague for a drink at the Red Lion, commonly known as 'Poppins' because it was in Poppins Court – now demolished by the *Express* organisation. Junor, breaking his own rule because he was entertaining the cartoonist Carl Giles (for whom all rules were broken) at the same pub, caught sight of Carew and his companion. The next day Junor summoned Carew and rebuked him, someone who should have known better, for leading a younger man into bad ways. In fact it had been Carew who, against his own sense of office discipline, had been persuaded into making these innocent-enough expeditions. Moved by the injustice of life, Carew said: 'I've shot better men than you.' Shortly afterwards, Carew left the paper.

Junor possessed a strong sense of the value of money. Though he liked walking from Waterloo Station to Fleet Street, in bad weather he would take the number four bus. On these bus journeys he would often be accompanied by a less energetic colleague – sometimes more than one – who also lived in Surrey. If Junor paid the colleague's fare, he would remember it. 'It's your turn to pay today,' he would say firmly.

He had strong views about extravagance with the company's money and proffered detailed advice, or instructions, to young journalists about the correct way to entertain politicians or other 'contacts' in restaurants. 'First of all,' he would say, 'get hold of the menu before your guest. If there is a Table d'Hôte menu say in decided tones: "I don't know about you, but I'm going for the Table d'Hôte. Of course you have what you like." It is a very brave and unusual guest,' Junor would add, 'who will then go on to the A la Carte. However, if there is no Table d'Hôte menu, as there frequently is not these days, order, to begin with, avocado pear or melon or a bowl of soup. Your guest will not dare to order oysters or smoked salmon. Then go for a main course where the vegetables come with it. If no vegetables come with it, order one vegetable only. Vegetables in restaurants are scandalously over-priced. If you must have vegetables, order only one. There is never any need to order potatoes. Potatoes are fattening. There should be no need to order anything else. Now, wine: the basic rule is to have nothing to do with wine lists or wine waiters. Say in decided tones: "I'll have a bottle of the house, or the carafe, wine." Red or white, as your guest prefers. But never, under any circumstances, order rosé. Only poofs drink rosé.' Poofs, as Junor called them, played a disproportionately large role in his demonology.

But he had his kindly side. A member of the *Sunday Express*'s staff was detected falsifying his claim for expenses. He had defrauded the company for years. His method was simple and beautiful. He would list various items but refrain from adding them up to produce a total. He would have the claim signed by Junor or one of his 'executives'. Having secured the appropriate signature, he would then add a few items of his own, add up the total correctly and proceed to collect a larger sum than he would have collected if he had done the addition in the first place. He was dismissed. Junor, however, went out of his way to find the fraudulent journalist a job with another paper.

A young Scottish journalist, a single man, joined the paper. Having made some inquiries about whether he was properly settled in London, Junor said: 'I hope you're not sending your laundry back to your poor old mother in Aberdeen.' The journalist assured him that he was doing nothing of the kind, that his arrangements for laundry were perfectly satisfactory. Junor remained unconvinced. He had got an idea into his head. Once this had happened, it was difficult to remove the idea. 'It is very wrong to send laundry home to your old mother,' Junor said, warming to his theme. 'You must buy yourself some drip-dry shirts, and wash them yourself. I will get you an advance on expenses to enable you to purchase shirts, so that you do not impose upon your poor old mother.' Whereupon Junor picked up the telephone and instructed the accounts department to advance money to the journalist concerned for the acquisition of drip-dry shirts.

Altogether he was interested in clothes, and how much they cost. He was given to saying things like: 'They have some very good shirts in the sale at Meakers.'

He once noticed a young journalist wearing a pair of buckskin shoes. 'How much did those shoes cost?' he asked. Ten pounds, he was told: this was in 1959. 'Ten pounds?' Junor was, or pretended to be, horrified. 'Here you are, a young man, with a wife, and a little baby, and a mortgage too, I've no doubt, and you're on the NUJ minimum, and you chose to spend ten pounds on a pair of shoes. You're not being fair to your wife or your little baby.' The journalist remained unchastened, but happened to possess several pairs of cheaper shoes, previously purchased. One day he was wearing a pair of these cheaper shoes. 'How much did those shoes cost?' Junor asked. Two pounds, he was told. 'Let me give you a piece of advice,' Junor replied. 'The greatest mistake an ambitious young journalist can make is to buy cheap shoes.'

He had a harsh side. Once, at half-past five on a Friday afternoon, he was discussing Sunday's possible leading articles with a leader-writer. He suddenly buzzed someone on the 'intercom': it was clear that he was speaking to the Foreign Editor. The conversation was audible in his office.

'Have you read Sam White's column in the *Standard*?' Junor asked.

'Not yet, John, I'm afraid.'

'What time is it?'

'I don't follow you, John.'

'I asked you what time it was.'

'Half-past five, John.'

'Your watch agrees with mine, I see. And what position do you hold on this paper?'

'I'm not quite with you, John, I'm sorry.'

'I asked you what position you held on the *Sunday Express*.'

'I'm Foreign Editor.'

'The Foreign Editor of the *Sunday Express*, at half-past five on a Friday afternoon, has not yet read Sam White. May I suggest you read the column to which I refer, which may contain ideas that may interest you or your gifted correspondent in Paris. And, when you have read it, would you be so kind as to give me a buzz.'

It is doubtful whether Junor would have spoken in quite this way if someone else had not been present in his room.

In similar circumstances he would address A. J. P. Taylor, then under contract to provide a certain number of leader-page articles a year, as follows: 'Alan, I want you to begin this piece with the beaches in August 1939. I want the sand and the sunshine and all the nostalgia you can put into it. Think of a popular song, if you can. Don't rush into the piece. Spend a long time on the build-up. And put it on the train so that it reaches me by three this afternoon.'

Junor had various journalistic maxims: 'An ounce of emotion is worth a ton of fact'; 'No one ever destroyed a man by sneering'; 'Always look forward, never back'; 'Everybody is interested in sex and money'; 'When in doubt, turn to the Royal Family'; 'It is not libellous to ask a question' (the last much followed in his column, one of whose favourite lines was: 'I do not know the answer to this, but I think we should be told').

His despotic methods were a protection to younger journalists, or some of them. One might be bullied by Junor, but not by anyone else: 'Around this office there are various people called executives. If they ask you to do something, as they may, never refuse, but simply tell me. I will then tell you whether to do it or not. And if you do do something, and if by chance I don't know about it, just put in a black [a carbon copy] with my secretary. I like to know what's going on.'

One of his 'Cross-bencher' columnists made the mistake of working through Thursday night and producing his column at a quarter to eleven or so on Friday morning. He persisted in this error, which enabled Junor to indulge in bullying. 'This column is piss-poor,' he would say. 'I see no method of salvaging it. You must re-write it completely, and have sandwiches for your lunch in the office.' This columnist's younger successor would write the column on Friday morning instead, finish shortly after one, have a convivial lunch and present the finished piece to Junor at about half-past three. He might grumble ('No one's ever heard of Iain Macleod') but the time was too far gone for major alterations.

Generally, however, he was flattering to his journalists. This did not mean that he would go on to print their contributions. Broadly he had three categories of assessment, 'good', 'very good' and 'brilliant'. 'Good' articles seldom went into the paper; 'brilliant' ones might even be excluded. 'There is only one word to describe your article' Junor once said to a young journalist, 'brilliant. You know, if I were going to use it I wouldn't change a single comma. Unfortunately Alan Taylor has just come up with a piece, completely out of the skies, brilliant too, though not so brilliant as yours, but unfortunately we've got to use it because Taylor is under contract to us to produce a certain number of articles a year.' The last part of this, about Taylor's obligation to produce a certain number of articles, was true; the other part, about Taylor's piece appearing by surprise, out of the blue, was almost certainly untrue, for Taylor never had an idea of his own about *Sunday Express* pieces, being given clear instructions beforehand by Junor (whom, incidentally, Taylor privately described as 'a blockhead').

Junor deserves a footnote in constitutional history. He was the last editor to appear before the Bar of the House of Commons to apologise for breach of privilege – for, precisely, a contempt of the House. It happened early in 1957. The case derived from the imposition of petrol rationing after the Suez operation in 1956. Under the rationing scheme, local or constituency political parties, together with doctors and other categories, were to be given an increased allocation. A *Sunday Express* leader said, not altogether unfairly, that MPs were giving themselves special treatment ('The tanks of the politicians will be brimming over'). Junor comported himself with some dignity at the Bar. Throughout the affair he received no support from Lord Beaverbrook, who was always a coward under frontal attack from the politicians.

Junor fell out with Beaverbrook over support for Harold Macmillan in 1963. Junor was not inclined to give uncritical support. He resigned, and was replaced, for a short time, by the late Derek Marks. Subsequently Arthur Brittenden was the heir apparent. But Macmillan retired and Junor made his peace. Though he had briefly been a tenant of a cottage on Beaverbrook's estate in Cherkley, his general policy was to give the old bugger (as he called him) a wide berth. He preferred to leave the deciphering of Beaverbrook's often incomprehensible instructions to the late Robert Pitman.

Pitman once referred to sexual intercourse in the mornings. This was at a Saturday lunch at the Cheshire Cheese in Fleet Street. Junor said: 'No one has sex in the morning.' He was a dogmatic man and a great journalist. He was married and had two children. Though large and rubicund, he drank in moderation. His hobby was sailing.

SIR OSBERT LANCASTER

4 August 1908 –

OSBERT LANCASTER was famous for creating Maudie, Countess of Littlehampton, together with a supporting cast, who appeared in a pocket cartoon he drew in the *Daily Express* from just before the Second World War to the end of his life. He was also an illustrator of books, a designer of stage-sets, an historian of architecture, an underestimated writer of English prose, a wit, a dandy, a compulsive clubman and, as he freely admitted, a most tremendous snob.

He was born in Elgin Crescent, Notting Hill, then a redoubt of the Edwardian professional classes; during his childhood the family (he was an only child) moved to Sheen Lane, not far from Richmond Park. His father was killed in the First World War in 1916. His mother, to whom he inevitably became closer, was a strong-minded woman with an interest both in art – she had been a pupil of the Victorian painter G. F. Watts – and also in obscure religions. The Lancasters came from King's Lynn. His paternal grandfather was a self-made businessman with one house in Putney and another in Norfolk. His maternal grandfather, a financier, had a somewhat grander house in Dorset. This grandfather (Manger by name) was the descendant of refugees from Marburg.

He was sent to Charterhouse, where he was not at all happy, but where, in the tradition of the school, he was encouraged to develop his talent for drawing and painting. At school he was a friend of Ronald Cartland, who became an MP and was killed in the second world war; Cartland introduced him to the novels of Aldous Huxley. He left school comparatively early ('not under a cloud,' he would emphasise) and spent some months at the Byam Shaw Art School, where he was happier. He was happier still at Lincoln Coilege, Oxford, where he perfunctorily read History and, even more mistakenly, English Literature. His chief interests were the *Cherwell* magazine and acting in the University Dramatic Society. Like others of his generation, he was patronised by Sir (as he later became) Maurice Bowra. He stayed on for a fourth year and scraped a fourth class degree.

His mother's ambition was for him to become a barrister, because at the time of his birth she had been told by a medium (or someone in that line of business) that a glittering legal career lay before her son. Accordingly Lancaster joined the Middle Temple, where he found the Law even less congenial than History or English Literature. 'I acquired a number of incomprehensible volumes on Torts.' Having taken one look at an examination paper on Real Property, he left to see a Marx Brothers film. His legal studies, such as they had been, were interrupted by an attack of coughing up blood; tuberculosis – then a greater scourge than it is today – was suspected; and he was packed off to a sanatorium in Switzerland. On his return to England he joined the Slade School and found his vocation, or part of it.

He married in 1933. His wife Karen (so christened 'because her mother had read one of those awful Scandinavian folk-tales') was the daughter of Sir Austin Harris, a City banker of cautious disposition and some eminence. On the eve of the wedding Lancaster's mother, according to him, advised his bride: 'Now, dear, I want you to promise me that you won't let Osbert be tiresome. I know what those Lancasters are like when given half a chance and I was always very firm with his dear father.'

Lancaster and his young wife lived to begin with in a Victorian flat in West Kensington. He earned a living by reviewing books, designing Christmas cards, posters and suchlike, and painting the occasional still life. He also formed a connection with the *Architectural Review* which came about partly through his mother's long-standing friendship with the mother of the editor (Hubert de Cronin Hastings), and partly through the presence on the staff of John Betjeman, who had become a friend at Oxford. The prevailing tone of the *Review* was determinedly modernist – it proclaimed the gospel according to Le Corbusier, of 'fitness for purpose' and 'international design' – but this tone was varied by both Betjeman and Lancaster. Lancaster wrote a monthly column decorated with drawings, and an occasional feature article. This period saw the publication of two of his best books, *Homes Sweet Homes* and *Pillar to Post*, potted and witty histories with drawings of, respectively, English interior and exterior domestic design.

He also formed his connection with the *Daily Express*. This too came about through his friendship with Betjeman, who had begun a series of articles for the paper purportedly tracing the rise of civilisation from early times, and entitled 'Man into Superman'. Unable to do justice to the earlier period and knowing Lancaster's interest in archaeology, Betjeman suggested that his friend should write the pieces instead. The arrangement worked satisfactorily; in particular, Lancaster got on well with the then Features Editor of the *Express*, John Rayner. One evening after dinner Lancaster mentioned to Rayner how much he admired the small column-width cartoons which appeared in the French papers, and wondered why the English papers had never tried the same kind of thing. Rayner encouraged Lancaster to try his hand at them, and on the first day of 1939 Lancaster began his career as a pocket cartoonist.

The *Express* at that time, it should be remembered, had an aura of glamour and smartness which it was to lose some years before the death of Lord Beaverbrook in 1964; certainly the paper did not recover from Beaverbrook's death. Part of the paper's success lay in its ability to persuade ordinary readers that, even though they might not actually be sharing the lives of the rich, the powerful and the successful, they nevertheless had a seat in the front row of the stalls, so to speak. Lancaster's pocket cartoons were a minor but important ingredient in the recipe.

In 1940 he joined the News Department of the Foreign Office. From 1944 to 1946 he was attached to the British Embassy in Athens. He remained a lover of Greece, which was his favourite country for holidaying in, despite the Greek food. After the war he resumed his career as cartoonist and architectural writer, adding stage design to his accomplishments. One of his happiest productions in this period was *Drayneflete Revealed* (1949), a parody of that kind of local history which was then becoming popular. In his book Lancaster demonstrated his gifts not only as a topographer but also as a literary pasticheur: take, for example, the following attempt at the verse of the eighteenth century:

> Th' enamelled meadows that can scarce contain
> The gentle windings of the limpid Drayne
> Full oft have seen me, wandering at dawn
> As birds awaken and the startled fawn
> Leaps from her mossy bed with easy grace
> On catching sight of my indulgent face.

And so on. (When the late Robert Pitman of the *Sunday Express* was teaching English at the Sloane School, Chelsea – Pitman was a schoolmaster before becoming a journalist – he placed this poem, unattributed, before his pupils, and received several grave expositions on it.)

The comparison with Beerbohm, another Carthusian, is inevitable. Oddly enough, Lancaster, like Beerbohm, possessed German connections – though Lancaster himself had little sympathy with or liking for Germany. Maybe this exotic strain led him to overplay the part of English clubman. His blue eyes bulged and blazed (poached egg-like eyes were a distinguishing feature of Lancaster cartoons). The eyebrows were raised in real or feigned astonishment. The moustache was military in cut. His relative lack of height – the head and torso were those of a taller man – added to his formidable yet somehow comic aspect. He was given to saying things like: 'They blackball like hell at the St James's' (one of his four clubs – the others were Pratt's, the Beefsteak and the Garrick – until it was disbanded and amalgamated with Brooks's). Or, of his Anglicanism: 'I don't mind incense. I'm not keen on birettas. I am prepared to tolerate Reservation.' He described his parish church as 'tremendously high: I fancy the Vicar is slightly overplaying his hand' and categorised his brand of churchmanship as 'high and dry'.

He was fascinated by clothes, both his own and other people's. He had a particular liking for, and knowledge of, military uniforms. He believed that people should dress the part: 'Tycoons should not look like seedy intellectuals, nor left-wing politicians like well-nurtured stockbrokers. The only exceptions I would admit are certain eccentric peers of ancient lineage who are justified by long tradition in shambling about disguised as out-of-work jobbing gardeners.' He had an aversion to shoes with pointed toes, shirts with embroidered monograms and brown suits. He liked dressing-gowns (of which he had several), smoking jackets, hats, carnations, walking-sticks, umbrellas and dinner-parties at which dinner jackets were worn: 'I can't see the point of saying "don't dress, just put on a dark suit". If you are going to change, you might as well do it properly.' He claimed to have inaugurated pink shirts, shirts with collars attached and suits with two buttons instead of three. He described his style of dress as 'trad: I am fascinated by the past but I don't live in it'.

His working routine was to paint in the morning, wearing only a dressing-gown, to lunch at one of his clubs and to arrive at the *Express* in mid-afternoon, where he would scan the latest edition of the *Evening Standard* for likely ideas for his cartoon. Though highly professional as a cartoonist, he had no great regard for editors and newspaper 'executives' generally. His objection to them was that, far from issuing instructions, they had few if any ideas and liked to be told what to do. His work completed, he would retire with a friend or two from the *Express* to the public bar★ of the King and Keys, where he would drink a dry martini on whose correct preparation he had instructed the barman. He was attached to this cocktail. When embarking on a day's sightseeing in Greece or the Greek islands, he would take with him a supply in a thermos flask.

His first wife died in 1964. They had two children, a boy and a girl. For most of his first marriage he lived in an early Victorian house in Henley-on-Thames. He married secondly, in 1967, the journalist Anne Scott-James, and lived, to begin with, more in London: later he and his wife lived in the same village as Richard Ingrams in Berkshire. His passionate interest in social distinctions and their manifestations led some people to identify him as a High Tory or at any rate as an old-fashioned Conservative. In fact he was impatient of politics and politicians; he was, if anything, an old-fashioned Liberal. He 'placed' himself firmly as a member of the pre-1914 metropolitan professional class – a class, he used to say, as extinct as any lost tribe. He wore his learning lightly. He provided not only instruction but pleasure for over forty years.

★ This bar was destroyed when the pub was modernised.

IAIN MACLEOD

11 November 1913 – 20 July 1970

IAIN NORMAN MACLEOD was a Conservative politician who was the party's finest orator since 1945 and who possessed an unusual capacity to inspire young people. It is often asserted that, had he lived, he would have become leader of the Conservative Party, but this is doubtful. On two occasions, in 1963 and 1965, he had been nowhere in the contest – not even seriously considered. Certainly at the time of his death, when Edward Heath was the new Prime Minister, he had reconciled himself to a permanently Butler-like status in the Conservative Party.

He was the son of Norman Macleod, general practitioner, of Skipton, Yorkshire, and Annabel Ross. Both his parents came from the Isle of Lewis. Macleod regarded himself as a Yorkshireman when he was watching cricket – Fred Trueman was one of his heroes – but as a Scotsman for the rest of the time. He was educated at Fettes, where he played cricket and rugby for the second teams, and at Gonville and Caius College, Cambridge, where, though he continued to participate in these sports, he spent most of his time playing bridge and going racing at Newmarket. He took a second in History.

After leaving Cambridge he worked for the playing-card and bank-note manufacturing firm of De la Rue, having been introduced to it through his bridge connections. He did not last long there because of his habit of falling asleep at his desk: he had usually sat up all night, playing cards. The parting was amicable. Thereafter Macleod subsisted as a professional gambler, though he talked about reading for the bar.

In September 1939 he enlisted as a private in the Royal Fusiliers, and was posted to an OCTU. In April 1940 he was commissioned as a second lieutenant in the Duke of Wellington's Regiment. Almost at once he was sent to France. In the retreat to Dunkirk, he was ordered to put up a road block near Neufchâtel. He constructed it out of large logs. A German armoured vehicle crashed through the block and one of them shattered Macleod's leg. This injury was the start of his disabilities.

In January 1941 he married Evelyn (Eve) Blois, daughter of the Reverend Gervase Blois and the Honourable Mrs Blois. Macleod was always quite proud of his wife's comparatively exalted social connection. They had two children, Torquil and Diana. In June 1952, when the children were eight and ten, Eve collapsed with meningitis and polio, and was at first paralysed from the waist down. She recovered the use of one leg and the partial use of the other, but she could not afterwards walk unaided. Though Macleod and she had their ups and downs, they fortified each other partly on account of their similar disabilities. In 1971 she was created Baroness Macleod of Borve, the title Macleod would have taken if he had ended his days, as he expected to do, in the Lords.

In 1943 he was sent to the Staff College at Camberley, where, he later said, he first became ambitious: he realised he could 'take on first-class people' and defeat them. In 1944 he participated in the Allied landings in Normandy. Demobilised, he unsuccessfully contested the Western Isles as a Conservative. He joined the Conservative Research Department through the good offices of a Conservative organiser, Sir (as he later became) William Urton, whom he had met in the Army. Enoch Powell and Reginald Maudling were at Central Office at the same time.

In February 1950 he was elected for Enfield West. Two years later he became Minister of Health after making a parliamentary attack on Aneurin Bevan. He was Minister of Labour from December 1955 to October 1959, Colonial Secretary from October 1959 to October 1961, and both Leader of the House and Chairman of the Conservative Party from October 1961 to October 1963. He then, with Powell, refused to join Sir Alec Douglas-Home's new Cabinet, and was editor of the *Spectator* from December 1963 to December 1965.* He rejoined the Conservative Front Bench in 1964. He was Opposition Spokesman on Steel from 1964 to 1965 and Treasury Affairs from 1965 to the 1970 election. From June 1970 to his death a month later he was Chancellor of the Exchequer.

He had to a remarkable degree the capacity to inspire not so much fear in others as a certain apprehension. Usually the people who felt about him in this way did not know him well or at all. They knew his reputation, in which political cunning and political callousness mingled in roughly equal proportions. Had he not been a champion, a first-class, an international player of bridge? Did he not, now that his bridge-playing days

---

*For information on Macleod's appointment, see 'Sir Ian Gilmour', p. 50 at pp. 52–3.

were over, play chess, but play it against himself rather than against proper flesh-and-blood opponents? Manifestly Macleod was 'after something'. He thought not one but two – or three or four – moves ahead. Clearly he was someone with whom one had to watch one's step, mind one's tongue, not give anything away. So went one conventional estimate of Macleod which persisted until the end of his life.

I first met him in 1955. The then president of the Cambridge Union asked my advice about visiting speakers for a forthcoming debate in which I too was to take part as a preliminary turn. The debate was to be broadcast on the Third Programme. Even so – perhaps because of the austere atmosphere into which our words were to be cast – the president was anxious to obtain the best performers available. Though a professing Tory, he was not, as I remember, greatly interested in politics as they operated from day to day. Who, he demanded to know, were the two best political speakers in Britain? I thought briefly and replied: 'Iain Macleod and Michael Foot.'

Both Macleod and Foot accepted the invitation. At the dinner before the debate I was placed next to Macleod. He turned to me and inquired the subject I was reading. (By which I do not mean that he simply asked the question. He turned the entire upper half of his body. Though the disability which made this and similar manoeuvres necessary became worse as the years went by, it was noticeable even then, in 1955.) I said I was reading Law. The answer seemed to please Macleod. At any rate he did not appear displeased. Nor did he respond with one of those long silences which, as I was later to discover, were a feature of his conversation. Nevertheless his response was startling.

'Ha,' he said, like a Victorian stage villain.

It may have been 'Ah' but, owing to Macleod's high-pitched, strangely bell-like voice, it sounded 'Ha'. 'Are you from Scotland, by any chance?' he went on.

'No, Wales.'

'Pity. If my son were anxious for a political career I should send him to the Scots bar. He could then join either party – doesn't matter which – and, if he were any good at all, become a member of the government straight away. There is always an acute shortage of Scottish law officers.'

This prescription for political success in either party slightly shocked me; and I wondered whether Macleod's critics were not right after all.

I did not see him for another eight years. In 1963 I was writing the

'Cross-bencher' column and acting as political correspondent on the *Sunday Express*. A rumour was current that Sir Winston Churchill would shortly be offered honorary membership of the House of Commons. I telephoned Macleod, who was then Leader of the House. He confirmed that the story of Sir Winston's possible honorary membership of the Commons was in circulation but correctly thought that nothing would come of it. I reminded him that we had met some years previously. He said, whether truthfully or not, that he remembered the occasion well and had greatly enjoyed the debate. I suggested another meeting. He was enthusiastic. We arranged to have lunch.

Later I mentioned casually to my editor, John Junor, that I was shortly to have lunch with Iain Macleod. Junor showed alarm. 'Iain Macleod never does anything without a reason,' he said. 'He's after something.'

If Macleod was indeed 'after something', he successfully concealed his intentions. Presumably he hoped merely to do himself some good, and perhaps the Macmillan government as well. He may have realised by this time that he had made a mistake in not laying a claim to a major department when he left the Colonial Office. He undoubtedly did realise that the posts of party chairman and Leader of the House were hard to mix. But on the whole he was happy enough. He was bitter only about his recent biography of Neville Chamberlain. I said I thought it had been grudgingly and meanly reviewed. Macleod, I am sure, felt the same. He would not have been human if he had not felt so. Throughout the time I knew him, however, he would go out of his way not to appear complaining or self-pitying; and it was so on this occasion. He was bitter not with the reviewers but with himself. 'It was a bad book,' he said. 'I made a great mistake in writing it. It made me no money, and it has done me a lot of harm.'

For the next year we saw each other fairly regularly, every two months or so, usually at lunch. Though Macleod always claimed to be interested in good food and wine, he never seemed to me to be greatly concerned about what he was eating or drinking. His drinking habits were American. He liked large, strong drinks before the meal (gin in the middle of the day, whisky in the evening) and afterwards seemed happy enough to drink water, though it required no effort to persuade him to drink wine instead. But he never fussed about it. There were, however, problems, embarrassments even, connected with his health.

What was one to do about the long silences which punctuated any conversation with him? For no apparent reason he would detach himself, withdraw, and at these moments he would not look preoccupied, still less serene, so much as angry. Numerous Conservatives, especially the party workers whom Macleod met during his period as chairman, found these interludes disconcerting, as well they might.

Their discomfiture was aggravated by Macleod's lack of small talk. It was not that he liked talking about great themes or his deepest convictions. On the contrary, he seemed embarrassed by such conversation, though he was adept – none more so with the possible exception of Lord Hailsham – at larding his conference orations with references to hope, greatness and duty. But in private he was, like most practical politicians, happiest with political shop-talk: who's up or down, in or out, what the opinion polls really mean, Randolph Churchill's latest enormity. Of small talk as usually understood in the Conservative Party, however, he had little. He showed no interest in one's garden, car or children's education. It could I suppose be argued that this indicated something more fundamental than an aversion to small talk: that is, an egotism which dismissed everything outside himself and his political concerns as of no importance. Anyway his lack of small talk made it no easier to know what to do when his silences came down like a fog.

They were caused, as was obvious enough, by intense pain. The course to follow, as I discovered by a process of trial, was either to remain silent too, which Macleod did not seem to mind at all, or else to carry on talking as if nothing had happened. The course not to follow was to say something like: 'Are you sure you're quite all right?' or to send for a glass of water.

For Macleod hated to be reminded of what everyone called his ill-health. In fact the phrase was unapt. He was for practical purposes a semi-cripple. Though he could walk unaided, the simplest operations – going upstairs, entering a car, sitting down at a table – gave him painful and obvious difficulties. When it was clear that one could make his life easier, whether by carrying a bag, opening a door or shifting an inconveniently placed chair, to what extent, if at all, should one do so? I decided to behave as if he were physically normal. I may even have gone too far in this direction and neglected, say, to open doors which in the usual way I would have opened. If this was the case, as it may have been, the fault was probably good. Nigel Fisher, his biographer, told me after his death that there was nothing he disliked more than to have a fuss made of him.

Whether in his physical state he could ever have become Prime Minister is a difficult question. Certainly Roosevelt was more severely handicapped than he; and Kennedy, as Macleod would occasionally point out, suffered greater pain. There seems no doubt that he would have been able to carry out all the ordinary duties of the Prime Minister without undue strain. It does not follow, however, that the Conservative Party would have been prepared to choose or elect a partial cripple as their leader. Of course the public – not just the majority of people but the *Panorama*-watching, *Times*-reading, political commentary-perusing public – had no idea of how lame and shrunken, hunched and bent he really was.

On television he invariably appeared a man at the height of his powers, as in a sense he was. His shoulders, true, may have seemed a trifle high, but nothing out of the ordinary. His inability freely to move his head and body worked to his advantage: the immobility conveyed an impression of directness, sincerity and strength. At the party conference, again, he could make his speech standing behind a long table and thus partly concealed from view. And he was rarely filmed for television while moving about or getting into or out of aeroplanes. Whether this omission was a deliberate one by the producer or higher authority I do not know.

What I am sure of, however, is that writers in the press went out of their way to make light of his troubles. I did so myself. After all, Macleod made light of them as well. On balance I believe the conspiracy of silence, for this is what it was, was justified. But I am not certain. (Similar conspiracies often operate in regard to politicians who drink to excess, which Macleod did not.)

Some amateur psychologists might I suppose urge a connection between Macleod's disability and his enthusiasm for sport. How unsurprising, and yet how sad, that the afflicted should look up to the young, the healthy and the strong! But from my observation of him I am sure that his zest contained nothing of this element. Conflict, competition rather, always excited him: violence, power and physical grace did not. He was almost as interested in horse- and greyhound-racing as in cricket, rugby football and athletics. (Indeed, according to Fisher,* betting at the dogs, together with betting on bridge, used to provide him with part of his income.)

His interest was ... I was about to write 'technical' but it was not really technical either. As in other areas, he never showed much concern with

---

*In conversation. It is not in his biography.

how things were done. Results, winning and losing, were what mattered. And, because of this, sport was additionally attractive, for it allowed him to exercise his exceptional memory. Who won the Derby in 1927? Macleod could tell you; would tell you, given the slightest encouragement. There was a sense in which sport was a vehicle for his own vanity, for a display of his own mental powers.

His approach to politics was in some ways similar. To Macleod the Conservative conference was not an opportunity to test feeling in the constituencies, to renew or refashion alliances, or to meet old friends. It was the occasion when he made his great speech. He was always supremely and usually justifiably confident of his oratorical powers. 'I don't know how I do it,' he would say. 'I suppose it's mainly the voice. Some people can do it; others can't. I can. Just like Nye,' he would usually add.

He had the same confidence about his administrative skills. His view, which he expounded to me several times, was that in any country, certainly in Britain, there was only a small number capable of assuming the highest responsibilities. He generally cited Lord Cudlipp (as he became), Lord Beeching and himself. Specialised knowledge was not necessary. Nor was general education. Nor of course was social position. What counted was 'ability', which remained undefined. Macleod's view was that, as with the elephant, you could recognise it when you saw it.

This confidence about both his administrative and his speaking abilities made him seem attractive rather than arrogant. As far as his political career was concerned, however, the inner certainty worked to his disadvantage. It was not merely that fellow-politicians and, in particular, party workers found him conceited, which they frequently did. More important: Macleod refused to intrigue on his own behalf. In 1963–65, true, a group of Conservatives including Ian Gilmour, Humphry Berkeley, David Howell and David Rogers, his research assistant, tried to build up support for Macleod with a view to his eventually becoming leader of the party. But he always seemed to me more grateful for their friendship and admiration than hopeful of any substantial political advancement as a consequence of their endeavours. By this time, admittedly, hope – of the leadership, that is – had been sadly diminished. But for most of his career Macleod held the belief that talent such as he possessed would find its inevitable and just reward.

The consequence of this belief was not only that Macleod refused to intrigue for himself, which was probably laudable, but that he neglected to keep himself even moderately well-informed, which was certainly regrettable. The *Spectator* article of January 1964, in which he told of the struggle for the Conservative leadership, was a splendid piece of journalism, a classic of its kind. It added a new phrase, 'the magic circle', to the vocabulary of British politics. It told us much about the Conservative Party's operations which we did not previously know. It also told us something about Iain Macleod. The fact, as he admitted, was that for the two crucial weeks before the elevation of Lord Home he had rather less idea of what was happening than most political journalists. If R. A. Butler disqualified himself during the events by his pusillanimity, then so did Iain Macleod by his ignorance.

It was perhaps surprising that Macleod settled down as contentedly as he did as editor of the *Spectator*, though looked at in another way – on the assumption that he realised, deep down, that his chances of the succession were over – it was not really odd at all. At this time, in 1963–64, I was still working for the *Sunday Express*. I tended to see less of Macleod than I had earlier in 1963. But during the spring of 1964 I heard that the then political correspondent of the *Spectator*, David Watt, was about to depart for Washington. I was kindly encouraged by him to apply for his job.

I wrote to Macleod, he replied favourably and, after one friendly meeting, he suggested lunch at White's Club to complete the arrangement. White's was always important to Macleod. It filled much the same function in his life as his occasional weekend visits to Randolph Churchill, which were sometimes prolonged to the Monday or Tuesday. The club, likewise, appealed to his romantic view both of Toryism and of himself. When I arrived there at one o'clock he had a large dry martini in his hand and was seated before a television set which, surprisingly I thought, was situated on the ground floor, virtually in the bar itself. England were playing Australia. Macleod bought me a drink and said somewhat peremptorily: 'I forbid any further conversation until 1.30.' After that, however, he was gruff but friendly enough.

'How soon can you start with us?' he said, almost in a rasp, as if trying to give an imitation of Lord Beaverbrook, or at least of a tough editor, of few words, at any rate spoken ones.

I explained that I was on a three-month contract with the *Sunday Express* and could, if necessary, give in my notice that afternoon.

'You do that at once,' Macleod said decisively.

An editor's relationship with his political correspondent is almost always delicate. Admittedly it varies a good deal. The factors that can affect it include the nature of the paper; the existence (or not, as the case may be) of an overtly 'political' proprietor such as Beaverbrook; the character of the editor and his interest in politics; the character of the political correspondent; not least, the type of column he has been engaged to write. Columnists or even occasional contributors who write under their own names are rarely instructed to take a given 'line'. Editors are prone not so much to issue instructions as to steer writers away from subjects on which their views are considered dangerous or otherwise unsound. Suppose, for example, that a columnist and his paper are in conflict over the Common Market and that he wishes to write an article on the EEC. Don't you think (he may be told) that we've heard quite enough about the boring old Common Market for the time being? After all, we had a leader on it only the other day – last week, wasn't it? Couldn't you do us a strong piece on the Department of Industry instead?

Discussions of this kind never took place with Iain Macleod, in part because whenever possible he avoided discussions on the reasonable ground that they wasted time. When he came to the *Spectator* he abolished the editorial conference. Instead every member of the staff could come and see him whenever he or she chose. There was no need to knock. The editor's room would be open to everyone at all times. However, this was not perhaps such a valuable concession as it may have appeared at first sight, for Macleod's hours of work were from 10 or 10.30, when he arrived in a chauffeur-driven Daimler provided by the finance company of which he was a director, till one, when he departed for lunch. These hours suited my own habits well enough but were less convenient for those other members of the staff who spent the whole day at the office. Nonetheless I wished to see him regularly – weekly at least – because he was, after all, the editor, he knew a great deal about politics and he could tell me of any other articles in the week's issue whose subject matter might overlap my own. Actually the last reason was not very important, for the deputy editor, J. W. M. Thompson, was as well – if not better – apprised of the contents of the paper. But the other reasons for seeing Macleod remained valid. He was never less than wholly courteous.

'Come in, come in,' he would say.

'I was thinking of having a go this week at ...'

'Go right ahead and do it,' Macleod would reply, often before I had told him what I proposed to do.

This admirably illustrated both his quickness of mind and his vaunted speed of decision. Usually he was right about my projected topic; sometimes not. He never turned down an idea flat; and he was always reluctant to embark on what might turn out to be a lengthy discussion. At the beginning of our connection I made the mistake of trying to engage him in such talks during office hours.

'Ha, good to see you,' he would say with apparent enthusiasm. 'What can I do for you?'

'I was just wondering whether we could have a talk.'

At this the editor's expression would become troubled. The eyes would begin to flicker and dart and he would move his head from side to side. A talk could comprise so many things – resignation, family troubles, offers from other papers, difficulties of various kinds. Who could say where such a discussion might end?

'About what, exactly?'

'The state of politics, I suppose.'

My delimitation along these lines would do little to cheer up Macleod. Politics, he seemed to say, was the last subject he wished to discuss with his political correspondent.

'What aspect of politics?'

'Well, you know, your party, and how Alec's doing, and ...'

'Ha, Alec. Alec is a difficult case.'

Sometimes Macleod would add a few words about the difficulty of the case of Sir Alec Douglas-Home, the then Conservative leader; more often not; and we would part with mutual expressions of goodwill which would be renewed when we passed each other on the stairs or in the corridors of 99 Gower Street.

'Carry on the good work,' he would say, or sometimes, with even greater vagueness: 'Splendid, splendid. Nice to see you.'

Macleod, however, was sometimes uneasy about what I wrote. 'Oh dear,' he would occasionally lament on a Wednesday morning, 'must you really say that about Ted? Well, if you must, I suppose you must.'

Strangely, our one real row concerned dinner jackets. In the course of making some fairly obvious contrasts between Labour and Conservative conferences – the Tories had heavy leather baggage or even trunks, whereas the Socialists had battered suitcases, and so forth – I mentioned, in print, that of an evening the Tories lost no opportunity of getting into their dinner jackets. Indeed this was one of the reasons for their possession of such large quantities of luggage. From some cause these light-hearted observations on what Conservatives wore in the evenings infuriated Macleod.

'It simply isn't true,' he said, 'and you know it isn't true. Dinner jackets went out in 1939.'

I was not so much hurt as surprised, both by the vehemence of the response and, more important, by its flat contradiction of what went on at Conservative conferences. For the truth is that Conservatives, when gathered together by the seaside in the autumn, are forever putting on their dinner jackets. Agents' dinners, Young Conservative balls, South-West area receptions, to say nothing of private functions of one kind or another: the list, if not actually endless, often seems so. And at all these events dinner jackets were – are – worn. Why had Macleod failed to perceive this? And, whatever the truth of the matter, why was he so angry about it?

Maybe he thought his party was being traduced. He was always at pains to emphasise the unsnobbish and meritocratic character of the modern Tory Party, often citing his own career as evidence of this laudable condition. (One reason for his anger about the elevation of Sir Alec was that it seemed to cast doubt on this view.) But Macleod, as I have already said, attached considerable weight to his membership of White's and his long weekends with Randolph. In any event he himself certainly possessed a dinner jacket. I had seen him wearing it, and at Conservative conferences moreover. The episode remains mysterious, but it produced no lasting ill-effects as far as relations between Macleod and myself were concerned.

On only one occasion did he evince suspicion of my activities. In the 1965 election for the Conservative leadership he supported Edward Heath, though he was on closer terms with Reginald Maudling. (Macleod had possibly, in his younger days, been even closer to the third candidate, Enoch Powell: but in the period when I knew him the two of them had become somewhat distant from each other. 'Poor old Enoch,' he would say. 'Driven mad by the remorselessness of his own logic.') Like Macleod, I was closer to Maudling than to Heath. In fact I knew Heath hardly at all, a condition which has persisted. Unlike Macleod, however, I both hoped and believed that Maudling would succeed Home.

But I did not write in Maudling's favour, partly because I do not like writing articles of this kind, partly because few in the Conservative Party would have taken much notice anyway (or, if they had, might have voted for Heath) and partly because the Conservatives, in accordance with their practice of concluding unseemly or potentially damaging episodes with the utmost expedition, had allowed very little time for anybody to write anything.

On the afternoon of the result I saw Maudling in the Members' Lobby of the House of Commons. 'That was a turn-up for the book,' he commented in his affable way. He then said he was withdrawing from the contest. I returned to Gower Street with the news. Macleod was, for once, spending the afternoon in the office. He knew the result but not Maudling's plans, or lack of plans. I told him of the withdrawal after this, the first, ballot. Far from commending his political correspondent for zeal, he looked exceedingly angry: 'I hope you haven't been telling Reggie anything of what I've been saying. It could be very damaging,' Macleod added, to leave no misunderstanding on the point.

As Macleod had not said anything to me of any substance about the Conservative election, I was able to assure him with complete sincerity that on this matter I had been silent.

The spurt of suspicion and anger was untypical. The omission to confide in me over the election was, however, characteristic, at any rate of Macleod's dealings with myself. No doubt he was discreet to the point of taciturnity in part because he wished to be able to tell colleagues he had nothing to do with whatever it was his political correspondent had written. Perhaps again he did not want me to feel I was being pointed by him in any particular direction. Not that he was distant exactly. He was uninformative. The principal reason, I believe, was that he saw his period as an editor not as a continuation of politics by other means but as a respite from them.

In these circumstances it was natural for him to take more pleasure in his personal column 'Quoodle' and his articles of wartime and other reminiscence than in the leaders or the rest of the overtly political pieces in the paper. Macleod wrote most of 'Quoodle' in longhand – and sometimes in bed – on Saturday afternoons while watching sport on television. One of his engaging characteristics was to convince himself subsequently that all the items in a 'Quoodle' column had been not only thought of but actually composed by himself. This was a characteristic which he shared with both Kingsley Martin and Richard Crossman. In fact about a quarter or a third of the column (the proportion naturally varied from week to week) was contributed by other members of the staff. As a rough guide it is safe to assume that anything written about art, music, the theatre, the cinema, non-political books or the law, though not of course sport – the blind spot of most editors – was by someone other than Macleod.

Not that Macleod wrote as politicians customarily do. Real writers write in words; most literate people in ready-made blocs of words; and politicians, commonly, in whole prefabricated sentences or sometimes paragraphs. By this test Macleod was very close to being a real writer. Certainly he was a journalist of considerable technical accomplishment, being able to pen short and easily understandable sentences without producing a jerky or staccato effect. And, like most columnists, he had his favourite targets, notably Harold Wilson and Sir Hugh Greene, then director-general of the BBC.

His dislike of Wilson was, as he freely confessed, irrational. He simply did not care for the man. For George Brown he felt affection, for James Callaghan a growing admiration. 'The best man they've got is Jim,' he would sometimes opine, for no very clearly stated reasons. But he made no effort to understand Wilson. Wilson did not reciprocate. At least I never heard him say an unkind word about Macleod. Indeed he regarded Macleod with a wary respect. When he was elected leader of the Labour Party in 1963 he said Macleod would be his most dangerous opponent – that if the Conservatives had any sense they would choose him to lead their party. But Macleod was prone to dislikes of this kind. Another example was Roy Jenkins, who irritated him by his displays of aloofness during post-1967 debates on successive Finance Bills.

Sir Hugh Greene and the BBC were a different case. While Wilson was referred to as 'the little man' (though he was an inch or so taller than Macleod), the BBC became 'Auntie'. For Macleod to use this nickname at this particular time was in a way strange. The satire trade, though not perhaps flourishing, was still being plied with vigour and a certain amount of profit. Macleod claimed to disapprove of the protests which some of his colleagues had made in the earlier, 1961–64 period. Nevertheless he remained convinced that the BBC was dominated by the Left. This was inevitable, he said, because the Left were usually more intelligent and more politically conscious. It was only a result of chance that he was not on the Left.

In addition he had a genuine dislike of both monopoly and what he termed 'the nanny state'. This was paradoxical. For at other times Macleod would declare: 'I am a Tory.' He never, as far as I am aware, described himself as a Liberal who found himself in the Conservative Party for the want of any more comfortable niche. Furthermore, in his political life he was always happiest at those Departments which provided him with ample opportunities for 'action' – the Ministries of Health and Labour and the Colonial Office. He was rarely in practice averse to paternalism, or at any rate to interventionism. At the core of his political thought, nonetheless, there was ambiguity, as perhaps there has to be with any successful politician within the British system. He did, said and wrote many courageous things: but I am sure that by canonising him the young Conservative Left misunderstood his real political nature. Here is an example. Macleod was deploring to me the Conservative Party's growing opposition to comprehensive schools, which was at that time both a cause and a consequence of the hostility towards Sir Edward (later Lord) Boyle, whom Macleod liked. I asked him why he felt so strongly.

'More parents have children who fail the 11-plus than pass it,' Macleod replied. 'It is a matter of simple arithmetic. There are a lot of votes to be got from comprehensives, although even the Labour Party doesn't seem to realise it properly.'

Oddly, I did not and do not think he was being wholly sincere: not so much in his support for comprehensive education, which was honest enough, as in the reason he provided for that support. Once again the romantic, who loved declaiming and had been known to compose poetry – usually concerning Scottish islands, wind-swept moors and similar picturesque subjects – was playing at being the political realist, the cynic even.

When Macleod left the *Spectator* we resumed our old relationship, lunching every few months or so. He had enjoyed his spell there but was, I think, glad to be back in active politics, even the politics of opposition. He was at this time preoccupied with the tax reforms which he intended to carry out as Chancellor. He did not seem greatly interested in wider economic questions. Indeed Macleod was always cavalier about economic theory, regarding it as a branch of knowledge with which any intelligent politician could acquaint himself in a matter of weeks if he chose. His first and only Budget was widely pronounced 'disappointing' on account of its prudence and orthodoxy. I thought this myself at the time, though I was not altogether surprised by his cautious proposals. It may be, however, that if he and not Anthony Barber had been at the Treasury in 1970–74 we should not have reached the conditions of the middle-Seventies. Macleod would have tended to be vivid in speech, more subfusc in action. And, had he lived, he and not Mrs Margaret Thatcher might have succeeded Heath.

Such speculations are, however, profitless not only because they must lead nowhere but also because they do less than justice to the memory of Iain Macleod. He was more than a might-have-been, a politician who failed to climb the last rung – or even the last rung but one, if we except his brief spell at the Treasury. Not only was he the greatest Colonial Secretary since Joseph Chamberlain: more, he added to the gaiety of politics and, for a short time, of weekly journalism. Macleod in his role of realist might not have appreciated the epitaph. He used to say that he was interested only in power, that without power one could accomplish nothing. But the romantic Macleod would have liked the epitaph very well. For there is nothing more romantic, surely, than the man who lives to astonish a generation or two and then dies young or with promise not quite fulfilled?

HUGH MASSINGHAM

11 February 1905 – 26 December 1971

HUGH MASSINGHAM, the founder of the modern political column, was never a public figure. He did not participate as a 'political expert' or 'talking head' in radio or television broadcasts: partly because such programmes were in the 1940s and 1950s few and far between, partly because he had a stammer (though others have of course turned this and other oddities of speech to their advantage) but mainly because he regarded himself as a private person. His name was not printed even over the political column he wrote for the *Observer* between the end of the war and 1961. He was 'Our Political Correspondent'. But though Massingham wrote mainly as 'Our Political Correspondent' he had, as he explained in an article he wrote in 1963, a personal and immediately recognisable style:

> When I came back from the war and was asked to be a political correspondent – a job I did not want – political journalism had reached about its lowest ebb. The writing was undistinguished. Political correspondents were hardly more than valets, rightly despised by their ministerial masters: day by day, and week by week, they took down the insipid views that were given them from on high. The idea that a political correspondent should have an honoured place in the community, that he should be independent, that he should defy the gods if need be – in addition, that he should sharpen his pen and model himself on Swift – had seldom occurred to anybody. There were exceptions, of course, but on the whole political commentators when I came back to civilian life were a poor lot. Certainly nobody treated them very seriously. It seemed to me that to be a valet was not the ideal job for a person who thought of himself more seriously then than he does now. I therefore set out to write something quite different. Some people have said that I created a new formula. In fact I went back to something as old as journalism. I went back to my father, one of the most powerful political commentators of all time [H. W. Massingham, editor of the

Nation 1907–1923], and through him to the irreverent, laughing, sardonic denizens of Grub Street. This attitude naturally aroused the ire of the professionals on the Right and the Left of the House. To have a view of one's own, to treat them as if they were not sacred cows – what blasphemy!*

As a general statement of what Hugh Massingham did for political journalism – and, as we shall see, he did a great deal – this passage is true enough. Nevertheless it needs some qualification and expansion. For a start, the end of the last war is scarcely a suitable time at which to slice a section of British political journalism and examine it under the microscope. There was a shortage both of newsprint and of newspapermen, many of whom were serving in the forces. There was a censorship both imposed and, more important, self-imposed. If we are trying to assess Massingham's influence it is more useful to look at the period immediately before the war. It is probably correct that at this time the lobby organisation of political correspondents was at its most influential. And in a way it was to this that Massingham objected; this which he had in mind when he wrote of 'valets' and 'ministerial masters'.

'In a way' because Massingham did not object to the lobby organisation as such. He was not in any event a particularly assiduous attender anywhere at the Palace of Westminster. He preferred to do his work in restaurants, at his home in Vincent Square (where he had R. H. S. Crossman as a neighbour) or, more rarely, at the *Observer*'s office. Yet Massingham never broke lobby rules. Or rather, he did not break that rule to which lobby correspondents tend to attach the greatest importance. He did not reveal sources or quote politicians when he was not meant to quote them. He did not, in other words, see himself as someone who was out to break the system.

Indeed the system – at any rate as far as the non-attribution rule is concerned – is not peculiar to political journalism but general. It depends upon the common principle of human intercourse: 'I'll tell you what's going on if you promise to keep my name out of it.' Quite often, in fact, the principle works against the interests and also the desires of the politician concerned. He wants nothing more than to be mentioned, to be quoted, to have views of some description attributed to him. 'You can quote me on that, old boy,' he will say hopefully. Alas, he rarely is quoted partly because

---

* Hugh Massingham, 'Journalists and Politicians', *Aspect*, February 1963, pp. 12–13.

what he has said may not be striking, original or even moderately sensible, but partly because lobby journalists have grown into the habit of never quoting anybody.

The change that Massingham introduced was not of reporting convention or technique but of manner, tone, style. He refused to accept politicians at their own valuation. And the vehicle he used was the political column, quite short, of 800 words or so, and undivided into sections or items. He employed the normal lobby correspondent's argot, though even here elegance kept breaking through:

> It is difficult enough, as ministers have been sharply reminded in the last few weeks, to work out a detailed plan for a year ahead ... The question is whether these methods will get the active cooperation of the rank-and-file of workers. Have they not been tried already? Would the Government, in fact, succeed along these lines even if it were able to give a guarantee of the Promised Land, sparkling with neon lights, crawling with charabancs, in four years from now? It is very doubtful. For nearly two years the Government has been issuing exhortations, edicts, proclamations, appeals, plans, promises and reproofs without any noticeable effect ... The old trade union discipline has broken down, and ... the TUC – distracted and bewildered – no longer dare advocate any changes which might offend some of its sections. Now and again, I understand, one of the bolder spirits has raised the question of a wages policy, and those dread words have had much the same effect as an oath dropped at a meeting of the Elders of the Kirk.*

Truly everything changes, and everything remains the same. For if Massingham was no innovator in the technique of news-gathering, nor was he the first political columnist. He freely acknowledges this in the autobiographical passage quoted above. Yet one wonders not exactly whether he was being over-modest but whether he had read the past entirely right. In the 1930s the best-known columnists were foreign affairs experts – A. J. Cummings, for instance. Even if they were not experts, they devoted most of their time to agonising about foreign policy. Writing in parallel, so to speak, the foreign reporters – Sefton Delmer, F. A. Voigt, Hugh Greene, William Forrest, Vernon Bartlett – were read with an avidity withheld from their successors today.

* *Observer*, 2 March 1947

It is not that the standard of foreign coverage has gone down. If anything, the case is the other way. It is rather that the 1930s were peculiarly obsessed by foreign affairs. Not only was the international situation menacing but the belief existed that Britain could do something about it. And the diplomatic correspondents, like the foreign reporters, had a position if not in society then at least in their own newspapers. Today the relative positions of the diplomatic and political correspondents have been reversed, owing partly to a decline in British power and to a consequential insularity but mainly to the disposition of prime ministers to take over control of foreign affairs – and then to continue to deal with those journalists whom they know, or can manipulate, best.

Massingham himself, moreover, rarely showed indignation, whether about topics of the day or about individual politicians. His work was, on the surface, tolerant, sceptical, civilised, amused. If we are looking for an eighteenth-century parallel it is surely with Addison rather than with Swift. Such a style of writing can, unless handled with judgment and discretion, easily appear flippant, facetious, cynical. Or it can say by implication, as Addison after all said: 'This is the way of the world. Those who wander from it do so at their peril.' From this second fault, if it is a fault, Massingham was wholly free. In this regard the comparison with Addison breaks down. 'Whatever is, is right' was never among his maxims. He was more prone to the first fault – flippancy.

This was perhaps inevitable. There are some readers who demand solemnity on all occasions, especially if their own trade or profession happens to be involved. Journalists are as sensitive as anybody – worse, possibly, than politicians. But politicians are bad enough. It was natural that Massingham should have been accused from time to time of treating weighty matters with less than a due seriousness. But what is surprising is not how often but how seldom this accusation was made, and how much more seldom it was made with any kind of justification. With artistry, Massingham rarely strayed on the wrong side of the line that divides lightness of touch from a mere flippancy. Such discernment, such sureness of taste, is not wholly a matter of technique, craftsmanship, tricks of the trade. Values and beliefs also enter into the business.

Massingham's convictions were never obtrusive but they were nonetheless strong. Like all radicals, from Charles James Fox to Aneurin Bevan, Massingham believed in the people. This belief is simpler to recognise than to define. It is easy to caricature and mock it, as Malcolm Muggeridge did, or to attack and denounce it, as do those who say: 'So you'd bring back hanging?' or: 'Then you really think that Enoch Powell ought to be Prime Minister?' Massingham's concern, however, was not so much to ask questions about populism and democracy as to avoid both sentimentality and statistical bloc-thinking.

He was not only the son of H. W. Massingham but the brother of H. J., naturalist and editor of the *Countryman*. He went to Westminster School and started to write as a shipping clerk in Liverpool. He soon gave this up, however, and worked briefly for the *Manchester Guardian*. He then came to London, where he set himself up as an investigator of social conditions, going first to South Wales, then to the East End. The latter expedition produced the sub-Orwellian *I Took Off My Tie* (1936).

A novel he published in 1945, *The Harp and the Oak*, provides us with some useful signposts to Massingham's political attitudes – to his belief in the people, his relish for oddness and eccentricity, the delight he took in the overblown, the theatrical and the fake. But it is worth remarking that none of the various works of fiction he wrote is concerned either with politics in the narrow sense or with broader questions of social policy. He never attempted to write the great political novel. In his books, division bells do not ring imperiously, smooth black cars do not glide between Whitehall and the Queen Anne house in Berkshire, champagne is not sipped at embassy receptions, and the glib and unscrupulous journalist does not climb into bed with the under-secretary's wife. But then again, there is little in the books about the toilers in the field with whom he had such sympathy. We cannot go to his novels and catch that authentic atmosphere compounded of strong tea, dust and sticky labels, scribble, scribble, like Gibbon himself, and the dusk gathering as the canvassers homeward plod their weary way.

Yet, there was no question about it, even as a political journalist he was different. The difference can perhaps best be expressed by saying that he carried with him a whiff of another world, gayer, more gossipy, more malicious even, certainly more frivolous, than that of Fleet Street or Westminster. What was it? Brighton, perhaps, or the theatre or old bohemian London. Not that Massingham was in the least loud, flamboyant or pushful. As a man he was notably shy. Yet his overcoat sometimes had a velvet collar, and he wore his grey hair long and with sideboards well before this became either fashionable or conventional. The photograph on the back cover of the Penguin edition of *The Harp and the Oak* shows a thin, apprehensive and somehow unhappy face. The picture may have been misleading when it was taken. Certainly it did not foretell Massingham in his later years.

He was a big man with a massive head which, because of his height, did not appear disproportionate. He generally seemed to be, not laughing, but smiling to himself. At party conferences or on other occasions when he was out of London he found difficulty with telephones, with the paraphernalia of journalism. Or he said that he did. Often people with a certain amount of charm, and Massingham had a lot of it, will exploit others, at any rate in small matters. Probably with Massingham there was both a real and a pretended helplessness, or a helplessness that had begun as partly assumed and ended as mainly real. James Margach of the *Sunday Times* remembered Massingham's difficulties in communicating with his office from a party conference.

'How do I get in touch with them in London, J-J-Jimmy?' Massingham asked.

'You see that little box over there?' said Margach. 'Well, you go into it, and pick up the receiver, and the girl on the hotel switchboard will ask you what number you want. You tell her, put the receiver down and wait in the box. Then in a few minutes she'll ring you back with the number you want.'

'But, Jimmy, I don't *know* what number I want.'

Yet it would be wrong to conclude that he was inefficient or lacking in perception in the less physical aspects of newspaper work. For instance, David Astor remembered that when the *Sunday Times* began serialising the memoirs of generals and other notabilities Massingham was the first, virtually the only, member of the *Observer*'s staff to perceive the danger to the paper. He maintained that the *Observer* also should be carrying out the same improving work. His advice was not taken. Still, throughout most of this period, from the end of the war until the early Sixties, dealings between Massingham and his editor were harmonious enough, as these always delicate and often difficult relationships go. He would bring in his copy and wait apprehensively for Astor to smile. When the smile appeared, as it usually did at some point, Massingham would sit back, smile too, look benign, relaxed. He considered that part at least of his work was done. Nevertheless there were troubles. One of them concerned expenses:

Lunch is an important occasion in a political commentator's life. It should, no doubt, be a rather pleasant interlude and so it is if one is on the staff of the *Daily Express* or the *Daily Mirror* – opulent newspapers, ruled by journalists who know the facts of life. Unfortunately, I had such a limited expense account that it would hardly have fed a sparrow ... I was mostly paying for everything out of my own pocket.*

What was more serious was that Massingham eventually became not so much disillusioned, for he was never illusioned, as simply bored. We have already noted his disposition to see politics as a form of theatre. Now, in the late 1950s, the exuberant men – Lord Woolton and Hugh Dalton – were gone. Aneurin Bevan had become a respectable figure and was shortly to die. Others who had provided Massingham with much gentle amusement – Clement Attlee, Sir Stafford Cripps and Herbert Morrison prominent among them – were no longer part of the political play. R. A. Butler, true, was still present to provide delight with his crab-like movements and left-handed indiscretions, and for a time Massingham reposed the highest hopes in Lord Hailsham as a comic character almost in the Woolton class. 'There's this extraordinary Hailsham chap that I've discovered,' Massingham would say to Astor with glee. Alas, he was disappointed of his expectations. Hailsham let him down and became almost like any other politician. Things were not the same as in the old days of the Attlee government and the Bevanite revolt and the rows on the National Executive Committee when Dr Edith Summerskill's hat – one of the Massingham stock properties – would bob with a terrible fury and she would find herself quite unable to pronounce the horrid words 'Ian Mikardo', calling him 'that man in the brown suit' instead.

And there was another aspect to Massingham's loss of interest. Astor decided that something different was called for from a weekly essay, however witty, elegantly composed or well-informed. Massingham had never been particularly interested in 'policy'. The idea of painstakingly guiding the readers of the *Observer* through, say, the latest White Paper on housing filled him with not the least enthusiasm. When negotiations to enter the Common Market began in 1961 he was appalled, and who shall blame him? 'I can't possibly write about that sort of thing,' he said to a friend.

There was, however, one striking exception to his lack of zeal for the exposition of detailed policy. This concerned defence. Virtually monthly from 1957 onwards, he devoted his column to the potentially disastrous consequences of Duncan Sandys and his reliance on the nuclear deterrent

---

*Hugh Massingham, art. cit., *Aspect*, February 1962, pp. 11–12.

The hand of George Wigg lay heavy upon these pieces, though owing to Massingham's gifts as a writer the touch was not as ponderous as it might have been. Throughout Massingham's journalistic career, indeed, Wigg was one of his most valuable informants. One can only look back with something approaching awe to the number of rambling expositions, well-laced with sergeants' mess asperities and arcane military simile, which he must have endured over the years. As always with Wigg, however, there was gold in the dross, if one could but find it. Massingham, like other journalists, must have felt as if he were allowing a corporation dust cart to be emptied over his head in the hope, maybe vain, of discovering somewhere in the rubbish a diamond ring. It was strange, to say the least, that he found no mention in Lord Wigg's autobiography.

Above all, however, Massingham was suffering increasingly bad health. In 1961 he left the *Observer* for the *Sunday Telegraph*, then something of a pioneering enterprise. His departure was lamented by many but went unrecorded, as far as I have been able to establish, by the *Observer* itself. When he gave up his column it was as if he had never been or disappeared or become a non-person.

But in 1962–4, while on the *Sunday Telegraph*, he had a wonderful revival, an Indian summer. The Vassall case made the ink flow once again. The Profumo affair was even more to his taste as material for column-writing. Until the succession of Harold Wilson, and some months beyond, he wrote articles on a fairly regular basis which were as amusing and perceptive as anything he had contributed to the *Observer*. The bravura characters, admittedly, were no longer about, though Massingham did his best with George Brown:

> There is no doubt whom the Tories would like. In fact some sharp-eared observers who have recently passed through Smith Square swear that they could hear Mr Iain Macleod and his attending angels deep in prayer and supplication in the chapel that is supposed to exist at the top of the Conservative Central Office, 'O, Lord,' they are reported as chanting, 'we don't ask for much. Just give us George Brown and we'll do the rest.' *

Or again:

> As we know, Mr Brown is a mercurial person. He is now up and now down, now poor, earthy, humble George and now a mighty eagle,

---

* *Sunday Telegraph*, 3 February 1963.

soaring through the heavens and lord of all he surveys. There is also a curious Walter Mitty side to his character. Sometimes he is Mr Florence Nightingale Brown, whose soothing touch has brought comfort to many a fevered brow. Sometimes he is that old salt Admiral of the Fleet Lord Brown of Trafalgar – no Vassall fan is he – whose rough countenance and even rougher ways conceal a most tender and constant heart. The only trouble is that one never knows what part Mr Brown is going to play next.*

In their combination of wit, fantasy, disrespect and fundamental affection these passages are typical of Massingham. But before going on to give some examples of his earlier – and, in the opinion of some critics, better – work, it may be as well to say something of his style considered technically. We have already seen a little of his character, appearance, background, habits and beliefs. All these avail nothing without technical proficiency, without craftsmanship. And Massingham was a superb craftsman. Some of his articles and columns are better than others. He had his ups and downs. So do we all. But he never turned out anything that was shoddy or ill-designed.

On the whole he did not take as his weekly subject a single topic or a solitary point of dispute between the parties. Nor did he 'angle' his articles in any surprising fashion. He would sometimes produce an apparent paradox, such as that the Labour Party (this in the early Sixties) was being transformed into the party of Empire, and that Mrs Barbara Castle might shortly be expected to join lustily in 'Land of Hope and Glory'. Generally he would examine the political situation through a wide lens, looking at it from the point of view, in one week, of the Labour Party and, in the next, of the Conservatives. 'Let us, this quiet Sabbath morning,' he would begin, 'see what all the fuss is about, and try to put the matter into some kind of perspective.'

The advantage of this method is that one is most likely to give satisfaction to the maximum number of readers. People who are interested in politics will read an article on the general political situation, especially if it is amusing, well-informed and laced with character-sketches. They may pass by on the other side if a piece is on a subject in which they feel no interest, or which they consider unapt for the particular week. 'Why,' they

---

*Ibid.

may ask, 'is he writing about the Labour Party's boring policy statement when he should have been writing about the great spy row?'

The disadvantage of the approach is that, though the writer is less likely to make mistakes, to get the timing wrong, a sharpness of focus is lost. Moreover, the method can over the years become monotonous not so much for the reader – readers, like editors, are natural conservatives, and prefer what is familiar – as for the writer. Though Massingham made occasional expeditions into the outfield for by-elections, he rarely varied his pace, length or direction. It was both a strength and a weakness.

He aimed at a careful informality, never pompous but never crude. He eschewed Latinisms, thereby losing in authority and power what he gained in familiarity and ease. He could write in short sentences without ever appearing abrupt. His metaphors and allusions were usually taken from the Bible, from hymns – the simpler the sentiments, the better he was pleased – and from popular sayings, proverbs, turns of phrase. He preferred 'although' to 'though', 'that' to 'which', 'as if' to 'as though'. He sometimes used the colon but almost never the semi-colon. His favourite form of punctuation, the comma and full stop apart, was the dash. He used this both to indicate parenthesis and at the end of a sentence where a comma or a colon might have served instead. His attitude towards language was nicely illustrated by his treatment of the Labour candidate at Hampstead in 1950:

> Mr Hawkins, the Labour candidate, is unlikely to quicken any pulse – poor, solemn, long-winded Mr Hawkins, who can never answer a question in six words when 1,600 will do almost as well, who never says but always states, who never needs but always requires. And Mr Hawkins, God bless and save us all, is a schoolmaster.*

As a chronicler of the troubles of the 1950s he was unequalled, despite – maybe because of – his suspicion of revisionism. His message was usually that the party would somehow muddle through more or less intact. It is hard to choose an example of his work during these years because many of the controversies are forgotten today, and most of the points of detail were no more than that even when they were first raised. So here are Massingham's observations on the resignation of Aneurin Bevan, Harold Wilson and John Freeman in 1951, partly because the similes he used about

---

*Observer, 19 February 1950.

the Labour Party's disposition to quarrel were repeated many times in the following years, and became something of a Massingham trade-mark:

> The effect of all this should be to produce panic and bewilderment throughout the Labour movement, but people forget that the course of true love has never somehow run quite smoothly in the Labour Party. It resembles one of those apache dances where the man looks adoringly into the eyes of the beloved, only to throw her half way across the room. Listening to the fearful cries, noticing the damaged eyes, the vivid splashes of blood, the onlooker is apt to think that the lady would prefer to be at home, quietly knitting. But this is to misunderstand the real meaning of the scene. The lady is used to it. So is the Labour Party, in which the mating season is traditionally ushered in to the merry sound of broken glass.*

Massingham's influence really involves two separate through connected questions: the influence he exerted on his contemporaries and successors in the press; and the influence he, and others like him, exerted on politicians and the public.

If this were about the development of the political column rather than about Hugh Massingham, Henry Fairlie, who wrote in the *Spectator* in the 1950s and in the *Daily Mail* in the 1960s, would occupy almost as much space. For what he did was to introduce into the political column, not so much facts, as ideas and a sense of history. He admired Massingham, he accepted the comic element in politics and he sometimes wrote in this vein himself, as amusingly as Massingham: but he also acknowledged that politicians were mainly serious and honourable people, engaged in work of the highest importance.

Of course other columnists, notably Bernard Levin, have disputed this view both directly and by implication. If, they say, politicians are mainly serious and honourable – which they rather take leave to doubt, on the whole – it is no business of the columnist to inflate their pretensions still further by continually telling them so. The business of the columnist, they maintain, is to expose and deflate. So of course it is; and we should be careful before concluding that differences of general attitude necessarily govern every single article a columnist writes.

But all recent columnists, whatever their methods, and to whatever

---

*Observer, 29 April 1951.

degree they may vary then, can plausibly be attacked on the same grounds. They sneer; are too literary; pretend to be above the battle; concentrate on the 'Westminster hot-house'; neglect the 'great issues' of peace and war; do not tell us about pollution, the population explosion, the energy crisis or whatever happens to be the latest fad; do not tell us about anything; tell us too much; trivialise; are irresponsible. Some of these criticisms are contradictory – for instance, that columnists go into both too much and too little detail.

This brings us to the final question of influence. 'Whom,' people politely inquire, 'are you trying to influence?' The short answer is that you are not always, or even usually, trying to influence anybody at all. Why on earth should you? Why should political writing alone be assumed always to have some ulterior purpose? It is surely enough to try to tell the truth as you see it, and to persuade people to read it. From his experience of the 1930s and 1940s George Orwell concluded that for an overtly political writer this was an impossible attempt. Malcolm Muggeridge has echoed him. It was Massingham's supreme achievement to prove both Orwell and Muggeridge wrong. He wrote about politics, every week, for two decades, telling the truth as he saw it.

G. E. MOORE

4 November 1873 – 24 October 1958

GEORGE EDWARD MOORE was the greatest English moral philosopher of the twentieth century. Both his father Daniel and his paternal grandfather George were physicians. His mother, Henrietta Sturge, came from a family of Gloucestershire Quakers; the Moore household, however, was not Quaker but Baptist. At twelve Moore would importune passers-by near his home, Hastings Lodge, Sydenham Hill, Upper Norwood, and ask them about their relationship with God. He was converted to agnosticism by his brother Thomas (later to become the poet T. Sturge Moore), who tended to dominate him in his youth and who was, according to Moore, 'a far readier talker than I and far more fertile of ideas'. Daniel Moore married twice, and had one daughter by his first marriage, and three daughters and four sons (of whom G. E. Moore was the second) by his marriage to Henrietta.

In 1872 Moore's parents moved from Hastings in Sussex to Upper Norwood in order that their sons should attend Dulwich College nearby as day boys. He was taught mainly the Classics at school and in 1892 went up to Trinity College, Cambridge, to read the same subject. In 1894 he was placed in the first class of Part I of the Classical Tripos and in 1896 in the first class of Part II of the Moral Sciences Tripos.

He was a Fellow of Trinity from 1898 to 1904, a university lecturer in Moral Sciences from 1911 to 1925, editor of *Mind* from 1921 to 1947, Professor of Philosophy at Cambridge from 1925 to 1939 and a visiting Professor in America from 1940 to 1944. He published *Principia Ethica* (1903), *Ethics* (Home University Library, 1912), *Philosophical Studies* (1922) and *Some Main Problems of Philosophy* (1953).

The most famous of these books was the first. It became the credo of the Bloomsbury Group. J. M. Keynes, however, wrote that he and his friends tended to take out of the *Principia* what suited them: that they used its reflections on love, truth, beauty and personal relationships as justifications for their own activities, whether sexual, literary or artistic, and that they disregarded its sterner injunctions on duty and obligation. In any case, Moore's influence was as much personal as philosophical. He was a genuinely disinterested man. Though he was musical, and sang Schubert and Beethoven songs, he lacked fancy, and had a literal approach. He was guileless, and something like a child.

In 1950 – five years before he was awarded the Order of Merit – his reputation was probably at its height, together with those of the other Cambridge figures of his time, Bertrand Russell, E. M. Forster (both, like Moore, then still living) and J. M. Keynes. In the following thirty years, though biographies and diaries concerning Bloomsbury poured from the publishers, the reputations of the group's founders and forerunners tended to go down: partly through a decline of faith in Cambridge rationalism and partly through the revealed activities of Guy Burgess, Donald Maclean, Kim Philby and Anthony Blunt, all of whom had been members of the Apostles Society at Cambridge. Moore had likewise been an Apostle and had ground out some of his ethical ideas at meetings of the Society. To make the connection between Moore's teachings and what was commonly called treason* was no doubt both fanciful and unjust, but the connection was made, by, for example, Sir William Rees-Mogg in a leading article in *The Times*.

In 1955 I came to know him. Even then, I had some notion of Moore's philosophical importance, both in general and in relation to Bloomsbury, though I had not read his *Principia Ethica*. I knew his views that goodness was a simple, unanalysable quality, like redness, that personal relations were of the highest importance, that we should strive after love, beauty and truth. I did not, as it happened, accept all of it, but this by the way. What I did not realise was the personal awe in which he was held.

Everyone, I later discovered, had been in fear of his disapproval. Bertrand Russell said that Moore was the only man of whom he had ever been frightened. All this I did not know at the time. Whether, if I had, I should have behaved any differently towards him, I am not sure. As it was, I did not thrust my views upon him. But I was certainly not afraid to open my mouth in his presence.

Nor was my wife afraid of him. She it was who was responsible for my knowing him at all. What happened was that shortly after I left the

---

*Burgess *et al.* had never been technically guilty of this crime, owing to the absence of a state of war between Britain and Russia, though there is room for argument about the legal position during the period of the German-Soviet pact.

university we married. We decided to live in the town. My wife's job was there. And I, being about to be conscripted into the RAF, had no job at all (though, before being called up, I put in a stint at Chivers's jam factory, progressing from Christmas puddings to jelly creams). For accommodation she discovered a converted stable, no more than a doll's house really, at the bottom of Moore's garden. He – or, rather, his wife, Dorothy – had another young married couple lodging in the principal house on the Chesterton Road. Moore had a bed sitting-room at the front of the house; Mrs Moore had one at the back. By this I do not mean that their conditions were cramped or uncomfortable. The Chesterton Road house was large and Victorian. But the fact remains that England's greatest living philosopher, already the recipient of the OM, was living in a bed sitting-room and taking in lodgers.

Mrs Moore married Moore when she was a student. By 1955 she was in her sixties. She was Scottish, had thick glasses and smoked a pipe, as also did her husband. She called him 'Bill' when talking to him and 'Moore' to outsiders as in 'Moore says such-and-such ...' When the weather was fine he would walk about the garden and Mrs Moore, sitting at a back window, would superintend his progress through opera glasses. This procedure was necessary because of her short sight and because Moore was liable to fall over. He would occasionally lose his balance, while striking a flower with his walking-stick. I thought him inconsistent when, some years later, during a visit by my wife and me, he rebuked our three-year-old son for tearing up some flowers in the garden.

His wife took a kindly, maternal and somewhat bossy interest in her tenants. She once insisted on selling us a gate-leg table for £10 on the ground that it was genuine Jacobean. We never discovered whether it was or not. Sometimes she would invite us to tea with Moore and herself. Mrs Moore was voluble, and he confined himself to interjections. She was once talking about a table that some of their previous tenants had bought. Odd how everything to do with Moore seems to come down to tables.

'You see,' she explained, 'they wanted it to have tea on.'

Moore stirred.

'No, no, dear,' he said. 'That's not quite right. Coffee too.'

Occasionally the entertainment was more formal. Tenants, past and present, would be invited to dinner. Moore insisted on grinding the coffee. Afterwards he pressed us to Marsala. My exchanges with him were about politics rather than philosophy. He admired James Griffiths. I agreed up to a point but said I thought the we-who-have-toiled-in-the-bowels-of-the-earth routine could be overdone. Moore looked uncomprehending. To him, Jim Griffiths was a good man; he perceived goodness in Griffiths; there was no further argument.

Moore was short, slim, blue-eyed, an inhabitant of fairy-land. He was addicted to hot baths, which he generally had around lunch-time. I do not think he was lonely: his most frequent visitor was Casimir Lewy, the philosopher. The only person about whom I ever heard him speak unkindly was his brother, T. Sturge Moore.

'I wanted to kill my brother,' he said to me. 'He is the only man I have ever wanted to kill.'

'Why was that?'

'You see, I hated him. I have never hated anyone so much as I did my brother.'

Mrs Moore, on the other hand, had a particular detestation of Bertrand Russell.

'Bertie Russell,' she said several times, 'is a bad lot.'

On my asking for further and better particulars, she would merely reply: 'He has caused a lot of unhappiness in his time.'

I suspected she was envious of his greater affluence and popular fame compared to Moore: but this may have been unfair of me.

She continued to send us Christmas cards after our departure, and we – to be exact, my wife – reciprocated. We visited her and Moore several times after leaving Cambridge in 1957. I wish I had talked to him more, but I do not think he would have been very interested. All I can really say is that I was G. E. Moore's lodger.

MALCOLM MUGGERIDGE

24 March 1903 –

THOMAS MALCOLM MUGGERIDGE was the son of H. T. Muggeridge, a city clerk who lived in Croydon, was active in local Labour politics and was Labour MP for Romford from 1929 to 1931. He came from Penge, Muggeridge's mother from Sheffield. Malcolm Muggeridge was educated at Selhurst Grammar School, Croydon, and at Selwyn College, Cambridge, where he read, to begin with, Chemistry and Zoology, did badly in his examinations in these subjects, and was awarded a pass degree in English, being placed in the second class.

He read science because it was the only subject which, according to him, his school taught to a sufficiently high standard to secure entry to Oxford or Cambridge. He went to the university, so he also claimed, solely to please his father, who had ambitions for him as a Fabian intellectual. He further claimed that he was unhappy at Cambridge and made only one friend there, Canon (as he was later to become) Alec Vidler. But his letters to his parents at the time, and his activities in the College Boat Club and elsewhere, do not wholly support this subsequent sombre view. However, children often pretend to their parents that they are happier or more contented than they are so as not to hurt them. We may choose to take Muggeridge's word for his unhappiness at Cambridge.

This was an illustration of one of his frequently asserted beliefs: that memory was a more truthful guide – to one's own state of mind, at any rate – because, though memory was often fallible, it did not intentionally lie, whereas contemporary 'evidence' was frequently designed for no other purpose than to mislead.

On leaving Cambridge he contemplated taking holy orders but was not greatly encouraged in this course by his friend Vidler. Instead he became a teacher. He was the then equivalent of a supply teacher. And he taught, chiefly English, at a missionary college in India and, from 1927 to 1930, at the Egyptian University in Cairo.

In 1927 he married Katharine (Kitty) Dobbs, whose mother was the

sister of Beatrice Webb (Aunt Bo). He did not invite his parents to the wedding. His father would presumably have been proud to witness him soldering a connection with the Fabian aristocracy, and Muggeridge admitted as much afterwards: his mother was largely uninterested in high or, come to that, low politics. When reproached in later life with being ashamed of his parents, with social climbing or, at least, with lack of consideration, he would reply that the thought of inviting his parents had simply not occurred to him and that, in fact, he remained both fond and proud of his father throughout his life, though he came to think of him as being as deluded in his way as Aunt Bo in hers.

It was from Egypt that he started contributing stories or articles to the *Manchester Guardian* which appeared anonymously, though by-lines were then much less common than they subsequently became. In 1930 he joined the staff of the *Guardian* in Manchester, where he made friends with A. J. P. Taylor, who was at the university, with Kingsley Martin, who was a fellow-leader writer, and with Ted Scott, who was C. P. Scott's son and had sent Muggeridge the original letter of invitation to join the paper (though the good word had been put in by Arthur Ransome, who had met and been impressed by him in Egypt).

Muggeridge considered C. P. Scott a humbug. He was clearly disillusioned by liberalism, though at this stage from the point of view of the extreme Left. Nor, so he claimed afterwards, did he much take to Kingsley Martin: though Martin puts in his first appearance in Muggeridge's *Diary* in 1950. Martin, Muggeridge said, was both self-seeking and dishonest. He retailed several times the story of how George Orwell, lunching with Muggeridge in a restaurant and finding himself seated opposite Martin, insisted on changing their table because Orwell found the spectacle of him so repellent.

In this Manchester period Muggeridge wrote his first lengthy published works, *Autumnal Face*, a novel, and *Three Flats*, a play (produced by the Stage Society). Muggeridge had a certain fondness for the stage and for appearing on it himself: as the Gryphon, he cavorted with Sir John Gielgud in Jonathan Miller's television version of *Alice*. He particularly liked dressing up as a clergyman and, in old age, was delighted when an amateur production near his home in Robertsbridge provided him with the opportunity for so doing. He had earlier appeared as a clergyman in the Peter Sellers film *Heavens Above*.

This period also provided Muggeridge with one of his longest-serving jokes, built around the phrase 'It is' – or 'is greatly' – 'to be hoped', as in, 'It is greatly to be hoped that men of good-will and moderation will come together, and wiser counsels yet prevail.' What precisely, Muggeridge would ask, was 'it'? Who was doing the hoping? And suppose the men of good-will and moderation, assuming there were any, obstinately refused to come together, and that wiser counsels, so far from prevailing, were spurned? What then? What indeed! He would illustrate this by a sentence, apocryphal or not – who can say? as he would put it – from a *Guardian* leading article of the time: 'One is sometimes tempted to believe that the Greeks do not want a stable Government.'

He was offered the post of *Guardian* correspondent in Moscow, and accepted it with delight, intending to make a new life in Russia. He and Kitty sold all their possessions before embarkation. But he was soon disillusioned, by the harshness and incompetence of the regime, by the cutting or softening of his dispatches to the *Guardian* and by the procession of Western luminaries who came to be gulled. He always lumped these people together as 'liberals', irrespective of whether they were Western Communists, fellow-travellers or genuine liberals, and never gave Bertrand Russell adequate credit for seeing through the Soviet system some years before Muggeridge saw through it himself. He would get out of this and similar dialectical difficulties by saying that Communism was a perversion of – or a natural progression from – liberalism. In any case, we were all in the West doomed, 'done for', as he liked to say.

He left the *Guardian* and, with Kitty, went to Geneva to work for the International Labour Organisation. His task was to collate statistics about co-operative movements. As the figures were provided by the national Governments concerned, and were not verified (which would, in any case, have been difficult), Muggeridge saw that he was producing chiefly lies. When he raised this with his superior, he met with an unsympathetic response. This spell, together with his experiences in Moscow, strengthened his life-long suspicion of 'facts'. He occasionally saw Ramsay MacDonald walking, who would say, rolling his Rs, 'the mornings are for myself'. Muggeridge thought him absurd.

For most of the time Muggeridge was bored, unhappy and in poor health: until late middle-age he suffered from indigestion, insomnia and bronchial trouble (aggravated by heavy smoking), but in his sixties and seventies he became remarkably healthy. He attributed this change not so much to his latter-day abstemiousness as to his greater inner composure:

as he would put it, to the conquest of the Will by the Imagination. What made the strongest impression on him in Geneva, apart from the futility of the whole exercise, was the remark of a journalist in a bar: 'I sometimes wonder whether I'm licking the right boots.' This seemed to him to summarise power and the attitude towards it.

In the next year *Winter in Moscow* appeared, which annoyed the Left without catching the fancy of the Right. And his novel *Picture Palace*, about the *Guardian* under Scott, was withdrawn by the publishers, Eyre and Spottiswoode, after the paper had threatened legal action. Though Scott ('old Savoury' of the *Accringthorpe Courier* in the book) was treated unsympathetically, his son Ted ('young Savoury') was not. Ted had died in a boating accident, which had moved Muggeridge almost more than anything in his life. Young Savoury died likewise, of a heart attack on a long country walk. Muggeridge implied in the book, what he felt both at the time and afterwards, that C. P. was somehow responsible for Ted's death – that the egotistical father had drained the life out of the son. It was almost certainly this implication which aroused the ire of the Scott family and the threat of legal action, rather than (as Muggeridge's admirable biographer, Ian Hunter, suggests) the charge of humbug against the *Guardian* for being subsidised by its louche sister-paper the *Manchester Evening News*. The attempted withdrawal was by no means effective, and copies of *Picture Palace* could occasionally be picked up in second-hand bookshops. But the episode left Muggeridge with a lasting contempt for liberal pieties about freedom of speech or of the press.

Money was short and, seeing an advertisement, he applied for the job of assistant editor of the *Calcutta Statesman*. To his surprise, he was successful. He was on his travels again. His second period in India was less happy, or more miserable, than his first. He took a dislike to his English colleague on the paper, Wordsworth, a descendant of the poet and the father of Christopher Wordsworth of the *Observer*. His chief friends were four Indian intellectuals and a painter, Amrita Sher-Gil, whose mother was Hungarian, and with whom he had a serious love affair. Otherwise he occupied himself mainly with morosely trying to write a Life of Samuel Butler for which he was contracted, and which appeared in 1936, to the dismay and indignation of Butler-followers, then not uncommon.

However, Wordsworth lent him money when he was in trouble, and was repaid with a couple of disdainful and dismissive references in his autobiography. Throughout his life he had the disposition to attack any individual who had helped him or any institution that had harboured him; he admitted this trait cheerfully enough, saying it was the way he was made. For example, Lord Montgomery, whom he met through Churchill's Minister, P. J. Grigg, took a fancy to him and, after the war, provided him with several exclusive pieces of news which duly appeared in the *Daily Telegraph*, as, of course, Montgomery had intended they should. Yet in his writings he treated Montgomery, certainly not with hostility, but with a genial contempt. Perhaps he was right to do so. Personal friendship can be a corrupting relationship. Loyalty, to person, institution or country, is often an ambiguous virtue. But Muggeridge seemed to go out of his way to demonstrate these truths when the demonstration served no useful purpose.

Yet he was not invariably ungrateful. He always spoke warmly of Hugh (later Lord) Cudlipp for employing him as a columnist on the *Sunday Pictorial* when he was barred from the BBC and other organs of opinion on account of his attack on the Queen in the *Saturday Evening Post* in 1957.

Moreover, he was in other respects the kindest of men. He tried to imitate Swift in doing good to individuals and doing it by stealth. He was particularly generous to fellow journalists who were down on their luck or had been simply imprudent. Several times he lent money to Maurice Richardson – though he was not alone in this. One Christmas Eve, again, another, younger journalist, a neighbour of Muggeridge in Sussex, was flung into Brixton prison owing to his contempt of court over some bankruptcy or Inland Revenue proceedings. His wife found herself without food, money or presents for the children. Muggeridge organised the entire Christmas and paid for it himself.

In the mid-1930s, however, he was in no position to pay for much. Living in London with Kitty, he joined the 'Londoner's Diary' staff of the *Evening Standard*. He was paid £1,000 a year. This was by no means bad pay for those days, though Harold Nicolson, doing an identical job five years before Muggeridge, was paid four times this salary. Muggeridge was as unhappy in the job as Nicolson had been. The Diary was one of Lord Beaverbrook's favourite personal vehicles: 'Ya gotta say ...' 'We duly said it,' Muggeridge recorded later. He was expected to be suitably attired, and turned up for work in Shoe Lane in a suit and a hat and with a rolled umbrella. Not that the work was onerous: two paragraphs a day from each of the several contributors was the average.

It was here that Muggeridge learnt of the unreliability of the cuttings kept in the paper's library, and consulted daily by the Diary staff. An error, once implanted, could never be corrected: instead it would grow, small accretions transforming it into a pearl of misinformation. Once, as an experiment, Muggeridge wrote that Mr So-and-so was 'fond of music'. He had no idea whether this was true or not. But the story grew, until it was implied that no concert was complete without the presence of this personage. As far as Muggeridge was aware, he could not tell the difference between the 'Hallelujah Chorus' and 'God Save the Queen'. The editor of the column was Robert Bruce Lockhart, who recorded these impressions:

> Malcolm Muggeridge, the author of an anti-Bolshevist book on Russia and of a suppressed novel on the *Manchester Guardian*, joined us today. Clever, nervous and rather 'freakish' in appearance. Holds strong views (18 September 1935) ... is rather pro-Fascist yet stands strongly for individual liberties. Hates the big press proprietors (29 October) ... A wasted day. Gave luncheon to Muggeridge. He wants to retire to a farmhouse near Battle (which his mother-in-law will buy for him) and write his books. He will have only about £400 to do it with. But he is only 32 and I advised him strongly to take the risk (24 January 1936) ... Went to lunch with Muggeridge at the Jardin des Gourmets. Had a long talk ... about his future. He is not happy and wants to get out. Thinks it is ridiculous that people like himself and me should not be consulted about anything and should have our stuff 'subbed' by some half-educated nitwit (8 February).*

Though this last extract indicates that Muggeridge was not as devoid of ambition as he subsequently claimed, he left London and the *Standard* and moved to Whatlington in Sussex, to a house which was more than a cottage but lacked amenities. Water had to be drawn from a well, groceries fetched on foot from Battle. He lived by writing articles, and his regular work was reviewing novels for the *Daily Telegraph* at £5 a week.

He was urged to leave the *Standard* by Hugh Kingsmill – Kitty, H. T. Muggeridge and Vidler apart, the greatest influence in his life. He met Kingsmill (Hugh Kingsmill Lunn) through Kitty, whose father had worked for Kingsmill's father, Sir Henry Lunn. No teacher had previously inspired Muggeridge. Kingsmill filled this need. He denounced 'dawnism',

---

The Diaries of Sir Robert Bruce Lockhart, ed. Kenneth Young, 2 vols (1973–82), vol. I, pp. 329, 330, 339, 341.

that belief in the perfectibility of man which originated in the French Revolution and the Romantic Movement. And he drew the distinction, which was to remain with Muggeridge for the rest of his life, between the Imagination and the Will. The Will was the source of lust and the urge to exercise power, the Imagination of love, friendship and literature. Kingsmill helped fix Muggeridge's literary tastes, Shakespeare, Johnson, Cervantes and, above all, Blake. There was a third friend, Hesketh Pearson. a former actor, a more commercially successful author than Kingsmill (or Muggeridge at this stage) and, like Muggeridge, something of a woman-chaser. Their conversation was chiefly literary: around the Hastings area, in various country pubs, at the Horseshoe in Tottenham Court Road and in the Authors Club.

By this time he and Kitty had four children, three boys and a girl, and, though money was short, he was leading the kind of life he liked, despite his illnesses and depressions. In 1981 he said to a friend that book-reviewing was the most agreeable way of earning a living through journalism – a by no means universal opinion. But he also said in his later years that, having once dreaded the arrival of a parcel of half-a-dozen or so novels for review, he could not look on a new novel in its dust jacket without experiencing apprehension and disgust.

He liked to rise early and make himself a pot of tea. Early morning tea was always a matter of high concern to Muggeridge – as cigars were to Evelyn Waugh – and when he found difficulty in obtaining it in America after the war he felt deprived. He wrote in the morning, ate a light lunch, walked in the afternoon, and wrote or read between tea and supper, after which he would talk to Kitty or to friends and retire to bed early. This was his ideal regimen, which he maintained, more or less, at Whatlington in the late 1930s and at Robertsbridge from the 1960s onwards. There was a difference between the earlier existence and the later, when he was abstemious.

'I was never an alcoholic,' he used to say, 'but I was a bit of a boozer.'

He had never taken the slightest interest in food or wine as such: 'My dear boy, I simply liked getting drunk.'

He gave up drink – his favourite tipple was whisky – not, according to him, because of moral or religious considerations but because he wanted to carry on writing for as long as he could: 'My dear boy, the same decision will come to you some day.'

He gave up smoking because, writing one day in the 1960s in an

American hotel, he left the room to fetch something and returned to find it full of smoke and overflowing ash-trays. The sight and smell revolted him, and he successfully resolved never to smoke again.

Though he was tolerant of the drinking habits of others, providing his guests at Robertsbridge with sherry, beer and, sometimes, table-wine (though never spirits), he had a puritanical impatience with any manifestations of gastronomy or epicureanism. As Anthony Powell noted – his closest friend in the years immediately after the war, and his literary editor at *Punch* – he had a similar impatience with aesthetic matters generally, even where literature was concerned: he was liable to become angry over what he considered to be over-emphasis on form or style.

But, though abstemious in his later years, he was no ascetic, nor did he pretend to be one. In his seventies he continued to eat eggs, which, like tea, were somehow important to him. Typically he would lunch off home-made wholemeal bread, butter, cheese, salad, stewed fruit with yoghurt and dried fruit (sultanas, raisins, dates). He would later consume a hearty tea.

Until he was well into his fifties he was an enthusiastic, promiscuous heterosexual. Indeed, he described the decade itself, the 1950s, as a descent into the abyss, from which he emerged through the love of Kitty. One of his last serious affairs was with the wife, now dead, of a newspaper proprietor. Charles Wheeler remembered an exchange with him when he was in America, where Wheeler was the BBC's Washington correspondent:

'When you reach the age of sixty you have to decide whether to be a saint or a sod, and I've decided to be a saint.'

'What sort of progress are you making?'

But Muggeridge had always possessed a lively sense of sexual guilt, brought about not so much by infidelity as by dissatisfaction with the sexual act itself, at once transient, absurd and a source of lies. This sense of guilt emerged in a product of the Whatlington period, the minor masterpiece *In a Valley of this Restless Mind*. This book was intended by the publishers to be a modern version of William James's *Varieties of Religious Experience*. No one could have been less suitable to produce such a volume than Muggeridge, who possessed a contempt for abstraction and for apparently logical argument, both of which he considered to be frauds productive of nothing but misery and conceit, epitomised by Oxford and Cambridge in general and Bertrand Russell in particular. Instead he wrote a kind of personal *Pilgrim's Progress* through the London of the late 1930s. He was searching for God.

This image of the search recurred in his writings and conversation. It was usually employed for comic effect. He would illustrate his search vigorously, getting up and looking around, whether on television or in his sitting room. He might be searching for news. News, where is it? Give us this day our daily news! Or for power. Power, give me power, but what is it, where is it? Or he might pretend to be Sir William Haley, searching for enlightenment, 'taking book after book off his library shelves, with his library steps, climbing all over the shelves like a little monkey. Enlightenment here? No good. Try another book'. Or he might pretend to be Clive James, the Australian searching for culture. 'Culture under the bed? No. Behind the curtains? No good. Try somewhere else.' (James was one of his most effective hostile critics.)

In a Valley ... was a victim of the year before the war; his other minor masterpiece, *The Thirties*, a victim of 1940: neither received the praise it should have done, though Waugh reviewed the former favourably. Muggeridge made strenuous efforts to join up in the expectation, even the hope, that he would be killed. After writing an article about his difficulties in enlisting, he was invited to join the newly-formed Intelligence Corps as a private, which he did, completing *The Thirties* in barracks at Aldershot. He was commissioned, asked to stay away from one officers' mess on account of his (to his seniors) disturbing conversation and eventually dispatched via Portugal to Lourenço Marques as a British agent. He was more successful in this role than his quixotic account in his autobiography led one to suppose, being responsible for, among other things, the capture of an enemy agent and the sinking of a submarine.

But he was still depressed, and tried to commit suicide by swimming out to sea and drowning himself. He turned back. (It was an attempt identical with Waugh's as related in *A Little Learning*.) Ian Hunter, in his biography of Muggeridge, left open the question of whether the attempt was genuine or not. Certainly Muggeridge said to a British newspaper after the war that it was a put-up job, intended to deceive the enemy agents. But Hunter, a most conscientious biographer, was in error when he wrote that there was no reference to the incident in Muggeridge's diaries. On 30 March 1946, sailing to America, he recorded:

Sometimes think how agreeable to die – talk of an iceberg evoking a picture of a boat going down and providing an opportunity to go down with it; or, walking up and down the deck and vaguely considering slipping overboard in the dark night, only to recall my abortive suicide in Lourenço Marques, the awful struggle with the waves, the shivering resistance to death when it came to the point, the lights of Peter's Café shining along the shore, so remote, so desirable, and floundering naked in the mud afterwards.*

He ended the war in Paris, where he protected several people – some genuine allied agents, others merely unfortunate – from the revenge of the Resistance and its hangers-on. He also secured the release and safe conduct of P. G. Wodehouse, who might have been in serious legal trouble owing to his misunderstood broadcasts to Germany earlier in the war. Muggeridge was greatly taken with a phrase used by an English barrister dispatched to supervise the affair. Wodehouse, he advised, should be 'removed from the jurisdiction' without delay, and from the jurisdiction he was duly removed. Muggeridge was awarded the Croix de Guerre and the Légion d'Honneur – not the signs of an idle or incompetent intelligence officer.

When the war in Europe was over he simply discharged himself. He was technically, no doubt, a deserter, but in due course his official discharge arrived. In the meantime he had found work as a leader-writer for the *Daily Telegraph*. The then editor, Arthur Watson, asked only one question of substance: whether he believed in private enterprise. After some hesitation Muggeridge said that he did, and was engaged. In 1946 he was off again, to Washington, fascinated by the greatest power in the world. He started by displeasing the authorities at the *Telegraph* and ended by pleasing them. After his return he was made deputy editor of the paper.

In the late 1940s and early 1950s he was renowned, or reviled, as an implacable enemy of the Soviet Union. He still worked part-time for MI6, and was interviewed as a possible Conservative candidate. In 1953 he was appointed editor of *Punch*. Other editorships – of the *Spectator*, the *Sunday Times* and the *Daily Mail* – were dangled before him at this time. He would have accepted the *Mail*'s offer, more firm than the others, if he had not already been contracted to *Punch*. Here he brought in 'big names', such as P. G. Wodehouse, complained that the paper was 'too well-written' – that it was not sufficiently contemporaneous – and devoted much time to his cartoonists Leslie Illingworth, Michael Cummings and Norman Mans-

* *Like it Was: the Diaries of Malcolm Muggeridge*, ed. John Bright-Holmes (1981), pp. 211–12.

bridge. The circulation went up and then down. A cartoon of an enfeebled Churchill, to coincide with his eightieth birthday celebrations as Prime Minister in 1954, caused much offence to the paper's regular readers. In 1957 he left, with relief: he said afterwards that it was his one job which he had really hated.

He had already become a national figure because of his work as an interviewer for the television programme *Panorama*: his first interview was with Billy Graham. He became notorious for his reflections on the Monarchy in the American *Saturday Evening Post*, though he had said much the same in an earlier piece, 'Royal Soap Opera', in Kingsley Martin's *New Statesman*, which had caused no great stir. He remained ungrateful to Martin for publishing him in this period, though he felt, or spoke, differently about Hugh Cudlipp. He contributed to the *Statesman* until 1970, when Richard Crossman discouraged him on the ground that there were plenty of places where his work could appear, but the *Statesman* was not, or should not, be one of them; however, Anthony Howard often printed him in 1972–8. Crossman's predecessor, Paul Johnson, used to pay tribute to Muggeridge's journalistic generosity and fecundity: when Johnson was barren of an idea for an article or an item in his 'London Diary', Muggeridge would provide several.

In his later years he acquired several younger disciples, notably Christopher Booker and Richard Ingrams. He wrote and broadcast much on Christianity, but became bored with the company of too many Christians, and liked to engage in gossip about politics and journalism with other companions. But he was genuinely religious, and claimed to have undergone several mystical experiences in his life, though, on examination, they turned out to be moments of conviction that the universe was one and that he was somehow part of it. He had a crucifix on his wall but despised organised religion, as he despised theology. For a man who claimed not to be part of this world, as he did, he was surprisingly at ease in it.

ANTHONY POWELL

21 December 1905 –

ANTHONY DYMOKE POWELL was an author who wrote the most highly regarded novel sequence of the post-1945 period, *A Dance to the Music of Time*. He was also a conscientious literary journalist, an occupation in which he took some pride (at any rate in conversation with other journalists), saying that book-reviewing was a difficult craft that should not be underestimated. Though on the surface no one could have appeared less Welsh, he regarded himself as a Welshman.

His father was Lieutenant-Colonel Philip Powell of The Welch Regiment. Some of his ancestors came from Pembrokeshire and Radnorshire. However, Philip Powell's father was a doctor, a sportsman and a part-time soldier (the last two interests predominating) from Melton Mowbray in Leicestershire. His mother, Anthony's Powell's paternal grandmother, came from a Leicestershire brewing family. Philip Powell had joined his regiment not because of his Welsh connections but because a friend of the family, a senior military figure, had recommended it as being both 'good' and cheap. The former merit was not obvious to the officer who, in 1939, hastened Anthony Powell's progress into the Army, on Powell's own insistence. 'Easily get you into a funny regiment like that,' the officer said. 'Everyone wants to go into London regiments.' This caused Powell some amusement, tinged with annoyance.

Powell's mother was Maud Mary Wells-Dymoke, the daughter of (by Powell's own account) a somewhat ineffectual barrister. His maternal grandmother, Laura Jefferson, was of Scottish descent. Powell's mother was strong-minded but self-effacing. His father was a difficult man, prone to bouts of depression and of rage. After his retirement from the Army he took the bar examinations and obtained a second – no mean achievement – but did not practise as a barrister for long.

Both parents were unintellectual but artistic. Powell early acquired an interest in and knowledge of painting and drawing which were to remain with him for the rest of his life. He was an only child. Owing to the vagaries

of his father's profession, he spent his childhood and adolescence in numerous places: Albert Hall Mansions, London (where he was born), Yorkshire, Aldershot, Cambridge and St John's Wood. At ten he was sent to a preparatory school in Kent, where he became a friend of Henry Yorke (Henry Green). Powell refused to enlarge on the horrors of the school, saying that other writers had already covered the general topic more than adequately. He passed easily into Eton.

Two of his mother's uncles had been there, but otherwise there were no family ties with the school. It cost his parents about £300 a year. Powell said afterwards that, though his parents were pleased that he was at Eton, they did not regard his presence there as in any way exceptional: they simply preferred to spend their money on school fees. Most of the boys, he said, were in the same position: neither he nor they were made to feel out of place by richer or grander boys. This was Powell's own account.

At school his closest friends were Hubert Duggan, on whom Charles Stringham in *The Music of Time* was loosely modelled (though Powell, like most novelists, was sensitive about charges of 'putting people into books'), and Denys Buckley, later a Lord Justice of Appeal, who bore no resemblance to Kenneth Widmerpool. He did not meet George Orwell and Cyril Connolly till later. The strongest influence on him – certainly his favourite master – was Sidney Evans, the drawing master, who helped Powell and others form the Eton Society of Arts. In the holidays he became an acquaintance of Christopher Millard, a neighbour in St John's Wood, who occupied a kind of shack at the bottom of a garden in Abercorn Place. Millard was a bookseller, a friend of 'Baron Corvo' and A. J. A. Symons, a homosexual, a queer fish generally – though then, as always, Powell himself was resolutely heterosexual in his tastes. He was taught history by Henry Marten, passed out ninth in the school and third oppidan, and went to Balliol.

This college was recommended by Tom Balston, a friend of his father's, who was later to give Powell a job at Duckworths, the publishing firm where Balston was a partner. At Oxford Powell suffered what he described as an intellectual recession. He was one of the few people who were honest enough to admit afterwards that they had worked hard but obtained a third. His Tutor, Kenneth Bell, whom he admired, said comfortingly that his degree would seem a matter of no consequence in a few years. Though Powell did not lead an over-active social life during this period, he visited

Lady Ottoline Morrell's Garsington through Henry Yorke – ever-present from his preparatory school to Oxford.

He knew Maurice Bowra too, 'inevitably', one is tempted to add. Towards the end of his time at Oxford, Powell told Bowra that he was fed up with, in fact did not like, the place and that he looked forward to starting real life in London. According to Powell, Bowra, as an Oxford don, on his way to becoming an Oxford institution, took these fairly mild observations hard and did not forgive Powell for making them, if he ever did wholly forgive him, for many years afterwards. It is doubtful whether Bowra felt as strongly as Powell supposed. The story illustrates one aspect of Powell's character: his hyper-sensitivity in social matters. Though he was always courteous, it could be difficult to feel wholly at ease with him, because there was the consciousness that one might unknowingly cause offence at any moment – do a Powell, so to speak, to Powell's Bowra.

He started work for Duckworths in 1926, and lived in lodgings in Shepherd Market, a locality to which he was drawn by reason of its association with Michael Arlen's *The Green Hat*. Subsequently, until he moved to Chester Gate, Regent's Park, he lived chiefly in Bloomsbury – in Tavistock Square, Brunswick Square and Great Ormond Street – though most of his social life was lived in Chelsea, and though he disapproved of the Bloomsbury Group's social and literary influence. (Admittedly the centre of gravity of high Bloomsbury lay somewhat to the north, in Gordon Square.) Several of the interests that were to figure in his novels were already in evidence. For instance, he joined the Territorial Army, keeping quiet about it to most of his friends and concealing his literary ambitions from his fellow-officers, though one of them said: 'This is Powell. He's a Senior Wrangler or something.' Again, he went to séances and played planchette, though more as an observer, as a disinterested seeker after truth or even as someone in need of an evening's diversion than as a believer – or someone with the need to believe – in the life beyond.

In 1934 he married Violet Pakenham, daughter of the Earl of Longford. He also knew Violet's elder sisters. Marriage into this large and talkative family, according to Powell, introduced him to numerous relations: he acquired a new way of looking at the world, or, perhaps, learned that there was another way of looking at the world. He had been an only child. Large families conducted their lives differently.

Violet wrote the 'Mary Grant' column in the *Evening Standard* (it was about shops and not to be confused with the column of the same name in *Woman's Own*, which consisted of advice to readers). Later Violet Powell wrote two interesting volumes of autobiography, *Five out of Six* and *Within the Family Circle*, together with other books. Though there was some trouble with miscarriages to begin with, they had two boys, Tristram Powell, the television producer, and John Powell, the journalist. Powell used to say that, owing to the first world war and to disapproval, or suspicion, of marriage on the part of his contemporaries' parents, the married state was one of which his generation had little direct experience. He also used to say that he had never regretted marrying Violet and would do the same again.

He was never greatly interested in the commercial side of publishing and, following a period of part-time working with the firm, and a refusal by his father to honour a half-promise to buy him into a partnership – a refusal which Powell did not regret, either then or later – he left Duckworths to become a film script-writer.

One of his greatest friends during the 1930s was Constant Lambert, the composer and conductor. He was also, as Hugh Moreland, the one character in *The Music of Time* to emerge as wholly sympathetic. Powell never took exception to the Moreland–Lambert identification, whereas he tended to object to other, similar exercises. Lambert was inclined to take bigger risks – anyway to be more exuberant – than Powell. Though Powell generally disliked ostentatious nonconformity, on the ground, among others, that genuine differences would appear more clearly if certain rules were observed, Lambert's unconventional side undoubtedly appealed to him. In addition, Powell liked Lambert's matter-of-fact approach not only to music (in which, ballet apart, Powell was largely uninterested) but also to the arts generally. Lambert accepted the arts as a normal part of life: they were not activities either to be regarded with undue reverence, as Powell's own parents had tended to regard them, or, on the other hand, to be used as a social weapon or adornment, as many of Powell's Oxford contemporaries had tended to use them.

The same pattern was discernible in another of his friendships, with Malcolm Muggeridge. As Lambert 'knew about' the arts, in which Powell was interested, so Muggeridge knew about politics, in which, however, Powell was less interested. He was impressed not so much by Muggeridge's instinctively political mind as by his lack of worldly ambition. The friendship reached its height in the immediate post-war years, after Muggeridge had returned from his stint as *Daily Telegraph* correspondent in Washington, when the Muggeridges and the Powells lived in London. Hardly a day seemed to go by when they did not see each other. When Muggeridge became editor of *Punch*, he took Powell there as his literary editor. The friendship terminated when, with Powell about half-way through *The Music of Time*, Muggeridge wrote a review in the *Evening Standard* saying, in effect, that Powell was wasting his time in writing a seemingly endless series of novels about worthless people in a doomed civilisation. Muggeridge had previously reviewed earlier novels in the sequence with approbation. Powell did not consider Muggeridge's comments helpful at the stage he had reached.

By the outbreak of war he had written *Afternoon Men*, *Venusberg*, *From a View to a Death*, *Agents and Patients* and *What's Become of Waring?*: the publication of the last virtually coincided with the outbreak of war, and accordingly it sold disappointingly. All the books have the Balzacian or Stendhalian theme of the young man making his way in the world, usually in London, though *From a View to a Death* – the funniest of Powell's pre-war novels, which retains its funniness today – is about a socially ambitious painter in hunting country. These novels were favourably received, though some reviewers attacked them for a frivolity which is not apparent today. Powell said that, re-reading them, he was struck by their tone of menace or impending catastrophe.

During the war (in which he served first as a regimental infantry officer and then as a liaison officer in Intelligence) he turned his attention to John Aubrey. He did this because he found novel-writing impossible in the military conditions in which he found himself. In this respect he was unlike Evelyn Waugh, who produced several novels during his period in the Army. Powell's studies of Aubrey produced two books which were published after the war: a study, *John Aubrey and his Friends*, and a new edition of *Brief Lives* which is still one of the best available.

Powell's post-war life fell into two parts: the first, when he and his wife lived near Regent's Park and he was engaged in literary journalism and the opening volumes of *The Music of Time*; and the second, when he and his wife lived at The Chantry, near Frome, and he wrote the bulk of *The Music of Time*. The Chantry was a pretty, conveniently-sized, early-nineteenth-century house which had belonged to the Fussells, an old family of ironmasters. It had a lake in a wooded valley which Powell said reminded him of Conan Doyle's *The Lost World*. In his seventies he would walk down to the lake and back again up to the house, a good mile, with some rapidity and without any difficulty. He did not smoke, drank moderately and remained brisk in his movements even when he was old. Indeed, in his middle seventies he could easily have passed for a man fifteen years younger.

He showed no jealousy of younger writers and was a friend and admirer of Kingsley Amis. Once he and Amis were having a radio discussion about Powell's novels, with Amis in effect interviewing Powell. Amis was asking Powell specific questions about named books. The producer came from behind the glass panel into the studio and asked the two novelists to talk in more general terms about The Novel. Powell, according to Amis, said: 'No, we're not going to do it the way you want. We're going to do it the way we want. And if you try to make us do it the way you want, we're going to get up and walk out.' The producer retired. Amis used to tell this story to show how awkward – even offensive – people of Powell's class and generation could be if provoked.

But Powell was a determined and disciplined man. He combined these characteristics with a tendency either to take offence himself or to worry, often needlessly, about whether others had taken offence. He had a particular liking for making curries, and for cats.

SIMON RAVEN

28 December 1927 –

SIMON ARTHUR NOËL RAVEN was a writer, known chiefly for his novels, in particular for his sequence *Alms for Oblivion*, which was compared, sometimes to its advantage (by Auberon Waugh, for example), to the sequences of Anthony Powell and C. P. Snow. It was a chronicle of English upper and upper-middle class life with a background of a public school, Cambridge, the Army and literary London. All the people in it were rather nasty. Indeed, Raven specialised in nastiness, in conveying, usually in no very subtle manner, the smell of decay. He was particularly adept at writing about sexual corruption. Personally, however, he was nice. 'Simon really is very sweet when you get to know him,' people would say.

He was born in 1927 in a Welbeck Street nursing home. His paternal grandfather had been a self-made industrialist who had left close on a million pounds which, however, was divided among ten children. But the inheritance was sufficient for Raven's father to do no work. His mother came of a family of long-established Cambridge tradesmen. He was brought up in Surrey stockbrokers' country and attended an expensive preparatory school (60 guineas a term before 1939) in the same county. In 1941 he won the top scholarship to Charterhouse. At school he deplored 'keenness' and the house spirit, but worked hard academically and won a classical scholarship to King's College, Cambridge. He also played in the cricket XI with Peter May and James Prior.

This triumphant culmination to his school career, in scholarship and games, emboldened him sexually, and he seduced several younger boys. Rumours circulated, investigations were made, tales were told and in 1945 Raven was expelled, his parents being summoned to the school to remove him bodily from its environs. His expulsion for homosexuality – an episode to which Raven was to return to his writings on several occasions – did not, however, interfere either with his King's scholarship or, before he took it up in 1948, with his obtaining a national service commission in the Oxfordshire and Buckinghamshire Light Infantry. He was even admitted

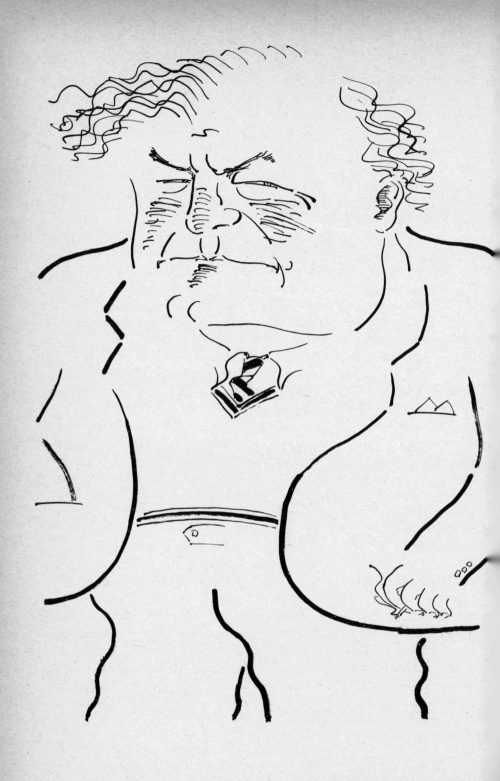

to the old boys' association. In fact Raven claimed to find his expulsion a social asset. When he said he had been expelled from school, people would reply: 'The usual thing, I suppose?' Raven would then proceed to tell the tale, which he had perfected over the years. Nevertheless, the episode gave – or played a predominant part in giving – him his detestation, to which he would recur almost as an all-purpose literary device, of Nosey Parkers, busybodies, tale-bearers, freelance moralists, and evangelical Christianity and its manifestations in general.

During his national service he was for a time in India. At Cambridge he enjoyed himself, got into debt but worked reasonably hard, though in the final part of the Classical Tripos he did less well than had been expected. He was nevertheless awarded a post-graduate studentship. And he had already begun to write: articles in the *Cambridge Review* (the dons' journal) and novel reviews in the *Listener*, where he was patronised by its literary editor, his friend J. R. Ackerley. But he became tired of research, he wanted a literary career, he also wanted money, and accordingly he rejoined the Army on a regular commission as a lieutenant in the King's Shropshire Light Infantry. This course was possible without trouble or pain because he had previously held a commission, even though as a national serviceman in a different regiment, and because he was a graduate.

Raven subsequently said that this decision to rejoin the Army was one of the few he had never regretted. We must take his word for it: still, it was odd. True, he had, or subsequently acquired, a somewhat romantic regard for the Army comparable to that of Evelyn Waugh: he loved and revered it as an institution but hated what it required him to do as a human being. For he was pacific and uninterfering not only by political inclination but by personal nature. He also disliked fuss. Moreover, tired of 'research' at Cambridge, he could almost certainly have earned a living of sorts as a literary journalist in London. At all events, he did not dislike his second period of Army life and saw active service of a kind in Kenya.

But there was trouble with cheques, with banks and with bookmakers; in 1957, after five years as a regular soldier, Captain Raven was presented by his commanding officer with the choice either of quietly resigning his commission and taking his leave of the KSLI or of undergoing a less quiet court martial for conduct unbecoming an officer and a gentleman. Raven chose the former, and embarked on the literary life with no greater stain on his character than that of being warned off the turf.

Before departing the Army, however, he had a piece of luck. He had returned to King's for a reunion dinner. The Provost, Noël Annan (formerly Senior Tutor of the College), told him he should be writing more, and promised to get in touch with his friend Robert Kee, then literary editor of the *Spectator*, with a view to obtaining work for Raven. Annan was as good as his word, and a parcel of books for review duly arrived from Kee. Thereafter, through the late 1950s and the 1960s, Raven wrote extensively for the *Spectator*, and showed himself to be not only an accomplished reviewer of books but a lively weekly journalist generally – though his contributions did not appear on a regular weekly basis.

His second piece of luck came in 1958. Hugh Thomas was editing a collection of essays to be entitled *The Establishment* for Anthony Blond, who had recently set up as a publisher. Thomas and Raven had overlapped at Cambridge, Thomas having been the junior and at Queens' rather than King's. The book he was editing had clearly to contain an essay on the Army. Who better to write it than Raven? His contribution, 'Perish by the Sword', was excellent, apart from some silly nonsense about swords. Raven took pains with it not only because he was a conscientious literary craftsman but also because he wished to make a favourable impression on Blond. He decided that his and Blond's fortunes were, or were shortly to become, linked – or, more simply, that Blond should henceforward keep him in return for a steady output of novels.

He wrote his first novel, *The Feathers of Death*, while living with his parents, who had by this time moved to Hunstanton in Norfolk. The book was a success and, having completed another novel, *Brother Cain*, Raven, understandably tired of Hunstanton, took himself off to London, to bachelor chambers – a kind of imitation Albany, though cheaper, in the Kensington area. Blond paid for several visits to Greece (one trip, to Hydra, was intended as a measure of economy). He was also generous in advancing sums of money to satisfy Raven's tastes for wine, brandy, restaurants, taxis and foreign travel. In 1960 Raven asked Blond for £250, a somewhat larger sum than those he had previously disbursed. He said Raven could have the money on condition he lived more than fifty miles from London.

He chose Deal in Kent because his brother taught at a preparatory school there. His routine was to rise at nine, breakfast at half-past nine and begin work at ten. Between then and one he would write about 2,000 words in longhand – a considerable output. He would lunch off a sandwich and a pint and a half of beer. In the afternoon he typed with two fingers what he had written in the morning: a more efficient typing technique, he said, would have impaired the process of revision. Between late afternoon and dinner time he read, either for pleasure or as part of his work, though in the summer he often watched cricket or played golf. After a hot bath at eight he would begin to drink seriously, consuming two large whiskies and soda. With dinner, cooked by his landlady, he drank most of a bottle of wine. With coffee he had a liqueur brandy. Afterwards he adjourned to his brother's residence, where he drank several brandies and soda and listened to the gossip about the school, which he always found interesting. The evening would end at his own lodgings with glasses of strong beer. Raven would make a note of those ideas which came to him towards the end of the evening: some of them withstood scrutiny in the morning and proved of value in his work.

In this manner Raven wrote not only the *Alms for Oblivion* sequence, together with other novels, but also radio plays and, more lucratively, television dramatisations, notably of Huxley's *Point Counter Point*, Trollope's *The Way We Live Now* and six Palliser novels, Iris Murdoch's *An Unofficial Rose* and Frances Donaldson's *Edward VIII* (or that part of it which dealt with events leading to the Abdication).

Raven was unfailingly polite and talked quietly in a somewhat high-pitched voice. He was tall and heavily built, with abundant curly hair, a slightly snub nose, a pinkish complexion and a tendency to sweat easily. He was fond of checked suits and ties that were striped, crested or otherwise indicative of membership of some group or association. He was a member of several cricket clubs formed for touring purposes as well as of the MCC and the Reform, the latter being a surprisingly staid choice for someone of his adventurous tastes. He seemed to be poised somewhere between the Regency and the Warren Street of the immediate post-war period. He combined the attitudes of the senior common room with those of the golf club.

In 1951 he married Susan Kilner who, as Susan Raven, was a journalist on the *Sunday Times*. The marriage was dissolved and there was one son. Raven remained on amicable terms with his former wife and was devoted to his son, whose separation was a source of sorrow to him. He did this boy only one disservice, which was to publish an embarrassing 'Open Letter to My Son' in the *Spectator* (compare William Rees-Mogg's 'Open Letter' to *his* son in the *Sunday Times*). People said of Raven that he could have been so much better if he had tried harder or been more serious or less interested in making money. It is doubtful whether he would have been a better writer if he had followed those courses or taken those attitudes. He was true to his nature. He was an entertaining and industrious writer, and a civilised and tolerant man.

MAURICE RICHARDSON

24 August 1907 – 25 September 1978

MAURICE RICHARDSON was a journalist with two inventions largely to his credit: the television column and the miniature novel review. He was the son of a successful stock-jobber who, after retirement, and some financial ups and downs, moved from a large house in Essex to another large house at Budleigh Salterton in Devon. Maurice Richardson used to recall that the house possessed not one but two billiard rooms. Though he was not a clubman (unless we are thinking of places such as the Colony Room in Dean Street), and though he was determinedly 'modern' in most of his literary tastes, the opulence of Edwardian England and its immediate aftermath was always at the back of his mind.

As a boy he read much, was good at games and acquired his lifelong devotion to reptiles, particularly snakes. He was educated at Oundle (where, he used to like to boast, he had received the most ferocious beating in the history of the school) and then at New College, Oxford. He started by reading Zoology but then switched to English and failed to take a degree. He used to say that he would have made a 'proper scientist', which he would have liked to be, if only he had been taught mathematics competently as a boy.

At Oxford he knocked out the coach of the university boxing club, or so he claimed, but afterwards relinquished his sporting interests and turned to social activities. He formed a friendship which was to last for the rest of their lives with the Byzantinist R. M. Dawkins.

After Oxford he earned a living as a journalist, a publishers' reader and a novelist, producing three books, *My Bones Will Keep*, *A Strong Man Needed* and *The Bad Companions*, which dealt, among other things, with the nationalisation of women. He pursued his interest in Freudian analysis – he underwent analysis twice in his life and would describe himself as a classic manic-depressive. He also joined the Communist Party. Politics, however, were not his natural subject, though he always liked to be regarded as a man of the Left.

In the war he joined the National Fire Service but was invalided out after falling off a roof. He later wrote a book about his experiences, causing offence to one of his fellow-fire-fighters, also in the literary trade, with his opening sentence: 'I joined the NFS to dodge the Army.'

Perhaps his most original and productive period came in the decade or so immediately after the war. He contributed to the magazine *Lilliput*, often writing virtually the whole of an issue himself under various pseudonyms. *Lilliput* was one of the 'pocket magazines' – the others were *Men Only*, *London Opinion* and the *Strand* – which, though they did not exactly flourish, kept going in the 1940s and '50s, and whose journalistic merits are insufficiently appreciated today. With the exception of the long-established *Strand*, they were considered vaguely indecent, because they contained, for those times, risqué cartoons, and a solitary photograph in every issue of a naked lady posing decorously, like one of Miss Phyllis Dixey's artistes. In fact they published much sound reporting and good writing, neither of a specially taxing nature for the reader. Richardson developed his interest in low life generally and the criminal classes particularly, about whom, however, he could be deplorably sentimental, rather as Lord Bradwell (Tom Driberg) was. He also invented a dwarf boxer called Engelbrecht, who belonged to the Surrealist Sporting Club, organised rugby matches on the moon ('The Day We Played Mars'), fought a hundred rounds with a grandfather clock and went wildfowling for ferocious witches.

In the 1950s he was the *Observer*'s first television critic and coined the phrase 'idiot's lantern' for the television set. In his brief, postage-stamp reviews, chiefly of crime novels, he stretched ingenuity to its limits in finding similes for the stock words. Thrillers would grip 'like a pair of delivery forceps', 'like Pierrepoint's farewell handshake', 'steadily, like a conscientious ant's jaw', 'blindly, like a baby's fist' or (this of a Dick Francis racing thriller) 'like Princess Anne's knees'. A plot would crack 'like an old pair of stays given by Agatha Christie to Oxfam'. Disbelief, instead of being suspended, would be strung up with a strong noose, hung in a closet with the door locked, or garotted. This kind of activity cost Richardson a good deal of effort, by no means well-rewarded, for book-reviewing is one of the surviving undemolished houses of old Grub Street.

In his late sixties, he could be seen plodding from the *Observer* and other offices with great piles of books. He once wrote that, when he surreptitiously read rubbish as a boy, he little imagined that he would later earn his living, or a large part of it, by reviewing the stuff. He did not of course read every book all the way through. That would have been impossible. But he was more conscientious than many of his fellow-practitioners. When he came to collect his books, he would usually suggest an expedition to a local pub. Though he was prone to spells of depression, he was gregarious. He also had bouts of abstinence. 'On the wagon,' he would announce tersely; and special forays had accordingly to be organised to those pubs which happened to stock the brand of mineral water currently favoured by him.

He was a big man who looked shorter than he was on account of his breadth. Like many of his physical type, he possessed quite delicate hands, smallish feet and a rolling gait even when absolutely sober. He could be charming and he could be garrulous. He also exuded a kind of menace: usually, to be sure, without intending to do so. Partly, no doubt, the feelings of apprehension he could arouse were due to his expertise as a boxer. He would sometimes wave his fists about in an alarming manner to demonstrate some pugilistic point. Partly also he caused unease because of his handsome but aggressive appearance. With his massive head and slightly protuberant, rather mad blue eyes, he resembled Randolph Churchill and, before the latter's death, was indeed frequently mistaken for him.

He moved effortlessly between Soho and Fleet Street, with occasional excursions to Hampstead and Chelsea. He was as much at his ease in the York Minster (better known as the French Pub) and the Colony Room (better known as Muriel's) as in El Vino (always known as El Vino's). He enjoyed dual citizenship, of Grub Street and Bohemia.

The area depicted above was, so to speak, his spiritual or proper home. The reality – even if he did find an occasional resting-place in Soho – was somewhat different. With his wife he once had a largish house in Golders Green. Pursued and harassed by the Inland Revenue, he was compelled to sell up and move to Suffolk. Jeffrey Bernard, another Soho habitué, was by chance a Suffolk neighbour of his at this time. They used to drink together at Sudbury on market days. The landlord of their chosen pub would charge 20p for a large Ricard or Pernod. He suspected that this was too little. Taxed, Richardson said: 'Oh no, my dear chap, this is simply rubbish from France. It makes people go blind in Marseilles. Gentlemen simply don't touch it. No, no, twenty pence is just right.'

Bernard and Richardson were once travelling in the buffet car of a train from Sudbury to Liverpool Street. Richardson announced in a loud voice: 'D'you know what I think I'll do this evening? I think I'll go to Ipswich and have a whore.'

On another occasion, involving not Bernard but someone else, Richardson espied his companion's full wallet and said: 'I'm taking a Chinese girl out tonight. Would you mind lending me a tenner?'

His companion complied with the request.

'I say,' Richardson said, 'would you terribly mind making that twenty?'

His companion complied again. The money was repaid shortly before his death.

Yet he did not have expensive tastes. He liked good food, good drink and the occasional – or, when the manic mood was upon him, the frequent – night out. But he was always in financial trouble. He had a special arrangement with the *New Statesman* whereby he was paid for his contributions immediately, in cash.

Still, he enjoyed life to the end. He did not behave as an old age pensioner of six years' standing. Indeed most people put him at around sixty. A few days before his death he attended the party at the Lyceum for the *Spectator*'s 150th anniversary, and danced vigorously. A few days before the party he had suffered a minor heart attack. It did not seem to concern him greatly. On the night of the party he had dined with a woman friend. ('Very good but rather expensive. Thank God she was paying.') Three days later he stayed with another friend in Tunbridge Wells. His host took him a cup of tea in the morning and found him dead. He had had a coronary during the night. He left Fleet Street a poorer place.

WILLIAM ROBSON

14 July 1895 – 12 May 1980

WILLIAM ALEXANDER ROBSON was Professor of Public Administration at the London School of Economics. He was the last of the old Fabians. He had been encouraged by the Webbs, had impressed Bernard Shaw and, with Leonard Woolf, had founded the *Political Quarterly*. For professional purposes he liked to be known, American-style, as William A. Robson. His friends called him 'Willie', as did his students behind his back. His numerous works were written on lined foolscap paper in green ink – often a sign of a certain mental imbalance, if not of positive insanity.

No one, however, could have been *saner* than Robson, though he was quick to take offence at slights, which were frequently real rather than imagined. His Professorship came late, in 1947. He did not chair any important Royal Commission or Committee of Inquiry, nor was he even appointed a member of those committees (such as the Franks Committee on Tribunals) to which he could have made a unique contribution.

His greatest work was *Justice and Administrative Law*, which was first published in 1928. In this book he refuted the claims of the nineteenth-century constitutional lawyer A. V. Dicey in at least three respects. He demonstrated that England did indeed possess a system, even though covert, of administrative justice; that, to protect the citizen, this system should be recognised, extended and regularised; and that, in essence, there was no difference between an administrative and a judicial decision – that there was no magic in the appurtenances of a court of law. Indeed Robson, though he was (perhaps because he was) a barrister of Lincoln's Inn who had practised for a short time, always showed an aversion to lawyers and their ways.

Justice and Administrative Law subsequently went through numerous editions, each more tedious and ill-constructed than the last. For though Robson was a good and clear writer ('your sentences are too long,' he once adjured his research assistant), he often had little sense of what to leave out. He had a particular affection for the post-1945 decisions of the War

Pensions Tribunal, presided over by Mr Justice (as he then was) Denning. Denning's broad approach, in this as in other types of case, was to say, 'Give him the money, Barney.' This was an approach which commended itself to Robson, who liked to regard himself as on the side of the underdog, though in progressive circles today his views would be stigmatised as intolerably élitist, managerialist, centralist and bureaucratic. The reports of the War Pensions Tribunal inevitably included accounts of medical conditions of a distressing nature. Robson insisted on passing on all the details to his readers, which, apart from other considerations, used up space. When asked why he did this, he replied: 'It adds human interest.'

This (in the best sense) journalistic side to Robson, his conviction that the reader's attention must be engaged, as demonstrated by his liking for medical details and short sentences, was not reflected in any regard for the trade or profession of journalism. When a research assistant announced his departure from the LSE to join the editorial staff of the *Sunday Express* as a feature-writer, Robson professed shock. 'But it is a popular newspaper,' he lamented, accurately enough. Inquiring the editor's name, and being told that it was John Junor (then unknighted), Robson was disbelieving. 'No one could possibly be called John Junor,' he said. 'It is clearly a pen-name. Pen-names,' he added sapiently, 'are much used in Fleet Street.'

Fleet Street, to Robson, expressed the dark and irrational side of English life. The BBC, on the other hand, sought the truth, even if inadequately. There was undoubtedly an establishmentarian side to Robson. It was expressed, for instance, in his fundamental admiration for the upper reaches of the civil service. He had been an Assistant Secretary at the Air Ministry during the 1939–45 war. It was perhaps significant that his second book (1922), a product of his student researches, was entitled *From Patronage to Proficiency in the Public Service*.

Admittedly this admiration for civil servants, though he could be critical of them when the occasion seemed to demand it, was not entirely, or even mainly, a product of Robson's establishmentarian side. He believed in rational decision based on evidence; civil servants, as a class, seemed to him to make their decisions more rationally than politicians, among whom his acquaintance was surprisingly small for a man of his eminence who also desired to 'change things' broadly in a Socialist direction. Still, establishmentarianism came into his attitude. He took pride, for example, in his membership of the Athenaeum, and clearly liked mentioning that he had met Lord Hurcomb, say, at tea there on the previous day.

But in the conventional sense no one could have been less snobbish than Robson: 'Cyril Hurcomb' was a name to drop not because he was a peer but because he had been chairman of the British Transport Commission. Nor could anyone have been less adept at sucking up to those in authority. His reputation was that of an awkward customer. He had honorary degrees from French, Italian and other foreign universities. He was, for some reason, held in high esteem in Japan. His views on town planning, on local government, on public corporations and, of course, on administrative law were earnestly sought in far-away lands, to which he made frequent visits. Yet in this country he remained virtually unrecognised except among a small group.

He never received any public honour. Several of his colleagues at LSE suggested to Sir Harold Wilson that Robson should be made a life peer, but nothing came of the attempt. (Robson was, like others much less shrewd than he, an early admirer of Sir Harold, but later turned against him.) This lack of recognition would not have mattered if Robson had not minded about it. But he did mind: he was hurt and felt excluded. He was not like his former colleague R. H. Tawney, who, on being offered a peerage by Ramsay MacDonald, asked what harm he had ever done the Labour Party.

The suspicion in which Robson was held in Labour circles was partly the result of the Conservatives' London Government Act, 1963, which abolished that old Labour keep the LCC. In the late 1950s he had established the Greater London Group at the LSE. The Group gave evidence to the Royal Commission on London; many of its proposals were incorporated in the subsequent Act. Robson was not one to follow a party line.

But his prickliness did not make things easier for himself. His research assistant once mildly questioned his method or style of setting down footnote references, hazarding that it might be preferable to follow the conventions employed in Sir Ivor Jennings's constitutional works. Robson became quite angry. 'Why,' he asked, 'should Jennings be considered superior to Robson?' The embarrassed research worker tried to explain that he meant no more than that the Cambridge University Press (the publishers of Jennings's major works) set a high standard in these scholarly matters, that their example might be worth considering, perhaps following, and that he had intended no judgment as to the relative merits of Jennings and Robson as constitutional authorities. Robson remained unmollified, indeed distinctly cross. Later the research assistant was told that Jennings and Robson had not been on the best of terms when they had both been on the LSE staff in the 1930s and that Robson was jealous of the public recognition and acclaim which subsequently came Jennings's way.

Both Robson's prickliness and his unfulfilled desire for public recognition may have had something to do with his being a Jew. He neither paraded nor concealed his Jewishness: he simply made no reference to it: it seemed to play no part in his life. He was born in North Finchley, the son of a Hatton Garden pearl-dealer. His father died when he was fifteen, and he left school without having taken any public examinations. He started work as a clerk with the Graham White Aviation Company, which owned Hendon Airport, and quickly became assistant manager of the airport. His experience led him to publish in 1916, at twenty-one, *Aircraft in War and Peace*. By this time he had enlisted in the Royal Flying Corps, in which he served as a fighter pilot in France.

His first book impressed Bernard Shaw, who brought him to the notice of Sidney and Beatrice Webb. They decided he should go to the then new LSE, and waived the normal entrance requirements in his favour. Thereafter, apart from a spell in Sir Henry Slesser's chambers and war-time service in the Air Ministry, the LSE was Robson's professional home.

His room was just down the corridor from Michael Oakeshott, Harold Laski's improbable successor. One gained the impression that Robson did not approve of Oakeshott: whether he disapproved more of Oakeshott's levity as a person or of his obscurity of style as a writer is difficult to say. Oakeshott wore corduroy jackets and cultivated a generally raffish air: Robson, dark-moustached, three piece-suited, pipe-smoking, green-ink scribbling (this last his one superficial eccentricity), gave forth an aura of Fabian earnestness and Fabian industry. He could work very hard partly because he was very healthy. He had fenced in his youth; he swam, walked and played tennis until he was into his eighties. His occasional jokes would be signalled by a crinkling of the nostrils, as if he were trying to imitate a rabbit.

His tendency to overload later editions of *Justice and Administrative Law* with excessive detail notwithstanding, he was a believer in not writing to the fullest extent of one's knowledge. Keeping something in reserve, he used to say, not only added a mysterious authority to the prose but also enabled one to mount a counter-offensive should one's conclusions or views be challenged by some ill-disposed critic. He believed too in going to the original sources. This was not specially difficult, admittedly, in the line of work in which he was engaged, as law reports, Hansards, white papers, blue books and the rest were – are – usually obtainable readily enough. Still, he was more scrupulous than some academics and most journalists about not accepting second-hand summaries as evidence.

He would enter every idea or fact on a separate piece of paper, with a heading giving the chapter in which the information was likely to appear, and a reference in the bottom left-hand corner. Before writing, he would shuffle, cut, and re-shuffle these sheets as if they were playing-cards. By this means, he said, he perceived fresh patterns – and also avoided the charge of cribbing. He claimed that this method of research had been invented by the Webbs, who had bequeathed it to him. But others may have had the same idea too.

Though formidable, demanding and touchy, he was a kind man. He was one of the few LSE dons to maintain the tradition of hospitality to their research students. He and his wife, who was French and a distinguished 'cellist and teacher of the 'cello, would entertain, usually once a term, on Sunday evening, at their house in Westbourne Grove. Chairs would be disposed round the walls of the room. After ten or so minutes' desultory conversation, Robson or his wife would clap hands and there would be a general re-arrangement. After about an hour of sometimes musical chairs (for Mrs Robson would occasionally give a rendition on the 'cello) the party would adjourn for plain fare and cider cup from which all deleterious substances, including alcohol, had mysteriously been removed.

Though he was a difficult man to deal with, he had a touch of greatness.

NORMAN ST JOHN-STEVAS

18 May 1929 –

THERE was an element of mystery about his name and his father's name and occupation. His entry in *Who's Who* gave his name as Norman Antony Francis St John-Stevas. His parents were named as Stephen S. Stevas, civil engineer and company director, and Kitty St John O'Connor. His birth certificate, however, showed certain differences. On this his Christian names were given as Norman Panayea St John. His father's name was given as Spyro Stevas and his occupation as that of hotel proprietor. In a letter to the *Spectator* of 20 October 1979, which followed a Profile of him, St John-Stevas explained:

> My father like myself had a number of Christian names: St John is a family name of my mother's and she hyphenated it when she formally divorced her husband. My father's family has had a long connection with the Ionian islands. They were under British rule in the last century and I believe it was my great-great-grandfather who married into an Ionian family, so that I have Greek and Italian connections for which I am grateful. My father was by profession an engineer and graduated in engineering, but never practised and went into business in hotels and property.

Certainly St John-Stevas was closer to his mother, who was Irish and a Roman Catholic. The family home was in Gloucester Gardens. There were two sisters, one of whom, Juno Stevas, became an actress. St John-Stevas was sent to Ratcliffe, a small Roman Catholic school outside Leicester, where he was known as Norman Stevas. He then spent six months in Rome studying for the priesthood but discovered he had no vocation for it. Afterwards he went up to Fitzwilliam House, Cambridge.

Fitzwilliam was not then a college, properly speaking, though it afterwards became one. Its members could, however, play a full part in university activities. St John-Stevas was elected President of the Union and took a first in law. His contemporaries included Patrick Jenkin and Sir (as

he subsequently became) Geoffrey Howe. He then moved to the grander surroundings of Christ Church, Oxford, having also been offered a place at Oriel College. He became Secretary of the Oxford Union and obtained a second in the examination for Bachelor of Civil Law. He was called to the bar by the Middle Temple in 1952, two years before taking his BCL.

But he did not practise ('I never practised, only preached') and, after 1954, there followed ten years of academic legal work, at Yale, Oxford, Southampton and London; of journalism, principally with the *Economist*; and of book-writing. He produced *Obscenity and the Law*, an innovative work not only because, for the first time, the subject was dealt with comprehensively but also because the book was equally valuable to the lawyer and the layman. Roy Jenkins relied heavily upon it in his Private Member's reform – later much criticised – of the obscenity laws of that time. Above all, he began, under the patronage of the *Economist*, the standard edition of the collected works of Walter Bagehot, which, as the volumes appeared from 1965 onwards, excited admiration as much for its chaste and elegant typography as for its scholarly editing.

In 1951 he had unsuccessfully contested Dagenham as a Conservative. In 1964 he became Member for Chelmsford. In Edward Heath's Government he was Parliamentary Under-Secretary at the Department of Education and Minister of State for the Arts. He was Opposition spokesman on Education between 1975 and 1978. In this last period he was out of key with the then prevailing educational tune of the Conservative Party. He felt persecuted, or purported to feel persecuted, by his colleague and junior spokesman Dr Rhodes Boyson, to whom he referred as 'Beeson' and 'the Colossus', from the Colossus of Rhodes. Nevertheless, he generally managed to secure a standing ovation from the annual party conference. 'Did you hear my speech?' he would ask journalists afterwards. 'No? how very remiss of you. What *can* you have been doing? My reception was ecstatic – there is no other word for it, ecstatic. I look forward to reading a lengthy article on the subject.'

It was, however, a relief to him when he was made Shadow Leader of the House in 1978. It was a joy when he was made the real Leader of the House after the Conservatives victory in 1979. He had dreaded a return to Education. Nor did he want a department such as Environment or Health and Social Security: in fact, he was quite capable of mastering the required detail, but did not wish to make the effort.

When a journalist telephoned to congratulate him on his appointment as Leader of the House, he insisted on showing the journalist round his new offices. These were the offices of the Lord President of the Council, the most splendid in Whitehall. St John-Stevas was not, as it happened, Lord President but Chancellor of the Duchy of Lancaster, in addition to being Leader of the House. However, the Lord Presidency was associated with the Leadership of the House; and the actual Lord President, Lord Soames, wished to occupy the old Admiralty offices on account of their association with his father-in-law, Winston Churchill.

On this occasion St John-Stevas, having been offered lunch, insisted on being taken to Langan's Brasserie, a restaurant then much in the fashion, in preference to some quieter establishment. It was one of his eccentricities to specify the restaurant at which he was to be entertained. On the whole his hosts fell in with his wishes readily enough, though they might complain to their friends afterwards about his social – for they were social rather than culinary – demands.

He was also made Minister for the Arts, an area of life for which, despite his numerous affectations, he had a genuine feeling (he was passionately attached to Venice, where he would stay at a modest *pensione*). He had the reputation of being the best Minister for the Arts since Lady (Jennie) Lee. He once visited the Buxton Festival in Derbyshire, and suggested that his ministerial flag, the flag of the Duchy of Lancaster, should be flown at the theatre he was attending. The organisers declined to do so on the ground that a member of the Royal Family was attending the festival at the same time and that she had made no such request in regard to her own flag: in the circumstances, they considered, to fly St John-Stevas's flag alone would smack of disrespect to Royalty.

This was not, as it happened, a member of the Royal Family with whom St John-Stevas claimed to be on close terms. Nor were these claims vainglorious. He was a genuine friend of Princess Margaret, and deplored her persecution, as he saw it, by the newspapers. He knew even the Queen, partly through his connection with a courtier called Nevill. He also made a point of visiting successive Popes, who seemed to receive him civilly enough. He would write lucrative articles in the papers about his trips to the Vatican.

He was a good Leader of the House, with two achievements to his credit. First, he inaugurated a new system of parliamentary committees. The old system was built on the Public Accounts Committee, which dealt with past expenditure; the Expenditure Committee, which was supposed to deal with current and future expenditure, but often in fact did neither satisfactorily; various *ad hoc* offshoots of the Expenditure Committee; and the generally admired Nationalised Industries Committee. Broadly, St John-Stevas placed parliamentary committees on a departmental basis, so that a group of back-bench MPs would supervise a specific government department. He implemented this reform against colleagues (like Michael Foot on the Labour side and Enoch Powell on the back benches) who were opposed to powerful back bench committees on abstract constitutional grounds or, more numerous, who were opposed to them because they thought ministers' lives would be made more difficult or who simply did not care much one way or the other. In addition, he ensured that membership of the committees was not controlled by the party whips.

His diminution of the whips' power in this respect was connected with, or was a part of, his second achievement. This was to make it plain that, as a matter of constitutional principle, he was as much the House's representative in the Government as the Government's representative in the House. This principle was diluted when his successor, Francis Pym, was also made Minister in charge of 'government information'. Indeed, it was said at the time that St John-Stevas's refusal to do the bidding of the Conservative whips was the reason for his outright dismissal from the Government in January 1981.

The dismissal devastated him because he had imagined that he possessed a special personal relationship with Mrs Margaret Thatcher, whom he had supported for the Conservative leadership against Edward Heath in 1975. He attributed the dismissal to his having argued in Cabinet against Mrs Thatcher's and Sir Geoffrey Howe's economic policy. He had, moreover, delivered a lecture at the Conservative conference of 1980 in which he lamented the Government's emphasis on economics to the exclusion of other 'Conservative values'. But the real reason for his summary sacking was probably his habit of bestowing nick-names on his colleagues. They pretended to laugh but did not really like it. Here is a selection:

Margaret Thatcher – the Blessed Margaret, the Leaderene, Heather.
Sir Geoffrey Howe – Geoffrey Who.
John Nott – John Nit (also attributed to Sir Ian Gilmour).
Sir Ian Gilmour – Ion or the Seal, after the office, Lord Privy Seal, which Gilmour held.
Angus Maude – Ong-goose.
Cardinal Hume – Basil (pronounced Bayzil) Brush.

Towards the end of his period as Leader of the House St John-Stevas's getting people's names wrong assumed manic proportions. Thus:

Sir Tom McCaffrey (press officer to Michael Foot) – Sir Dick McTavish.

Fred Emery, then of *The Times* – Bert Emery.

Simon Hoggart of the *Observer* – 'That nice Rupert Hoggart. I do like him, don't you?'

St John-Stevas had a collection of about half-a-dozen dark overcoats with velvet collars. He was fond of purple shirts with white collars attached, heavily striped shirts and coloured handkerchiefs. He was commonly described as 'elegant'. Though he drank moderately by the standards of many Conservatives – or indeed Labour – politicians, he possessed a rubicund complexion which was not apparent on television. For Lent he always gave up port. He did not smoke. His letters or postcards were concluded with 'Blessings N.StJ-S.' He had two houses, one at Montpelier Square in Knightsbridge and the other, The Old Rectory, at Daventry in Northamptonshire. His London house was full of Victorian bric-à-brac and contained a harp. He was proudest of his conservatory. This house was somewhat lifeless – a bit like a museum. He had a close friend who was a merchant banker. He would often describe himself as 'celibate' or 'chaste'. He was personally kind, and sensitive to the feelings of others. He was both more serious and more sad than he was commonly assumed to be. He would, he said, have preferred to be the Master of an Oxford or Cambridge college rather than an active politician.

DAVID STEEL

31 March 1938 –

DAVID MARTIN SCOTT STEEL was one of the most skilful, determined and creative politicians of the post-war period. He was the eldest of the five children of the Reverend Dr David Steel, who was Moderator of the General Assembly of the Church of Scotland from 1974 to 1975, and of Sheila Martin. Scott was the surname of his paternal grandmother. His paternal grandfather was the manager of a grocer's shop and his maternal grandfather the headmaster of a primary school.

He was born in Kirkcaldy and spent his childhood in Buckhaven, Dumbarton and Edinburgh. When he was eleven his father was made the Church of Scotland's Minister for the East African Territories. The family moved to Nairobi in Kenya, where David attended the Prince of Wales School. This school was for whites only. His experiences in Kenya, fortified by his father's sympathy for the insurgents (which led some colonial administrators to contemplate asking for his withdrawal), were to be important in his later political life.

When he was fourteen his parents decided that he should take up the scholarship to George Watson's College, Edinburgh, which he had won shortly before the move to Kenya. At school he was active in the debating society and in the Edinburgh Schools Citizenship Association (a local, junior branch of the United Nations Association). For four years he did not see his father and saw his mother once: he spent his holidays chiefly with his mother's parents in Aberdeen.

In 1957 he went to Edinburgh University, and became a Liberal because he was impressed by the performance of William Douglas-Home as the unsuccessful Liberal candidate in the Edinburgh South by-election. He obtained two pass degrees: one, which took him three years, in general subjects, and the other, which took him a further two years, in law. (Though Steel did not shine academically, there was nothing mediocre or dilatory about this performance, as universities in Scotland are organised differently from those in England and Wales.)

However, he devoted most of his time to student politics, becoming President of the Student Representative Council and organising Jo Grimond's successful campaign for the rectorship of the university. At this period the university authorities were concerned about the rowdy and sometimes violent behaviour of students at rectorial installations, which had reached its apogee at a previous ceremony, at another Scottish university, Glasgow, when R. A. Butler had been struck by a flour bomb and been unable to complete his rectorial address. Steel was determined that there should be no repetition of such scenes, and promulgated instructions which insisted not only on decorum in behaviour but also on propriety, even conservatism, in dress: 'Men should wear lounge suits with white shirts, collar and tie. Dark blazer is a very suitable alternative. Women should wear appropriate dress, such as a suit, or a blazer and skirt.'

He had no vocation for the ministry and contemplated becoming an advocate, but was deterred by his lack of private means. He found a job as Assistant Secretary of the Scottish Liberal Party at £850 a year. Shortly before taking this post he had become prospective candidate for Edinburgh Pentlands. (Earlier, in his third year at the university, he had declined the offer to become prospective candidate for East Fife.) In 1963 Sir Alec Douglas-Home fought the Kinross and West Perthshire by-election on becoming Prime Minister and disclaiming his peerage. Steel organised the Liberal campaign. His candidate came a creditable second; and Steel found he got on well with the journalists from London who were covering the contest.

He was then invited to become prospective candidate for Roxburgh, Selkirk and Peebles. He accepted, causing some bruised feelings among the Edinburgh Liberals. He accepted subject to two conditions: that the Roxburgh chairman, who, he considered, was insufficiently sympathetic to working people in the constituency, should be removed, and that he should be allowed to fight three successive elections for the seat. Both conditions were met. In the general election of 1964 he failed to win by 1,739.

He then found a job, under a six months' contract, with the BBC in Scotland as a television interviewer and reporter. In December 1964 the Conservative Member for Roxburgh died. Steel was immediately suspended by the Corporation on full pay. He considered he had been unfairly treated, because he had not been formally adopted by the Roxburgh Liberals for the forthcoming by-election, and because an English Conservative in a comparable position, Geoffrey Johnson Smith of *Tonight* and other programmes, had been allowed to continue in employment. Steel's feud with the BBC lasted till 1970, when he presented *Songs of Praise* from his father's church at Linlithgow.

The Conservative candidate at the Roxburgh by-election of 1965 was Robin McEwen. He came of an established Border family. He had been educated at Eton and Trinity, Cambridge, where he had been outstandingly successful as an academic lawyer. Having practised at the bar in London, he had returned to the Borders to manage his estates. His brother Rory played the guitar and had been a founder-member of the 'Princess Margaret set'. Unhappily Robin McEwen, despite – perhaps because of – his exalted connections and his formidable intelligence, could not keep his temper. He could not keep it with his prospective constituents. He could not keep it with visiting journalists, by whom, admittedly, he was much provoked, notably by George Gale of the *Daily Express*. Gale, whose knowledge of agriculture was cursory, had discovered an obscure government disbursement to hill farmers known as 'winter keep'. Day after day he asked McEwen about the problems of winter keep. Daily McEwen became more irascible, until finally he could stand it no longer, and denounced the entire press. Steel, by contrast, was all calmness, civility and poise. He won the by-election decisively.

He began by 'shadowing' the Labour Minister Ray Gunter at Employment, a job he did not much like. He rose to national prominence when he drew sixth place in the ballot for Private Members' Bills. Lord Arran, an eccentric journalist-peer who had taken up the reform of the law on homosexuality, urged Steel to devote his Bill to the subject. Roy Jenkins, who was then Home Secretary, and Dick Taverne, his junior Minister, urged Steel to devote his Bill to the reform of the law on abortion. Steel agreed to take up the latter cause. He did not, as it happened, feel specially strongly about abortion, though he thought the law needed liberalising to give greater freedom to both women and doctors. But his Abortion Act won him a parliamentary reputation as a skilful tactician and a national reputation as a 'controversial' figure. As he had correctly calculated, the Act did him little harm, and some good, both with the Liberal Party and with his Roxburgh constituency.

As far as his constituency was concerned, he was – again correctly, as things turned out – more worried about his opposition in 1970 to the South African rugby tour in general and to the South Africans' match in the

Borders in particular: courageously, he demonstrated peacefully at the ground, and was spat at for the first and only time.

Steel had always been a supporter of Grimond in his strategy of 'radical realignment'. Indeed, he and Jeremy Thorpe were Grimond's only convinced supporters among Liberal MPs. In January 1967 Grimond told Steel privately of his intention to resign as leader. Both agreed that Thorpe was the best successor in view. In the ensuing campaign – which led to some rancour among Liberal activists, owing to the restriction of the franchise to Liberal MPs – Steel was Thorpe's manager. However, he was not happy either with Thorpe's leadership or with the Liberal Party generally. He had no enthusiasm for detailed resolutions on 'policy'. He did not believe that Thorpe's brand of political showmanship, which emphasised the Liberals' independence and their supposed ability to form a Government, met the problems of the party's strategy. His spirits rose after the party's by-election successes in the early 1970s. They rose still higher after the party's performance in the first election of 1974, when it polled 19 per cent of the vote. But the following two years were increasingly dominated by what became known as the Thorpe Affair.

In 1971, as Chief Whip, he, together with Lord Byers (present at Thorpe's insistence) and Emlyn Hooson, Q.C., interviewed Norman Scott about his allegations of a homosexual relationship with Thorpe. Steel concluded that Scott was an hysteric. However, he secured from Thorpe the promise that if the allegations – whether true or not – ever did become public, he would resign as leader. The allegations did become public, and Thorpe refused to resign. Steel, though angry, continued to believe in a 'not proven' verdict against Thorpe. He changed his mind after the publication of evidence of a payment of £2,500 made by Thorpe's friend, David Holmes. Thorpe was finally persuaded to resign by Clement Freud. Afterwards Steel's distrust of Thorpe increased.

John Pardoe, whom Steel defeated for the leadership of the party, was a political ally of his. Together, in the late 1960s, they had run the Radical Action Movement from Pardoe's house in Hampstead in an attempt to keep Grimond's ideas alive. Steel relied on his economic knowledge (though there were others, such as Denis Healey, who questioned it) and was moved when he lost his seat in 1979.

Since his first, and in some ways most difficult, speech as party leader – at the Llandudno Assembly in 1976 – Steel had based his view of the future on coalition or, failing that, on alliance. This view was unacceptable not only to numerous old-fashioned Liberals but also to a sizeable chunk of the radical wing. It was unacceptable to the Young Liberals in particular. Nevertheless Steel stuck to it. In 1977 he was given an opportunity to put his ideas into practice.

The Labour Government which had been elected in 1974, and led by James Callaghan since 1976, lost its majority on account of defeats in by-elections. Steel was anxious to help Callaghan, but equally anxious not to appear to be making the first move. He succeeded in depicting the Prime Minister as a supplicant. He was equally successful in persuading both his parliamentary colleagues and the Liberal Party outside to accept, or tolerate, the agreement to keep the Labour Government temporarily in office – the Lib-Lab pact. For there was never positive enthusiasm for the pact in either Liberal group. Steel secured acquiesence by making the pact a matter of confidence in his own leadership.

Most Liberals did not want to ditch Steel, but equally most Liberals wondered what their party was getting out of the new arrangement. Steel made various more or less innocuous demands of Callaghan which could be met without inconvenience. He did not demand proportional representation because he thought he would not get it. He did demand PR in the direct elections to the European Parliament not because he thought he would get it – he always thought it probable that the House of Commons would reject the proposal – but because it was a reasonable demand to make and because he had to be seen by his party to be demanding something. His object was to secure for the Liberals some share in government. His technique was to claim credit for the Government's successes, such as the diminished rate of inflation, but to disclaim responsibility for the Government's failures.

Nonetheless, the fear of most Liberals and the wisdom of most commentators before the 1979 election was that the party would be lucky to survive: partly because of the Thorpe Affair, partly because of the pact and partly because the voters would be voting against a Labour rather than against a Conservative Government. Steel did not foresee disaster but was worried nevertheless. As it turned out, the Liberal share of the vote fell from 18 to 14 per cent and the party's seats from 13 to 11. Steel was widely held to have fought an excellent campaign, and the opinion polls for the three-week period before polling day confirmed this view.

In the same year, 1979, Steel held the first of several informal conversations with Roy Jenkins, who was then still at Brussels. At this stage he had, perhaps surprisingly, not even met David Owen. It was disputed whether Steel positively discouraged Jenkins from joining the Liberal Party. What was not disputed was that it was Steel who first saw clearly that, if the two-party system was to be broken in Britain, four parties – two of them in alliance – were better than three. He committed himself to helping the new Social Democratic Party (then un-named) but said he could not commit his party. All he could firmly promise Jenkins and his allies was a share in the Liberal party political broadcasts, which he himself controlled. As with the Lib-Lab pact, Steel helped to create the Liberal-SDP Alliance by making the 'issue', as far as his party colleagues were concerned, one of confidence in himself as leader. He overcame most doubts – indeed, he triumphed – at the Llandudno Assembly of 1981.

He was married to Judy, who was less self-contained than he was. They had three children of their own and one adopted son, who was looked after by them when his fostering arrangements in the constituency had proved unsatisfactory. Their house at Ettrick Bridge consisted of three cottages that had been joined together. It was purchased in 1966, partly with the proceeds of Steel's journalistic and television earnings. Indeed, despite his early feud with the BBC – during which he worked happily enough for the commercial companies – he made a good proportion of his income from television, being much in demand as a presenter of religious programmes.

He was an Elder of the Kirk but liked driving fast cars. His other recreation was riding. He also enjoyed food and drink, especially claret and whisky, but retained a trim, youthful and somehow buttoned-up appearance. He once said: 'I like good food and decent wine as much as Roy Jenkins does, but I keep quiet about it.' He smoked small cigars – large ones if they were offered to him.

He could be impatient with his subordinates. One of them once left his room and omitted to close the door properly. He shouted: 'I don't mind if the door's open, and I don't mind if it's shut, but for God's sake make up your bloody mind.' He said this in his hotel suite when he was under some strain at a party assembly.

It was a matter of dispute whether it was the present writer or James Fenton (then of the *New Statesman*, and a friend and admirer of Steel's) who first wrote of him: 'He is not as nice as he looks.' But he was both a formidable and an honest politician, and he was an engaging companion. He was of medium height but, despite his slimness, appeared smaller than he was. The other odd thing about him was that one expected his eyes to be brown. In fact they were blue, like the North Sea on a good day.

A. J. P. TAYLOR

25 March 1906 –

ALAN JOHN PERCIVALE TAYLOR was our greatest popular historian since Macaulay and one of the best writers of English prose of this century. Much of this prose appeared in the form of journalism, of which he was rightly proud. He was also something of a hack. He was proud of this as well.

He was born at Birkdale in Lancashire, the son of a Manchester cotton merchant. Most of his childhood, however, was spent at Preston and at Buxton in Derbyshire. He liked to emphasise that he came of radical, dissenting stock. A collateral ancestor of his father's was killed at Peterloo. His maternal great-grandfather voted for 'Orator' Hunt at the Preston by-election of 1830, and received one of the medals struck in honour of 'the free and independent voters of Preston'. He was a solitary only child but got on well with and admired his father, Percy Taylor. Alan Taylor used to say that all Lancashire men were romantics and romancers – what later came to be called fantasists – and that Percy would never give Alan's mother an entirely truthful account of his movements when he had left the house. Percy was a Lloyd George Radical before the First World War but afterwards, unlike most businessmen, moved left, joining first the Independent Labour Party and then the Labour Party itself. He became a Labour councillor in Preston and was a member of the local strike committee during the General Strike of 1926.

Alan Taylor was sent to a Quaker preparatory school and then to another Quaker establishment, Bootham School, York. He read historical novels – the less imaginative they were, the better he liked them – and took up Gothic church architecture as his hobby. But he did not attend an Anglican service until he went up to Oriel College, Oxford. He soon tried to cry off chapel on the ground of atheism. The Dean said: 'Do come and talk to me about your doubts.' 'I have none,' Taylor replied. However, he always had an admiration for Quakerism, saying that it had provided him with the guiding principle of his life: 'I am no better than anyone else, and no one else is better than me.'

At Oxford his friends included Tom Driberg, later Lord Bradwell; Norman Cameron, the poet; and J. I. M. Stewart, the novelist and, as 'Michael Innes', author of detective stories. He called himself a Marxist and was a member of the Communist Party for a year or so. He left the Party because he was disgusted by its treatment of Trotsky and disappointed by its performance during the General Strike, when he returned briefly to Lancashire and drove a car for his father's strike committee.

Oxford history of that time emphasised medieval history, in which he was not much interested. When he reached the Glorious Revolution of 1688, his tutor said: 'You know all the rest from your work at school, so we do not need to do any more.' He picked up most of his knowledge of modern history from the works of Sir John Marriott. He was also influenced, as much in style as in history, by Albert Sorel's *Europe and the French Revolution*. Indeed, it was Sorel who first attracted him to the antithetical style. His first in 1927 surprised him. He thought, as he later put it, that he was clever-clever but not history-clever. He still had no ambition to become a professional historian and, on leaving Oxford, spent six unsatisfactory months in a solicitor's office.

On his return to Oxford, the then Regius Professor suggested that he should go to Vienna and work under the Professor there, an authority on Oliver Cromwell. When he arrived in Vienna he found that the Professor had lost interest in Cromwell, so Taylor worked on various aspects of nineteenth-century diplomatic history instead. Nineteenth-century European history remained his principal professional interest for the next thirty years. But his future was still not settled in his mind. He learned German and thought of becoming a foreign correspondent. He even took preliminary steps towards becoming an inspector of ancient monuments.

His Viennese Professor was invited to deliver the Ford Lectures at Oxford and, at dinner one evening, happened to find himself sitting next to the new head of the history department at Manchester, who was looking for a lecturer. Taylor's name came up, and he was duly appointed. (Taylor seemed to find his element of chance in his own life surprising – or at any rate worthy of comment. He did not appear to realise that other people's lives fell out similarly.) As a lecturer at Manchester, he made a great discovery: he could speak in public. He could hold the attention of an audience. And, unlike other orators, he was not even nervous beforehand. This discovery was comparable to that of Richard Crossman, made some ten years later in Crossman's case, that he could write English.

Taylor was always self-confident about his writing ability. His journalism too started in Manchester. His mentor was A. P. Wadsworth, the editor of the *Manchester Guardian*, who used to say to Taylor: 'An article in the *Guardian* is no good unless people read it on the way to work.' Taylor wrote commemorative pieces and leader-page articles. His models were Bunyan, Cobbett and Shaw. He advocated resistance to Hitler but also thought the National Government was more likely to support Hitler against Russia. So he opposed rearmament until there was a change of government. With the reoccupation of the Rhineland, he decided we must re-arm. On his applying for an appointment at Corpus Christi College, Oxford, the President said: 'I hear you have strong political views.' Taylor replied: 'Oh no, President. Extreme views weakly held.' He did not get the job.

Another, lesser influence on him at this time was Lewis Namier, who came to Manchester as Professor of Modern History (Taylor was never Namier's pupil). Taylor once made some point or other in a review. Namier asked: 'How did you know that? I worked on the topic for three weeks before I found it.' Taylor said he felt it must be so. Namier said: 'Ah, you have green fingers. I have not.' As an historian, Taylor was inclined to include things if he thought they made sense. He then presented them as matters of fact. An acquaintance once asked him whether he could supply a reference or an authority for Morley's observation to Gladstone that journalists, owing to their habits of mind and mode of life, were unsuited to the exercise of administrative responsibilities – Morley, of course, being himself a politically ambitious journalist. Taylor confessed he had not previously heard the story but said it sounded likely enough. It would be a pity to spoil it. 'Put it in,' he advised. His acquaintance duly put it in.

Namier thought there ought to be a special subject in the diplomatic history of the years before the First World War. E. L. (later Sir Llewellyn) Woodward was promoting the same cause in Oxford. Both helped to get Taylor a Fellowship at Magdalen in 1938. Taylor's best-known books were written in the next twenty-five years, in which he was a full tutorial Fellow of the College. The style of *The Habsburg Monarchy 1815–1918* (1941) was influenced by Malcolm Muggeridge's *The Thirties*. Taylor said that Muggeridge was the last literary influence on him: 'Since then my style has been my own. It has however changed with my writing instruments. With a pen you write words. With a typewriter you write sentences. With an electric typewriter, which I use now, you write paragraphs. In military terms: bow and arrow, musket, machine gun. I try to keep up a continuous fire.' In writing *The Habsburg Monarchy* he also learned a lot from Central European refugees, notably Hubert Ripka, the predestined successor of Beneš, and Michael Karolyi.

Taylor thought, and subsequently maintained, that the Second World War was the British people's finest hour, but himself played no more active part in it than serving in the Oxford Home Guard with Frank Pakenham, as he then was.

All Taylor's major books, with the exception of *The Origins of the Second World War* (1961), were written on the suggestion of other people – publishers or academic editors. In 1956 he was invited to give the Ford Lectures, an invitation he accepted with pride. Alan (later Lord) Bullock suggested the topic: Taylor's heroes, the men who had opposed official British foreign policy. The lectures appeared as *The Trouble Makers* (1957), his favourite book. Michael Foot called it 'the book in which you stabbed all your friends in the back'. 1956 was also the year in which he was elected to the British Academy; on the strength, according to the Oxford historian V. H. Galbraith, of the bibliography to *The Struggle for Mastery in Europe 1848–1918* (1954). (He resigned from the Academy over its treatment of Anthony Blunt.) And 1956 was the year in which he met and became friends with Lord Beaverbrook. The friendship came about partly because he gave a laudatory review to Beaverbrook's *Men and Power*, partly because he wrote to him asking a specific question about Lloyd George.

His relationship with Beaverbrook introduced him to the *Sunday Express*, for which he wrote frequent leader-page articles (they did not appear every Sunday, but more frequently than those of any other regular contributor). By the mid-1950s he had already written a weekly column in the *Daily Herald* and was a regular book-reviewer, notably in the *Observer* and the *New Statesman*. These latter pieces were re-published as books, five in all: they were later divided into two books, one on European history, the other on English. They can be re-read, and re-read again, both with enjoyment and for instruction. Much of Taylor's best writing was in his short essays, from which one could learn something not only about history but about English. Journalistically, however, Taylor was no *prima donna*. He did as he was told. His maxims included 'The editor is always right' and 'A good journalist is he who pleases his editor'.

He had also established himself as a television performer. He could talk straight to the camera for 25 minutes and 27 seconds (he was precise about the time) and hold an audience's attention. He wrote down his opening and closing words on postcards, but this was all. Richard Crossman was jealous not so much of Taylor's ability in this regard as of his opportunity to exercise this ability, considering that he would be able to perform with equal facility if only given the chance. Taylor further established himself as a lively performer in the early programmes of television argument, the BBC's *In The News* and, when this was withdrawn after pressure from the political parties, commercial television's *Free Speech*. (Taylor was an early supporter of commercial television.)

After 1956, which he regarded as his own *annus mirabilis*, came the first of his two main disappointments. He was not appointed Regius Professor of History at Oxford. The choice of the then Prime Minister, Harold Macmillan, was Dame Lucy Sutherland, but she turned the job down. Namier offered to urge Taylor's claims if he would promise to relinquish journalism and broadcasting. Taylor refused to accept this condition. Macmillan appointed instead Hugh Trevor-Roper, Student of Christ Church, later Lord Dacre of Glanton. Trevor-Roper was, in many people's eyes, as good a writer as Taylor, but his historical works were fewer. Taylor was understandably cross. However, he and Trevor-Roper preserved a wary respect for each other. They engaged in controversy over Taylor's *Origins of the Second World War*.

His second disappointment was that the History Faculty Board did not renew his university lectureship in 1963. It was to this, rather than the failure to make him Regius Professor, that Taylor referred when he later wrote of being 'slighted in my profession' at Oxford. He had then been a lecturer for ten years, having been re-appointed for a second term after the first five years. According to some observers of the Oxford academic scene, there was no reason – it would have been unusual – for him to be re-appointed for a third five-year term. Taylor, however, did not see matters in this light. As a gesture of protest, or in a fit of pique, he resigned his Fellowship at Magdalen, though there was no need for him to do so. Magdalen gave him a special Fellowship and, in 1976, when this terminated, an honorary Fellowship. But after 1965 his home was London, not Oxford.

Shortly before this he was engaged in the Campaign for Nuclear Disarmament. His models were John Bright and Richard Cobden. Taylor had specially in mind Cobden's quotation: 'I know the Blue Books as well as the noble Lord does.' Once again he experienced the intoxication of moving thousands, even if to little effect: 'CND was a last splutter of imperial pride. The Cuba missile crisis [of 1962] taught us better. No one cared in the slightest whether we had nuclear weapons or not.'

He was a short, slight man with a peering and somehow suspicious expression. He resembled a small creature of the field who was apprehensive of attack but would turn nasty in that event. His recreations were walking, architecture (specially church architecture) and music. At one period he smoked one, and only one, Gauloise cigarette, at tea-time. He looked a serious drinking man but was in fact temperate in his habits, indeed something of an ascetic in that he rose at seven, had a cold bath, walked much of the way to his office (latterly in the old *Evening Standard* building) or the London Library, lunched off cheese, biscuits and lemon juice – going out to lunch, he said, meant a wasted afternoon – and went to bed at ten. He shaved with an old-fashioned open razor. But he ate a hearty breakfast, often enjoyed a pint of beer on his walk home to Kentish Town and invariably shared a bottle of wine with his wife at dinner. He never visited the United States because, he said, they had neither good food nor good architecture. He was an admirer of Evelyn Waugh's writings but did not write much about Waugh.

He married, first, Margaret, a friend and benefactor of Dylan Thomas, a relationship which caused some worry and inconvenience to Taylor and gave him a lasting suspicion of the Welsh – not, however, extending to Lloyd George, whom he admired. He married, secondly, Eve, the sister of Anthony Crosland, who was both a concert pianist and a tennis coach: he and Crosland never got on and hardly saw each other. He married, thirdly, Eva, from Hungary. He had six children altogether and eight grandchildren. He used to say that a man had only a limited amount of love at his disposal and that most of his love had gone into his children.

He worked as hard as he did partly because he liked work and partly because of avarice. He was one of those men who believe – it is a form of madness – that they are going to end up in the workhouse, or whatever is its modern equivalent, unless they constantly earn money. He was modest about his abilities as an historian, saying once that he had made only one original discovery (it was of a minor document in an obscure nineteenth-century diplomatic dispute) in his entire life. But saying this required some self-confidence and -esteem on Taylor's part. His greatest historical discovery was probably in *English History 1918–1945* (1965). This was that the Labour, leftist or progressive view of English history between the wars was wrong and that the standard of living of most people, including working people, had increased. It was a typically perverse discovery. His most unappealing feature was his weakness for political thugs, from Lloyd George, through Churchill and Beaverbrook, to Stalin himself, with a passing nod in the direction of Hitler. Despite this weakness, he was a patriot, something of an English nationalist, with a genuine love for the countryside, the language and liberty. He never scorned the Whigs and continued to believe in progress. In this belief too Taylor was perverse to the end.

D. J. WATKINS
8 March 1894 – 26 December 1980

DAVID JOHN WATKINS was a Carmarthenshire elementary schoolmaster of reclusive habits but influence within a restricted circle. He was born at a small stone house called Lighthouse in Penygarn Road, Tycroes, and was accordingly sometimes known as 'Dai Lighthouse'. His family shortly acquired a slightly larger house, Bryntirion, almost directly opposite. On his marriage he rented an even larger house, Proskairon – the name, devised by a nonconformist minister who had been a previous tenant, was of Persian rather than Welsh origin – about a hundred yards distant on the same road. In 1937 he had built for him another house, Tregarn, directly opposite Proskairon. His periods of teacher training, war service and teaching in London apart, he spent his entire life in the same spot.

His father, John Watkins, was the winder – the man responsible for the raising and lowering of the cage of miners up and down the pit shaft – at the Rhôs Colliery, Tycroes. John Watkins and his relations possessed some local fame as pit-sinkers in a small way of business. John Watkins's wife, Catherine Thomas, came from Penybanc, a small village outside Llandeilo in Carmarthenshire. John and Catherine Watkins were illiterate in both Welsh and English, though John possessed considerable ability in practical engineering. Their children, in addition to David John, were Sarah Ann (known as 'Saran'), who suffered from epilepsy, was none too bright and married a Londoner, and Daniel, who was a miner and a local rugby player of, by all accounts, a simple and affectionate nature. Dan was killed in the Battle of Jutland.

D. J. Watkins was educated, to begin with, at the Tycroes Church of England School, though his father was a Calvinistic Methodist and his mother a Baptist. He could not read English until he was twelve. However, he passed 'the scholarship' – the then equivalent, in a sense, of the eleven-plus, though taken somewhat later – to the Llanelli County School for Boys, subsequently the Llanelli Grammar School, some twelve miles away. He travelled to Llanelli by train from Pantyffynnon, an important railway junction in the years immediately before and after the First World War, owing to its function of channelling the anthracite coal of the Amman Valley, Ammanford, and the villages around Ammanford (including Tycroes) towards the coastal towns of Swansea and Llanelli.

Watkins was frightened of his father, the colliery winder, who was neither scholarly nor gentle and had a disposition to resort to fisticuffs, as much with his contemporaries as with his children. He felt affectionate towards his mother, who was small and gentle, but pitied her for her ignorance, foolishness and superstition. Though he retained many of the characteristics of the peasant throughout his life – he possessed a strong sense of the importance of property, was close with money and regarded any attempt to deprive him of either his property or his money as equivalent to a physical assault – he was not one to romanticise about the characteristics and habits of rural Wales, as was the convention among patriotic Welshmen until quite recently.

However, though he was no romantic, his recollections of rural Wales before 1914 (or of an area of Wales that was partly rural, partly industrial, but neither urban nor suburban) differed markedly from those of Welsh socialists. People worked hard, he said, but there was always enough to eat: virtually every household kept chickens and a pig. Above all, people were happy. Happiness, he said, disappeared in 1914.

Though he was at ease with his past, he was not a countryman, nor did he possess his father's skill in practical matters. He was reluctant to undertake the simplest household tasks, such as inserting a screw or replacing a tap-washer. He did not attempt to do any cooking, which would, admittedly, have been considered eccentric in a man of his generation living in his part of the world. Though he ate meat, he could well have been a vegetarian. Like most Welshmen, he did not care for underdone meat, but he pushed this disposition to extremes, saying, if a touch of blood was in evidence: 'This tastes of the farmyard.' Throughout his life, indeed, he felt uneasy about the exploitation of animals, saying: 'What have the poor cows and pigs ever done to us?' He hated to visit a market place such as Carmarthen's because the cattle and sheep were so physically abused by the farmers. Yet he continued to eat meat, in small quantities, and overcooked.

At the Llanelli County School he determined to be a schoolmaster. He could probably have gone on to a university, but he was always unambitious, and settled for becoming a 'certificated teacher'. Having left school with the School Certificate, he worked for some time in a local coal-mine – as a labourer, not a miner – to raise the money to take him to the Teachers' Training Department of Bristol University. He made most of his lifelong friends in this Bristol period (the majority of them Englishmen), visited the music-hall and, having previously played rugby, appeared as a goal-keeper for the soccer team.

Physically he was an arresting man, six feet in height, something under twelve stones (though he later put on weight), with a large head and powerful chest, shoulders and upper arms. His legs were too thin and led to the nickname in his native village, in addition to 'Dai Lighthouse', of 'Dai coesau rhubarb', or 'Dai rhubarb-legs'. He was sensitive about this appellation, and became angry whenever it was mentioned, even when it was referred to as something that had belonged to the distant past. Even when he was not angry, his eyes changed, or appeared to change, colour in a disconcerting way, from hazel through green to grey. His hair was black and curly and grew in a peak. He had thick lips which did not create any impression of coarseness. His general cast of feature was Spanish, or Jewish. In his later years he resembled the conductor Otto Klemperer. Several times he was mistaken for a Jew by German prisoners or war who formed a football team to play the village at soccer during the Second World War and who would excitedly point him out to one another. (He could understand what they said because, with some other local teachers, he was learning German from a Jewish refugee who had settled in Ammanford.) So far as can be established, he had no Jewish blood. But he was always pleased to be mistaken for a Jew.

Apart from fire-watching at his school, he played no part in the 1939–45 war, taking the view, about which he was perfectly open, that he had done quite enough for King and Country in 1914–18. He was proud of the fact that he had joined up from the Bristol Teachers' Training Department and had not been conscripted. In all other respects he was unmilitary, neither wearing nor otherwise displaying his two campaign medals. He served as a naval chemist in Dover, London and France, where he remained for some months, though he would emphasise in conversation that he was never 'in the trenches' or 'in the front line'. His task was to instal in tanks devices for creating smoke screens. Quite why the Army was unable to perform this function on its own, without calling on the Navy for assistance, remained mysterious: but there it was.

His experiences in the First World War left him with not only a detestation of war in general but a suspicion of what he would variously call 'swank', 'pretence' and 'nonsense' – words that to him comprehended the virtues of the parade-ground, officer qualities, pageantry, the Royal Family, law courts, judges and Winston Churchill (though not R. A. Butler, whom he admired). This dislike of the ceremonial aspects of English life did not, however, lead him to celebrate the homelier traditions of his native land. 'Lot of talk' was one of his favourite dismissive phrases. Or: 'Jim Griffiths' – the local MP and a Minister in the Governments of 1945 and 1964 – 'has the gift of the gab all right, but what does he know about anything when you come down to it?' This was an over-severe criticism, though not without an element of justice, of a politician who virtually re-created the national insurance scheme and was an outstanding Colonial Secretary. But Watkins, for reasons that will appear, was suspicious of politicians.

The other effect of his war service was to make him liable to nightmares, which ceased only when he became very old. Though he had not himself been gassed, he would imagine he could not breathe, that something or somebody was at his throat. These nightmares were not only distressing to his family but dangerous both to them and to himself, for, still asleep, he would get out of bed. He had a particular penchant for attacking wardrobes, the more so if they were equipped with a looking-glass on the outside of the door. Seeing his own reflection dimly, he would imagine he was about to be attacked by an intruder – perhaps a German soldier – and would accordingly engage the wardrobe in combat. He accounted for several wardrobes in this fashion but luckily remained unharmed himself.

After the war he taught at an elementary school in Stratford, East London. He held no high opinion of the London teachers who were his colleagues, finding them (or so he claimed subsequently) lacking in conscientiousness. He was even more shocked by their frequent resort to the cane, for quite severe corporal punishment was then as common in State as in private schools. He never used the cane, though he had no objection in principle to slapping an obstreporous child, always on the leg. As a disciplinarian he relied on the menace of his size – he was remarkably large for a West Walian of his generation – and, above all, on his resonant baritone voice. As a singer, however, he was inept. As a speaker he never made any attempt to modify his Carmarthenshire accent, with every R pronounced, and short As, to the extent that 'plaice' would be pronounced 'plăce'.

He also played rugby as a forward for the London Welsh's first XV. He said later that he would 'never have got into the team if it hadn't been for the war'. He added that he had been 'knocked about terribly'. Certainly the middle finger of his left hand was permanently crooked as a result of being broken in the match against Llanelli. This was also one of the great eras of English forward play, and he was proud of having appeared against such figures as C. H. Pillman, A. F. Blakiston and W. W. Wakefield, even though 'they gave me a terrible time'. In fact he exaggerated the size of these formidable players, transforming them in his mind into the 15- and 16-stone monsters of the 1960s and '70s. The records show that they were of about the same height as he, though a stone to a stone-and-a-half heavier.

He left London because he could not afford to live there any longer. He was then a normal social beer-drinker, though he was careful to add that he was 'never a real boozer'. He returned to teach at Blaenau School, not far from Ammanford. There he met another teacher, Violet Harris, the youngest daughter of Dr Edwin Harris, a local GP. She was six months older than he. She had distinguished herself at the Llandeilo County School, carrying off numerous prizes and matriculating, but had been compelled to leave school prematurely owing to the early death of her father, which had left the Harris family, not destitute, but decidedly short of cash. Accordingly Violet Harris became an uncertificated teacher.

She was of medium height, pretty, with brown hair and blue eyes. Though personally shy, she possessed much social self-assurance, for in the Carmarthenshire of that day there was no intermediate class between the local doctor (who, in esteem, ranked above the vicar, minister, solicitor or schoolmaster) and Lord Dynevor in Llandeilo. Her natural language was English and she was a member of the (Anglican) Church in Wales. In addition, she possessed an antipathy both to the Welsh language and to what might be described as Welsh ways. It would be tempting to explain this antipathy, which sometimes verged on contempt, by saying that it was natural in a middle-class Welshwoman of her generation, born in 1893, well before Welshness became *chic*. However, her feelings were not wholly shared by her brother or two elder sisters (teachers all), who considered her attitude to Wales and the language 'silly'.

Yet she became engaged to D. J. Watkins, a most Welsh Welshman. She was attracted by his size, his black hair, his gentleness and his aura of danger. Her family did not wholly approve of the match and thought she could have 'done better for herself'. Her two sisters remained unmarried.

She possessed a hard, logical mind and an aptitude for Latin, mathematics and English grammar – all areas in which Watkins was never wholly sure-footed. Indeed, to the end of her life she spoke and wrote English both with a precision and, more important, with a knowledge of idiom which belonged to the Victorian governess. Watkins, on the other hand, thought in Welsh and then translated his thoughts into English.

Violet Watkins was also practical, capable of making a shirt or re-upholstering a sofa. She did not have her husband's literary or philosophical interests or his powers of memory, particularly for the ramifications of family relationships. But she was the more 'able' of the two. She did not put things off, find excuses for not acting. And she was not frightened of anybody or anything – with the exception of snakes and cows, for she had once been chased by a cow. She was not only industrious but kind. The two of them complemented each other wonderfully.

Their original intention had been to have four children; as indeed, in a sense, they did; but there was a miscarriage and two deaths in early infancy. In 1933 Violet Watkins had a fourth child, a boy, by Caesarian section, then a hazardous operation. He went to Cambridge and later became a journalist in London.

The same year produced another event of importance to Watkins and his wife. From Blaenau he had gone on to become headmaster of Llanedi, a small country school three miles from Tycroes. Following an adverse inspector's report, he was deprived of his headmastership, and given the choice of becoming headmaster of a small school in Pembrokeshire or joining the staff of Parcyrhun School in Ammanford as an ordinary teacher. He chose the latter and remained embittered for the rest of his life, often falling into rages, though these became less frequent as he grew older.

It is difficult to say whether his deprivation or dismissal was unjust. Certainly it was rare for a headmaster to be so treated, as it remains rare today. He claimed that the standards of the school were acceptable, given the material he had to work on – almost entirely the children of small farmers or of farm labourers. The episode left him with a permanent dislike of county councillors and of the Welsh Labour Establishment generally. In this respect he was at one with his wife, who voted Conservative, though he continued reluctantly to vote Labour.

But he did not participate in local activities. Instead he read, virtually continuously, for about forty years. He was neither a browser nor a book-collector. Though he subscribed to the *Hibbert Journal*, his basic diet was the Everyman's Library: he belonged to the pre-Penguin generation. He also read Balzac, Maupassant, Victor Hugo and Dumas in French. He tried to teach himself classical Greek, though without much success. With German, in which he had a teacher, he was more successful. He took the *Listener* in 1948-51, mainly for his son's sake, but he was not a reader of the weekly reviews. Likewise he began to take the *Observer* only in 1948, though he then read it for the rest of his life. His daily paper used to be the *News Chronicle*; after it died, he found no satisfactory substitute.

His pattern of reading is, or perhaps was, familiar enough. But his lack of knowledge of fashionable opinion, combined with a paucity of acquaintances with similar interests to his own, led him to form quite independent views. Nor were these views provincial or eccentric. He perceived the merits of Thomas Hardy as a novelist (Hardy's poetry he had not read) well before his reputation reached its present size. In the 1950s, when J. M. Keynes's ability as an economist went almost unchallenged, he had his doubts: 'Keynes [which he pronounced Keenz rather than Kanes] took his ideas from Alfred Marshall, but Marshall was the sounder economist. What Keynes is telling us to do is to live beyond our means. Any fool in the pub can say that.' Though he did not have an elegant mind, he possessed an instinct for detecting exaggeration, falsity and fraud, as much in writers as in the people he met.

After his retirement he became happier, partly because, with no schoolmastering to do, the memory of his Llanedi disgrace receded; partly because he had grandchildren by now; partly because he saw more people, who would drop in for a chat and a cup of tea. Though he smoked fifteen cigarettes a day, he drank, and then moderately, only at Christmas time, on his occasional trips to the sea-side or on his annual visit to St Helen's ground, Swansea, to see Glamorgan play the visiting touring team at cricket. Cricket was a game to which he was attached but which, like many equally enthusiastic Welshmen, he never properly understood as he instinctively understood rugby.

Like many people of pacific instincts, he became angry at contradiction and had a quick temper. His sense of humour was partly of the custard-pie variety, partly ironical. For instance, he had been at school with Dr Jeffrey Samuel, who subsequently married Dr Edith Summerskill and was a vice-president of the London Welsh Club. One Saturday, after his retirement, Watkins was about to accompany his son, who was casually dressed and tieless, to a match. 'Put a tie on, boy,' he said. 'Who knows? We might meet Dr Jeff Samuel.' It was impossible to tell whether he was being serious or making a Carmarthenshire joke directed at swank, pretence and nonsense.

He died on Boxing Day 1980 of being eighty-six, at home, in some discomfort but no pain, with his faculties intact. His last words were 'Never buy Japanese bonds', a reference to a recent financial scandal, and 'I could never manage gin-and-tonic', a reference to his inability, as he grew older, to deal with the metal cap of the solitary bottle of Gordon's gin which he would purchase at Christmas. He was buried at St Edmund's Church, Tycroes, in which he had been confirmed after his marriage so that he could accompany his wife to the Anglican Church with a clear conscience, with, as he would say, 'everything above board'.

AUBERON WAUGH

17 November 1939 –

AUBERON ALEXANDER WAUGH was certainly the most offensive, and probably the most industrious, journalist of modern times. In private he was of a kindly and benevolent disposition, and possessed beautiful manners, but he rarely allowed these aspects of himself to become known to his readers. The literary agent Pat Kavanagh said of him: 'Something seems to come over him when he sees a blank sheet of paper.'

He was the eldest son of Evelyn Waugh and Laura Herbert, and he had two brothers and three sisters. He was born at Pixton Park, Dulverton, Somerset, his maternal grandmother's enormous house. This lady was one of the few people of whom Evelyn Waugh was frightened.

Auberon Waugh went to school at Downside, where he was a classical scholar and was miserably unhappy. He asked his father to take him away, as Evelyn had asked Arthur Waugh to remove him from Lancing. At this time Auberon Waugh fancied a career in catering and hotel management, and Evelyn went so far as to consult his friend the manager of the Hyde Park Hotel, who replied civilly but non-committally. Evelyn advised his son not to embark on a career in the hotel business but to stay at Downside, secure entry to Oxford, do his national service in a 'good' regiment and then go up to the university. He also told Auberon (who was known by his family and friends as Bron) that, though personable and intelligent, he possessed 'a defective sense of honour' and that his objections to Downside would apply equally to any other public school to which – he was then sixteen – he might be sent.

In fact Waugh followed his father's advice, but his experiences at Downside left him with a permanent detestation of the public school system. He once contemplated buying a house in North Somerset, near Shepton Mallet, but desisted because he could not stand the thought of the proximity of his old school. He frequently referred, in conversation and writing, to the middle- and upper-class practice of entrusting children to ageing pederasts and sadists, and of throwing away good money – which

would be better spent on pictures, furniture or wine – in the process. His own son passed the eleven-plus examination and was destined for a State grammar school near Taunton (Waugh was by this time living at Combe Florey), but Somerset reorganised its secondary education at this period and the boy would have had to attend a new comprehensive school some miles away; so Waugh reluctantly paid for him to attend Taunton School as a weekly boarder. His wife Teresa shared his unfavourable opinion of boarding schools.

He did his national service as a subaltern in the Royal Horse Guards and was sent to Cyprus. One day he noticed an impediment in the elevation of the Browning machine gun in his armoured car, and resolved to investigate it. He moved to the front of the gun, seized it and wiggled it up and down, whereupon it started to fire bullets into him. He survived, but lost a lung, his spleen, several ribs and a finger. As he was lying on the ground, waiting for the ambulance, he said to his platoon sergeant, a parachutist from Bristol called Chudleigh: 'Kiss me, Chudleigh.' Chudleigh, however, did not spot the reference, and afterwards treated Waugh with suspicion and reserve. He retired with wounds in 1958, and thereafter received a disability pension from the Government: in 1982 it was of something over £200 a month. It was believed by some that he had been fired on by his own troops – similar stories were told about his father – and also that he had lost a testicle: but both these tales were convincingly denied by Waugh.

His injuries gave him increasing trouble in his early middle age. The cavity where his lung had been would fill up with fluid, which had to be drained surgically. He would attend the Westminster Hospital for this repeated operation, where he endeared himself to the nursing staff by his patience and good humour. He became a regular patient in the Marie Celeste Ward, where his friends would bring him champagne.

He went up to Christ Church, Oxford, with an exhibition in English but read Philosophy, Politics and Economics. He left the university after a year because he first failed and then neglected to re-take the requisite preliminary examinations. Waugh, though he enjoyed his time at Oxford, was sensitive about this part of his life, and did not talk about it much.

Teresa, whom he married in 1961, was the daughter of the Earl of Onslow. They had two sons and two daughters. The youngest, Nathaniel, or Nat, was born during the war between Nigeria and Biafra, which engaged Waugh's passion on the Biafran side, and inspired some of his finest polemical writing. He claimed to have christened his son 'Biafra', which led to charges of lack of consideration as a parent. In fact the boy was always called Nat; and Biafra was one of several names.

He began as a journalist in 1960 on the *Daily Telegraph*, and was briefly supervised by Kenneth Rose, which he did not much like. In the same year his first novel, *The Foxglove Saga*, was published. Though there were some charges, notably in the *Sunday Express*, that the book would not have found a publisher so readily if it had not been by Evelyn Waugh's son, it was on the whole well-received, and rightly so, for it was a very funny book. In the next twelve years Waugh wrote four more novels, of which the best was *Consider the Lilies* (1968), about an idle Church of England clergyman with a tiresome wife. It was one of the funniest novels of the decade and was never properly recognised or appreciated as it should have been. However, he gave up writing novels owing to a lack not of critical acclaim but of financial reward: writing them was not worth the effort. For most of the 1970s he indulged in spasmodic attacks on the Government (for not introducing a, to him, satisfactory public lending right scheme), on publishers and, above all, on public libraries. He made several threats to remove his own works from the shelves of the libraries as a gesture of protest.

As a journalist, he was happier with the Mirror Group, which he joined as a 'special writer' in 1964. He was once trying to write captions for a pin-up series in the *Sunday Mirror* called 'The ABC of Beauty' when Lord Cudlipp (as he later became) walked past his desk smoking a large cigar. 'Wonderful thing it must be to have a good education, Auberon,' he remarked. Nevertheless, Waugh had warm feelings both for Cudlipp and for Cecil King. During the Arab-Israel war of 1967 he was dispatched to Tel-Aviv, where, the *Mirror* had been informed, Mandy Rice-Davies, of Profumo Affair fame, had abandoned her job as a night club hostess in order to tend the Israeli wounded as a nurse. Waugh discovered that this was far from the case and that Miss Rice-Davies was hostessing away like anything. Reluctant to spoil a good story, he procured a nurse's uniform, persuaded her to don it and had her photographed, which, he considered, showed commendable enterprise.

In 1967 he was appointed political correspondent of the *Spectator*. This was an adventurous appointment for the then editor, Nigel Lawson, to make, for, though Waugh had written a column in the *Catholic Herald* from 1963 to 1964, he had neither any great liking for politicians as a class – an attitude he maintained – nor, at that time, any great reputation as a columnist. As things turned out, the appointment was a triumphant success, and Waugh must rank high among the paper's political correspondents.* He did not make the mistake of trying to imitate another columnist but wrote in his own way. He did not pretend to know more than he did. And he worked hard. He once turned up in the press gallery in his slippers because an important debate had unexpectedly arisen. Above all, in the Biafra War he found a cause which could engage his talent for polemic.

In 1970, however, he was dismissed. One Wednesday evening, doing the 'late turn' at the printers in Aldershot, he decided to cheer himself up by altering, in the week's Table of Contents or Index, 'George Gale' into 'Lunchtime O'Gale' – from the *Private Eye* character 'Lunchtime O'Booze', though in fact the *Eye* had its own nickname for Gale, which was 'George G. Ale'. Gale had written an article in that issue in which he made a mildly derogatory reference to Evelyn Waugh, but Auberon Waugh denied – and there is no reason to doubt him – that Gale's reference had any influence on his action: he was simply bored at the printers, and sought diversion. The next day Lawson dismissed him for industrial misconduct.

Waugh, with the reluctant support of the National Union of Journalists, then began an action for wrongful dismissal. The case was heard at the Marylebone County Court and, to everyone's surprise, including his own, he was awarded damages of £600. The judge was influenced by Waugh's having called witnesses who had testified that jokes were not unknown in the *Spectator*, whereas the *Spectator* had called only Lawson. In particular, there was no evidence that Gale had been annoyed by Waugh's action. The judge was also influenced by Gale's reference to Evelyn Waugh: 'Mr Waugh must have said to himself: "I will now play a little joke on Mr Gale." ' Unhappily this leading case was not properly reported.

Shortly after leaving the *Spectator* Waugh was engaged by *The Times* as one of its regular columnists, to write about things in general. (Indeed, that he had taken immediate steps to 'mitigate the damage' caused to himself by his previous dismissal was a point urged in his favour by counsel in the *Spectator* action.) In one of his *Times* columns he stated that it was an article of Moslem faith that the Prophet would come again born not of a woman but of a man. As a consequence, there were numerous protests

* Charles Curran, Henry Fairlie, Bernard Levin, David Watt, Alan Watkins, Auberon Waugh, Peter Paterson, Hugh Macpherson, Patrick Cosgrave, John Grigg, Ferdinand Mount and Colin Welch.

to the paper from Moslem diplomats; and an enraged mob at Rawalpindi burned down the British Council Library there. Waugh's contract was terminated, for which he blamed not William Rees-Mogg, the then editor, but Charles Douglas-Home, the then features editor. He continued to praise Rees-Mogg whenever the opportunity presented itself, and sometimes when it did not, but persecuted Douglas-Home, whom he called 'Charlie Vass'. (*Private Eye* called the Douglas-Home family Vass. This derived from transposed captions in a Scottish newspaper of Lord Home and one Baillie Vass.)

At this stage Waugh was living at The Old Rectory, Chilton Foliat, near Hungerford. He moved to his deceased father's house at Combe Florey partly because his mother was living there alone and was not in the best of health (she was later to die at fifty-six), and partly because he had acquired a dislike of various neighbours who had lately moved into large houses on the Berkshire-Wiltshire borders. They were chiefly youngish men, of his age, who had made money in the City in the property and financial boom of 1970–73. Waugh did not like people of this kind or, usually, their wives.

In 1970 he began the connection for which he was best known, with *Private Eye*, though good judges considered that he did his best writing for the *Spectator*, the *New Statesman* and *Books and Bookmen*. His journalistic output during the 1970s and '80s was prodigious. He reviewed books weekly in, successively, the *Spectator*, the *Evening Standard* and the *Daily Mail*; monthly in *Books and Bookmen*; and occasionally in the *Sunday Telegraph*. In addition to his *Private Eye* column, he wrote regular columns in the *Evening Standard*, the *New Statesman*, the *Spectator* and the *Sunday Telegraph*. He thought he did his best writing for the *New Statesman* because he was working against the grain of the paper – he saw himself writing for an unmarried comprehensive schoolmistress in Coventry. He also had a high regard for the then editor, Anthony Howard, not only because Howard ignored threats to cancel subscriptions on Waugh's account but also because he would say things like: 'I think we've heard quite enough about the horrors of the working classes for the time being, Bron. Could you think of some different subject this week?' Indeed, Howard once asked Waugh to provide a new column instead of the one he had written, and Waugh complied. Though he grumbled, he bore Howard no malice: quite the reverse.

At around this time Waugh discovered the delights of the 'freebie', or facility trip provided for journalists. He travelled the world in this fashion, and formed a particular affection for the massage parlours of South-East Asia.

He was of medium height, and tended to wear either a black pin-striped suit or a corduroy jacket. He was knowledgeable about pictures, furniture, wine and food. He made several attempts to give up smoking cigarettes. He disliked smoking cigars himself, and seemed uneasy when others smoked them. Some of his acquaintances thought that his attitude to cigars was a clue to his real attitude to his father. Thus, Evelyn Waugh smoked cigars, and the son disliked – or was frightened of – the father. Auberon Waugh simply said that he became irritated by the fuss his father made about cigars, and that there was a bogus side to him, as illustrated by his practice of being photographed seated at his desk writing with a steel-nibbed pen and inkwell, whereas in fact he used an ordinary (even if old-fashioned) fountain-pen.

There was certainly something a little eerie about the way in which he pursued his father's dislikes or vendettas, even when their subjects were safely in their graves: Churchill and Duff Cooper (though largely on account of their treatment of P. G. Wodehouse), and Cyril Connolly and, among the living, Stephen Spender, Lord Lovat and Peter Quennell. As a corollary, he treated his father's old friends well on the whole. He was extravagantly admiring of Graham Greene, and was always indulgent to his godfather Lord Longford. There was at least one exception in Anthony Powell, who maintained that Waugh formed dislikes of his father's friends because he had been frightened of his father. But the truth seemed to be simpler, which was that Auberon Waugh considered Powell's *Music of Time* tedious and overpraised – particularly by literary hangers-on.

His own dislikes, as distinct from those he inherited from his father, were sometimes capricious, sometimes based on reason (as with Patrick Jenkin and his ministerial campaign against alcohol) and sometimes founded in jealousy. This jealousy was never professional or financial but usually sexual. Thus, while Waugh honestly disapproved of Harold Evans's style of journalism, with its emphasis on 'graphics' and its 'Insight' features, he almost certainly pursued Evans as persistently as he did because he had had a *tendresse* for Evans's second wife, the journalist Tina Brown. His pursuit of Lord (Grey) Gowrie had similar origins: it went back to the early 1960s in Oxford, when the subject of both Gowrie's and Waugh's attentions had been Grizelda Grimond.

Waugh admired single-mindedness as a virtue in itself, almost irrespective of the end to which this quality might be directed. Thus he admired Norman Scott for his relentless and apparently purposeless pursuit of Jeremy Thorpe. This may have been a moral failing, but it went with an intellectual failing: that, once an idea had entered his head, he found it very difficult to get the idea out again, whatever the evidence or the reasons that might be adduced to the contrary. This was a failing which he shared with his friends Richard Ingrams and Richard West. For instance, Waugh maintained that Thorpe's second marriage would do him harm among the nonconformists of North Devon. (He was obsessed by the Thorpe case, wrote a good book about it and unsuccessfully contested North Devon for the Dog Lovers' Party in 1979.) He refused to accept that there was nothing in Protestant doctrine to discourage re-marriage after the death of a wife. Again, he believed that, once libelled, one could libel the libeller back with complete legal immunity.

Waugh was frightened of the law of libel, on which he considered himself something of an authority, and put his property in his wife's name to protect himself from successful actions. In fact he was shrewd about how far he could safely go and also lucky in his litigants, of whom there were surprisingly few.

He had a keen eye for the value of money but was a generous host. In *Who's Who* he listed his recreation as 'gossip' but in fact it was croquet, which he played at Combe Florey under his own slightly different rules. He also did some rough shooting. In private life he was of an equable temperament and an unselfish nature, particularly where children, both his own and other people's, were concerned. One hot Saturday his and his guests' children asked to be taken to the local municipal swimming pool. While his adult guests retired to bed in the afternoon, or read books in cool rooms, he supervised a large party of young children while sitting in the boiling sun and reading a book for review which was periodically splattered with chlorinated water.

He was a Roman Catholic but did not practise assiduously. His wife was an Anglican who took their children to the church only yards from Combe Florey House. In addition to Combe Florey, he – or, rather, his wife – had a farmhouse in south-west France, to which he would retire in August. He worked every day, and came up to London twice a fortnight (that is, twice in one week), when he would either take a day return or stay at the Sloane Club: his real club, the Beefsteak, provided no accommodation. He was unsnobbish in his choice of friends, who included, in addition to West and Ingrams, Patrick Marnham, Paul Foot, Geoffrey Wheatcroft, and Simon and Alexandra Ward. But despite his gentle manners he aroused fear in those who did not know him well.

His politics were not Tory but libertarian. He disapproved of heavy taxation, capital punishment, and attempts by Government to interfere with other people's pleasure, from drink to cannabis. He hated bossiness. Though he went out of his way to cause offence in his writing, he was often surprised and sometimes, though he always denied it, sorry that offence had been caused.

PEREGRINE WORSTHORNE

22 December 1923 –

PEREGRINE GERARD WORSTHORNE was a journalist, broadcaster and man about London. He was justifiably proud of his journalism, chiefly in the *Sunday Telegraph*, and enjoyed his social life, but was more doubtful about his broadcasting activities, which he considered undignified and potentially corrupting. (On one occasion, as will be related, his appearance in a television programme impeded his career.)

His father was Colonel A. Koch de Gooreynd, OBE, who assumed the name of Worsthorne, a village near Burnley, by deed poll in 1921 in order to fight the Farnworth seat in Lancashire. As A. L. W. K. Worsthorne, Conservative, he came a respectable second to Labour in the elections of 1923 and 1924. Koch de Gooreynd was Belgian by nationality but became an officer in the Irish Guards. His father, Koch de Gooreynd senior, was a financier who had bid unsuccessfully for *The Times* against the Astors. It was thought by some – such as Philip Hope-Wallace – that Worsthorne was partly Jewish on account of the Koch de Gooreynd connection. Worsthorne denied this. His parliamentary ambitions notwithstanding, Koch de Gooreynd junior was, according to his son, somewhat indolent and aimless by nature. In 1982, however, he was still alive, occupying a council flat in Chelsea, where Worsthorne would occasionally visit him.

Worsthorne's mother came of an old Lancashire Roman Catholic family with aristocratic connections: his maternal grandmother was the daughter of an Earl. When Peregrine Worsthorne was a small boy his mother left Koch de Gooreynd (by this time Worsthorne) and married Montagu, later Lord Norman, who became Governor of the Bank of England. She left her first husband partly on account of his purposeless attitude to life. She herself was active in good works, and was a councillor in London for some years. She too was still alive in 1982, occupying a house in Campden Hill.

Worsthorne had a brother, Simon, two years older than he, who was a scholar of music, was High Sheriff of Lancashire and lived near Burnley.

He preferred to emphasise the Lancashire Catholic elements of his descent. In 1955 he assumed 'the surname and arms of Towneley by royal licence, by reason of descent from the elder daughter and senior co-heiress of Colonel Charles Towneley of Towneley' (*Who's Who*). The existence of a father, a mother and two brothers with four surnames altogether – Koch de Gooreynd, Norman, Worsthorne and Towneley – confused many people, including Evelyn Waugh.

Worsthorne and his brother lived a life largely of their own, in a separate house, with their small staff of servants, away from their mother and stepfather Montagu Norman. The house was – or the two houses were – at Much Hadham in Hertfordshire. Norman did not object to his stepchildren as such but felt uneasy in the presence of all children. Worsthorne, however, did not feel unhappy or neglected: in later life he regretted only that he and his brother had not made better use of the opportunities – say, for ordering delicious meals – presented to them by their separate existence. Worsthorne also remembered his mother discouraging him from reading. If she found him with his head in a book, she would say, or imply, that there were healthier activities in which a small boy might be engaged. Worsthorne would recall these episodes without rancour, saying that his mother's attitude to 'book worms' was commonplace in those of her class and generation.

When he was eight, he was sent to a small, Roman Catholic preparatory school, Ladycross, near Seaford in Sussex. His mother removed him after a term on hygenic grounds: he had caught impetigo. He was then sent to Abinger Hill, near Dorking in Surrey, run on progressive lines which enabled boys to concentrate on their preferred subjects. Worsthorne preferred English and History to Classics and Mathematics. One of his school fellows was Edward Boyle. He remembered young Boyle raising his hand after the headmaster had read an extract from Macaulay's *Essays*.

'Yes, Edward, what is your question?'

'Not really a question, Sir, more an observation. I just wanted to tell you that with your voice you could fill the Albert Hall.'

Worsthorne was bullied by one boy in particular, who finally threatened to strangle him. He ran away, but made the mistake of going to the news cinema as soon as he had arrived at Waterloo station (in the 1930s and till well after the war, news cinemas were a feature of the main London stations). Then and later, he considered this a wholly reasonable course to take: he wanted to postpone the confrontation with his mother for as long as possible. However, when he did finally arrive home, both she and the headmaster, summoned from Surrey, took the view that his visit to the pictures indicated a certain lack of serious purpose about running away. Worsthorne used to say that this episode illustrated how little grown-ups understood children. Still, the bully was removed from the school as a result of this exploit.

Worsthorne would have preferred not to go to a boarding school at all. Both his father and his step-father had been to Eton. But Stowe, under the enterprising self-publicist J. F. Roxburgh, was felt to be a milder and kinder institution: 'Westminster, which then, as now, had day boys, would have been regarded as quite unsuitable socially,' Worsthorne wrote later. Yet the House in which he found himself contained a preponderance of boys whom he considered 'low' or 'common', users of brilliantine and talkers about 'Mum' and 'Dad'. He admitted afterwards that his attitude had been intolerably snobbish, though if he objected to them, they objected more vigorously to him. A tweed knickerbocker suit which was ordered for him by his mother, and whose making necessitated a visit by his tailor to the school, was the cause of particular ribaldry.

Owing to his aversion to Classics and Mathematics, he had done poorly in the Common Entrance examination, and was accordingly placed in a low form. However, he was invited to the salon run by the school's most fashionable master on account of his striking looks. 'I was a rather pretty boy ...' he wrote later. 'My looks were of the rather romantic, sub-Byronic kind.' He used to dress up for the occasion in a cloak and a floppy hat. Homosexuality was implicit but never rampant. Already interested in girls, he had only one physical experience of the homosexual kind. When he was fifteen he was seduced on the art room sofa by George Melly, who was also fifteen. In later years he appeared on a television programme with Melly. After the programme he was attacked by Melly's new young wife as a puritan and a kill-joy. Worsthorne said: 'It might interest you to know, madam, that you and I have more in common than you care to recognise. We were both seduced in our teens by George Melly.'

He did not get on with his housemaster, a bully with a close-cropped head who was an enthusiast for the Officers' Training Corps. The greatest influence on him was John Davenport, a war-time schoolmaster, who was afterwards to become perhaps the leading figure in post-war literary bohemia. It was largely through reading two books recommended by Davenport – Tawney's *Religion and the Rise of Capitalism* and Edmund

Wilson's *To the Finland Station* – that he won an Exhibition to Peterhouse, Cambridge.

A friend from school also went to Peterhouse: Colin Welch. Welch and Worsthorne were together at school, at Cambridge, in the Army and on the *Daily Telegraph*. Welch was a different kind of Conservative (some would have said he was a nineteenth-century Liberal) but the two continued to influence each other.

Worsthorne's Cambridge career was interrupted by the war. In 1942 he was commissioned in the Oxfordshire and Buckinghamshire Light Infantry and in 1944 became attached to Phantom, GHQ Liaison Regiment. He injured himself in training, spent some time at the Radcliffe Infirmary at Oxford and became a member of Magdalen College. It was in the Army that he met Michael Oakeshott, who influenced his political thinking, as Oakeshott influenced that of other Peterhouse products. (Oakeshott himself was at Caius.)

After his war service, Worsthorne returned to Peterhouse to complete his degree. In 1946 he became a sub-editor on the *Glasgow Herald*, where he stayed until 1948, when he joined *The Times* as a sub-editor and later as a leader-writer. He remained with *The Times* for five years before going to the *Daily Telegraph*. He was there for eight years, writing signed articles, as he had not done on *The Times*. Worsthorne used to say that he spent about thirteen years altogether in journalistic near-obscurity and that, to this extent, his life had not been at all privileged. In 1961 he joined the newly inaugurated *Sunday Telegraph* as deputy editor under Donald McLachlan's editorship. He also began writing a political column.

But the machinery of politics, grinding on week after week, bored him: the one part of the job that he enjoyed was taking Richard Crossman to lunch at the Connaught. He soon changed the style of his weekly article so that it dealt with ideas or opinions: generally one idea or opinion an article, expressed in a paradoxical manner. McLachlan advised him against making this change, saying that if he did he would be taken less seriously than as a more conventional political columnist. But in the succeeding twenty years and more, Worsthorne's weekly article was a notable feature of British journalism. His article was presented not as a column but as the principal article in the paper. It was said that this was because the *Telegraph*'s proprietor, Michael Berry (later Lord Hartwell), had an aversion to columnists. He thought they got above themselves.

Worsthorne was early taken up by Lady Pamela Berry (later Lady

Hartwell), which led some observers to conclude that he would in due course be made editor of either the *Daily* or the *Sunday Telegraph*. But Lady Pamela's protégés rarely secured preferment in this sense. In any event, Michael Berry had a suspicion of well-dressed, articulate and opinionated journalists such as Worsthorne, when it came to editing his papers. Worsthorne, however, wanted to be an editor. When J. W. M. Thompson was appointed editor of the *Sunday Telegraph* in 1976 in succession to Brian Roberts (who had himself succeeded Donald McLachlan), a friend said to him: 'I hope you're not at all bitter, Perry.'

'I am extremely bitter,' he replied. 'I have every reason to be. I have been absolutely reliable, never drunk or anything like that, and this is the reward I get.'

Worsthorne was always frank in this kind of way.

Three years earlier he had been suspended from his duties on the *Telegraph* after saying 'fuck' on television. In a discussion on the resignation from the Government of Lord Lambton, who had availed himself of the services of call-girls, Worsthorne had been asked what he thought the response of the British public would be. He replied: 'I shouldn't think they give a fuck.' This was intended by Worsthorne as a joke. It had been thought up in a taxi on the evening in question by him and Philip Hope-Wallace. The readers of the *Telegraph, Daily* as well as *Sunday*, were not amused. To propitiate them, Hartwell suspended Worsthorne. He considered he had been shabbily treated. He specially noticed how, in and around this period, certain other *Telegraph* journalists shunned and avoided him, as if they feared, as they probably did, that too close contact with him would prejudice their careers.

This episode apart, he might still have become editor. But he had a certain penchant for getting himself into scrapes. At around the same time, at a party conference at Brighton, he exchanged shirts with Vanessa Lawson (then Nigel Lawson's wife) in a crowded Wheeler's Restaurant. This happening was speedily brought to the attention of Lord Hartwell by a colleague, Patrick Hutber.

His friends included George Gale, Kingsley Amis and Maurice Cowling, the political historian. With Paul Johnson, Henry Fairlie (before he went to America) and John Raymond (before he died at fifty-three), they formed not so much a clique or set as a network or connection.

In 1960 Worsthorne gave Evelyn Waugh dinner at Boodle's, of which he was then a member (his clubs later on were the Beefsteak and the

Garrick). The object was to persuade Waugh to do some work for the *Telegraph*: in the end nothing came of it. In a letter to Anne Fleming, Waugh claimed to have been confused over Koch de Gooreynd and Towneley. Worsthorne, however, remembers Waugh betraying prior knowledge by asking for him at the club by his father's original name. When the existence of such a member was denied, Waugh complained: 'Is it not the custom when one gentleman invites another to dine with him in his club, for the host to take the elementary precaution of joining the club in the first place?' Worsthorne's account of subsequent events was that

> after dinner I offered Waugh a glass of port. When it arrived he complained that 'this is not the kind of port which Lady Pamela Berry would wish you to offer me'. To this I replied rather frostily: 'But it is not Lady Pamela offering it to you.' On hearing this Waugh pulled out his wallet and began sprinkling fivers all round him.

Though he was a kind man and a stimulating companion, he was adept at losing his temper if he considered such a course suitable. He once walked noisily out of a Granada Television *What the Papers Say* annual luncheon, shouting 'disgraceful', when the recipients (from *Peace News*) of an award used the occasion to make political speeches about British 'oppression' in Northern Ireland. He also left a dinner party at which Harold (later Lord) Lever was developing a comparison between Britain's economic problem and that of a small Manchester manufacturer whose outgoings were slightly larger than his receipts. Such a comparison, Worsthorne thought, was insulting to Britain. Lever was surprised by this behaviour.

He was attractive to women and had many women friends, in particular Moyra Fraser, the distinguished comic actress. His wife Claude, whom he married in 1950, was French. She was known as 'Claudie', pronounced in the French way. They had one daughter. Claudie had the gift of coining phrases in which idiom gone wrong nevertheless illuminated a kind of truth, as in: 'Perry, poor Perry, everything he touches turns to sackcloth and ashes.' They first lived in Kensington in a house which had been given to Worsthorne by his mother, but (as he admitted afterwards) he rashly sold it, and he and Claudie rented a flat. When the rent was put up to a level he could not afford, he appeared both in print and on *The World at One* lamenting the harshness of contemporary capitalism. He and his wife bought a small house in Fulham; they also had a house at Wivenhoe in Essex.

He liked black striped suits, striped shirts and red ties. He drank in moderation and smoked small cigars. He was a good tennis player but was otherwise uninterested in competitive sport. As a journalist, he was at his best in his lengthy travel diaries – many of them reprinted in *Peregrinations* (1980) – in which he appeared as a combination of Lord Curzon and Mr Pooter. He was a good man, and his company always raised people's spirits, but there was a touch of sadness in his blue eyes.

A Note on Sources

THIS is an account of published works which have helped me or might interest the reader seeking further information. But it does not pretend to be an exhaustive bibliography. Thus I have not included a complete list of, for example, William Robson's works on public law and administration because it would be over-long and because a lay reader would probably not be very interested in most of them. I have not, again, listed the novels of Kingsley Amis, Anthony Powell and Simon Raven because the books are well-known and readily available; likewise with A. J. P. Taylor. I have followed no rule except that of trying to help the reader.

Though KINGSLEY AMIS is one of our leading novelists, there is surprisingly little on him personally, but there are some informative autobiographical pieces in his *What Became of Jane Austen?* (1970), Penguin edn (1981).

The memoir of LORD BEAVERBROOK is substantially my piece 'My Days with Beaverbrook', *New Statesman*, 1 September 1972. The standard life of him is A. J. P. Taylor, *Beaverbrook* (1972), Penguin edn (1974). It is not perhaps Taylor's happiest production, being more adulatory and less pithy than his other books. Indeed, his enthusiasm for his subject is such that he cannot see it when Beaverbrook is behaving badly. Accordingly he does not gloss Beaverbrook's faults but presents them as virtues, so serving the cause of truth. Tom Driberg, *Beaverbrook* (1956) is by no means superseded by Taylor. The best picture of what Beaverbrook was really like in old age is C. M. Vines, *A Little Nut-Brown Man* (1968), a comic minor masterpiece comparable to *The Diary of a Nobody*. Beaverbrook's best books are *Politicians and the War*, 2 vols (1928–32), 1 vol. edn (1960) and *Men and Power* (1956). *The Decline and Fall of Lloyd George* (1963) is good, his posthumous *The Abdication of King Edward VIII*, ed A. J. P. Taylor (1966), less successful. *Politicians and the Press* (1925) is rare and scarce. He dispenses worldly advice in *Success* (1921), *Don't Trust to Luck* (1954) and *Three Keys to Success* (1956). His *Friends* (1959), *Courage* (1961) and *The Divine Propagandist* (1962) testify to the high regard which he entertained respectively for R. B. (Viscount) Bennett, Sir James Dunn and Jesus Christ. He also wrote *Resources of the British Empire* (1934) and *Canada in Flanders*, 2 vols (1916-17).

LORD BRADWELL's posthumous and largely completed autobiograpy *Ruling Passions* (1977) is entertaining, invaluable and, I suspect, largely true, though some reviewers thought he was indulging in sexual fantasies. It has a loyal Postscript by Michael Foot. As Tom Driberg, Bradwell wrote a diary-cum-selection of his *Reynolds News* columns entitled *The Best of Both Worlds* (1953). The worlds referred to are those of politics and journalism: but the frontispiece shows a dashing, smartly-suited Driberg with his homelier bride photographed on the terrace of the House of Commons after their marriage – one of the most mysterious episodes of modern times. His *Colonnade* (1949) is a selection from his 'William Hickey' columns on the *Daily Express* and has an informative Introduction on the trade of journalism.

ANTHONY CROSLAND was not ashamed to be a one-book man, the book being *The Future of Socialism* (1956), paper edn (1959), rev. paper edn (1964), reissued hardback (1980). Like many authors, he was extremely proud of having been translated into Japanese. *The Conservative Enemy* (1962) is a planned collection of essays, *Socialism Now*, ed Dick Leonard (1974), a somewhat looser collection of essays and speeches. He also wrote *Britain's Economic Problem* (1953) and, anonymously, the *Co-operative Independent Commission Report* (1958). There is a Bibliography and a Chronology in the memorial collection by other hands *The Socialist Agenda*, ed David Lipsey and Dick Leonard (1981), which also contains memoirs by Lipsey, Leonard and Lord Donaldson. Susan Crosland, *Tony Crosland* (1982) is a major work.

There is a wealth of biographical material on RICHARD CROSSMAN: *The Diaries of a Cabinet Minister*, ed Janet Morgan, 3 vols (1975-7) and *The Backbench Diaries of Richard Crossman*, ed Morgan (1981) *The Crossman Diaries*, ed with Intro. Anthony Howard (1979), paper edn (1979) expertly compresses the former work. Crossman, 'My Father' *Sunday Telegraph*, 16 December 1962 is illuminating, as is Susan Barnes (Susan Crosland), 'Richard Crossman' in *Behind the Image* (1974). His Introduction to Walter Bagehot, *The English Constitution*, Fontana edn (1963) must be one of the most famous of Introductions, but is fundamentally misconceived, being based on a – partly deliberate – misunderstanding of John P. Mackintosh, *The British Cabinet* (1962). A more balanced, revised view of prime ministerial government, though a view nevertheless disputed by Sir Harold Wilson, is to be found in his three Godkin Lectures, *Inside View* (1972), which is not surprising because they were largely written by Mackintosh himself. My favourite is *The Charm of Politics* (1958), a collection of his *New Statesman* book reviews which shows what a superb reviewer he was. His *Planning for Freedom* (1965) collects his longer essays on principles and policies. It aroused little interest when it was published, which, Crossman said at the time, demonstrated that literary editors were, as others were, more interested in people than in principles or policies. I have also found useful *Plato Today* (1937), paper edn (1963), and the underestimated though often reprinted *Government and the Governed* (1939), 5th edn (1969).

There is some autobiographical material on MICHAEL FOOT in his *Debts of Honour* (1980), Picador edn (1981), notably in the pieces on Isaac Foot and Beaverbrook. Simon Hoggart and David Leigh, *Michael Foot* (1981), paper edn (1981), appeared after I had written my brief life. His *Aneurin Bevan*, 2 vols (1962–73), is very good despite the hagiographical tone and despite – from another aspect, because of – the paucity of written sources, but his best book is *The Pen and the Sword* (1957), about Swift and Marlborough, in which Swift by no means has all the best tunes. His pamphlet *Parliament in Danger!* (1959) is worth looking at, and his laudatory monograph *Harold Wilson: a Pictorial Biography* (1964) is a collector's item. As 'Cassius' he wrote *Brendan and Beverley* (1944), which is rollicking, and as 'Cato' (with Frank Owen and Peter Howard) he wrote *Guilty Men* (1940), which is tendentious but was influential at the time.

There is a good profile of SIR IAN GILMOUR in the *Spectator*, 1 March 1980. See also a letter from Iain Hamilton, *Spectator*, 15 March 1980. His *The Body Politic* (1969) is about the British constitution and is learned, stimulating and original. His *Inside Right* (1977) has too many quotations in it.

There is much autobiographical material on DENIS HEALEY in his book about photography, *Healey's Eye* (1980). The best summary of his approach to politics, at any rate international politics, is his 'Power Politics and the Labour Party' in *New Fabian Essays*, ed R. H. S. Crossman (1952).

PHILIP HOPE-WALLACE thought that journalists should not write books because writing them – or, rather, not writing them – was a cause of unhappiness both to their prospective publishers and to themselves. His own *A Key to Opera* (1939), like many other books of its year, fell on stony ground owing to the outbreak of war. The posthumous selection of his journalism, *Words and Music* (1981), is excellent. It was made by his sister, Jacqueline Hope-Wallace, and has an Introduction by her (and Hope-Wallace's) friend, Veronica Wedgwood. Tribute to him was paid by Paul Johnson in the *Daily Telegraph*, 15 September 1979, Geoffrey Wheatcroft in the *Spectator*, 8 September 1979 and me in the *Observer*, 9 September 1979. Wheatcroft also perceptively reviewed *Words and Music*, above, in the *Spectator*, 1 August 1981.

For RICHARD INGRAMS I draw heavily on two profiles, one, anonymous, in the *New Statesman*, 3 December 1976, the other by me in the *Observer*, 8 February 1981. *Goldenballs* (1979) tells his story of the legal battle with Sir James Goldsmith. *God's Apology* (1977) is a sensitive account of the friendship of Hugh Kingsmill, Hesketh Pearson and Malcolm Muggeridge. An interesting curiosity is the thriller he wrote with Andrew Osmond as 'Philip Reid', *Harris in Wonderland* (1973). Harris is a recognisable portrait of Richard West.

Of the numerous profiles of ROY JENKINS which appear virtually monthly, probably the best and certainly the fullest is Anthony Bailey, 'Travelling Man', *Observer Magazine*, 8 March 1981. *Essays and Speeches*, ed Anthony Lester (1967), is a good selection from his speeches and his accomplished though usually bland journalism. His best books are *Mr Balfour's Poodle* (1954), about the House of Lords crisis, and *Sir Charles Dilke* (1958), in whose pages sex wars with politics and emerges victorious, over Sir Charles and Mr Jenkins alike. *Asquith* (1964) has its detractors but is a respectable piece of work. Jenkins's memoir of Hugh Gaitskell is one of the best things ever written on him: it is in *Encounter*, January 1964, in *Hugh Gaitskell 1906–1963*, ed W. T. Rodgers (1964) and in *Essays and Speeches*, above. His Tribune pamphlet *Fair Shares for the Rich* (1952) deploys the case for a capital levy and is rare and scarce, but his early views on fiscal policy as an instrument of egalitarianism may be studied in 'Equality' in *New Fabian Essays*, above.

I wrote to PAUL JOHNSON asking him for information on his early life but received no reply. I have made some use of a piece I wrote on him in the *Observer*, 22 October 1978. His collection *Statesmen and Nations* (1971) demonstrates his formidable and wide journalistic talents. The Introduction is an admirable essay on political journalism, which he defines in the broad sense to cover any writing on public affairs, domestic or foreign. His other collection *The Recovery of Freedom* (1980) is more consistently polemical, and explains, up to a point, his conversion to Conservatism or liberalism as the case may be. His most notable books are *The Offshore Islanders* (1972), *Elizabeth I* (1974) and *A History of Christianity* (1976).

There is a useful profile of SIR JOHN JUNOR by Iain Murray in the *Observer Magazine*, 13 December 1981. Selections from his column in the *Sunday Express* may be perused in *The Best of JJ* (1981).

SIR OSBERT LANCASTER has written two short volumes of autobiography, *All Done from Memory* (1963) and *With an Eye to the Future* (1967). The profile in the *New Statesman*, 1 December 1961, draws heavily on the first volume, as I do on both. The first volume was originally published in an autographed edition of 45 copies in 1953. There is an interview with Anne Scott-James (later Lady Lancaster) about his clothes in the *Observer*, 23 June 1963 and 'A Life in the Day of' piece in the *Sunday Times Magazine*, 20 September 1981. I have profited from his *Drayneflete Revealed* (1949), paper edn (1962), *Homes Sweet Homes* (1939), paper edn (1963) and *Pillar to Post* (1938), paper edn (1963).

The memoir of IAIN MACLEOD is substantially my 'The Leader the Tories Mislaid', *New Statesman*, 10 October 1975. Nigel Fisher, *Iain Macleod* (1973) is a fine piece of work in view of Macleod's disinclination to keep papers or to write any but the briefest of letters. (Cf. Foot's *Bevan* above.) His own *Neville Chamberlain* (1961) was reviewed severely but the adverse criticism, of which there was too much, should properly have been directed at Peter Goldman, who wrote most of the book.

The essay on HUGH MASSINGHAM is entirely my 'The Political Columnist's Craft', *New Statesman*, 16 January 1976. Massingham's own reflections are in the short-lived *Aspect*, February 1963. In the 1930s he embarked on an Orwellian life in the East End which produced *I Took Off My Tie* (1936). Like Orwell, he rendered London working-class speech in a grotesque written phonetic form and, like Orwell, but unlike Dorothy L. Sayers, he remained unrebuked for snobbery on that account. He wrote several novels, which he mistakenly regarded as superior to his political journalism, but none of them caused much of a stir: a good example is *The Harp and the Oak* (1945), Penguin edn (1948). He compiled *The London Anthology* (1950) with his wife Pauline.

The memoir of G. E. MOORE is substantially my 'I Was G. E. Moore's Lodger', *New Statesman*, 24 March 1978. Purely philosophical works apart, the fullest book on him is Paul Levy, *Moore: G. E. Moore and the Cambridge Apostles* (1979). Also informative are Bertrand Russell, *Autobiography*, 3 vols (1967-9) and Michael Holroyd, *Lytton Strachey*, 2 vols (1967-8).

We know more about MALCOLM MUGGERIDGE than we do about most monarchs, most Prime Ministers or even Evelyn Waugh. Two volumes of his autobiography, *Chronicles of Wasted Time*, have so far appeared, *The Green Stick* (1972), Fontana edn (1975) and *The Infernal Grove* (1973), Fontana edn (1975), and a third volume is expected shortly. In addition we have his Diaries, *Like it Was*, ed John Bright-Holmes (1981) and Ian Hunter, *Malcolm Muggeridge: a Life* (1980). These last two books provide corrections to the autobiography. There are numerous autobiograpical references in his other works, notably in *Tread Softly for You Tread on My Jokes* (1966), *Muggeridge through the Microphone*, ed Christopher Ralling (1967), Fontana edn (1969), *Jesus Rediscovered* (1969), *Christ and the Media* (1977) and *Things Past*, ed Ian Hunter (1978). His most deeply personal work, however, remains *In a Valley of this Restless Mind* (1938), reissued (1978). I have profited from two of his novels, *Picture Palace* (1934), about the *Manchester Guardian*, and *Affairs of the Heart* (1949), about postwar literary London, and also from *The Thirties* (1940), reissued (1967).

ANTHONY POWELL has written four volumes of memoirs under the general title *To Keep the Ball Rolling: Infants of the Spring* (1976), *Messengers of Day* (1978), *Faces in My Time* (1980) and *The Strangers All Are Gone* (1982). Some reviewers found them over-discreet but there is a good deal of quietly conveyed information in them nonetheless.

There is a lot of autobiographical information on SIMON RAVEN in the linking passages of his collection *Boys will be Boys* (1963), in his *The English Gentleman* (1961), Panther edn (1966) and in his *Shadows on the Grass* (1982). See also his 'Perish by the Sword' in *The Establishment*, ed Hugh Thomas (1959).

MAURICE RICHARDSON wrote about his childhood in *Little Victims* (1968): the title refers to him and his fellows at their preparatory school. Tributes to him were paid by Terence Kilmartin in the *Observer*, 1 October 1978, Julian Symons in *The Times*, 6 October 1978, Jeffrey Bernard in the *Spectator*, 7 October 1978 and me in the *New Statesman*, 6 October 1978. His posthumous collection *Fits and Starts* (1979) is a good representation of his journalism, except that it includes none of his television criticism. It has an Introduction by Symons but is anonymously edited.

Though he hardly ever stopped writing – books, articles, pamphlets, memoranda to committees, editorials in the *Political Quarterly* – WILLIAM ROBSON was, like Anthony Crosland or G. E. Moore, a one-book man: *Justice and Administrative Law* (1928) is his monument. It is reassessed by J. A. G. Griffith, 'Justice and Administrative Law Revisited' in *From Policy to Administration: Essays in Honour of William A. Robson*, ed Griffith (1975). There is a masterly obituary (anonymous, but in fact by Bernard Crick) in *The Times*, 15 May 1980. Other memoirs are by Griffith in *LSE*, November 1980 and by L. J. Sharpe in *Political Studies*, vol. XXVIII (1980).

There is a profile of NORMAN ST JOHN-STEVAS in the *Spectator*, 13 October 1979. His works include *Obscenity and the Law* (1956), *Walter Bagehot* (1959), *Life, Death and the Law* (1961), *The Right to Life* (1963) and *Law and Morals* (1964). The last three of these are quite short. He has also edited *The Collected Works of Walter Bagehot*, 11 vols so far (1965–).

DAVID STEEL is the subject of a workmanlike biography, Peter Bartram, *David Steel* (1981), and he has himself written fairly frankly on the Lib-Lab pact in *A House Divided* (1980).

A. J. P. TAYLOR writes about himself in 'Accident Prone' in *Politicians, Socialism and Historians* (1980). There is a good profile of him by Geoffrey Wheatcroft in the *Observer Magazine*, 22 March 1981, and a 'Life in the Day of' piece in the *Sunday Times Magazine*, 23 October 1977. Selected essays of his are conveniently available in two Penguins, *Essays in English History* (1976) and *Europe: Grandeur and Decline* (1967); the former was published simultaneously in hardback; the pieces in it have short, witty autobiographical prefaces. An autobiography is promised.

A good background to the life of D. J. WATKINS is Kenneth O. Morgan, *Rebirth of a Nation: Wales 1880–1980* (1981), a perhaps over-optimistic title. There is much interesting social history in the official account of the Welsh Rugby Union, David Smith and Gareth Williams, *Fields of Praise* (1980).

Autobiographical information about AUBERON WAUGH is scattered through his collections *Country Topics* (1974), *Four Crowded Years: the Diaries of Auberon Waugh 1972–1976* (1976) and *In the Lion's Den* (1978). The diaries are not completely made up, though claims to encounters with members of the Royal Family are invariably untrue. There are numerous references to him in *The Diaries of Evelyn Waugh*, ed Michael Davie (1976) and *The Letters of Evelyn Waugh*, ed Mark Amory (1980).

PEREGRINE WORSTHORNE has written about his schooldays in 'Boy Made Man' in *The World of the Public School*, Intro. George

MacDonald Fraser (1977). His jaunts abroad, with him appearing as a combination of Mr Pooter and Lord Curzon, are a substantial part of his collection *Peregrinations* (1980). His political view about the need for an élite or a ruling class is stated and re-stated, several times, in *The Socialist Myth* (1971). The account of his meeting with Evelyn Waugh is given, from his side and Waugh's, in *The Letters of Evelyn Waugh*, above, pp. 552–3.

Generally, *Who's Who* and *Who Was Who* are invaluable. A most useful book is *Who's Who of British Members of Parliament*, ed M. Stanton and S. Lees, vol. IV (Harvester Press, Sussex, and Humanities Press, New Jersey, 1981), which covers the years 1945–79 and is based not on *Who's Who* but on *Dod's Parliamentary Companion*. *Dod*, though neither as consistent nor, often, as full as *Who's Who*, sometimes provides information (on clubs, names of fathers, addresses, early marriages, and religions) not available in or suppressed by the contributors to the latter work.

INDEX

Abersychan County (Grammar) School, 74
Abortion Act, 170
Ackerley, J. R., 149
Adam, Corinna, 31
Addison, Joseph, 115
Afternoon Men (Powell), 145
Agents and Patients (Powell), 145
Aircraft in War and Peace (Robson), 160
Aitken, Ian, 11, 15, 16
Aitken, Jean (Noble), 9
Aitken, Sir Max, 9, 45, 86
Aitken, Rev. William, 9
Alms for Oblivion (Raven), 147, 151
Amis, Kingsley, xii, **1–8**, 51, 146, 204
Amis, Rosa, 1
Amis, William Robert, 1, 3
Annan, Noël, 150
Apostles Society, Cambridge, 125
Arbeiderbladet, Norwegian Labour paper, 58
Architectural Review, 93
Arran, Lord, 170
Aspect, 113n., 118n.
Asquith (Jenkins), 76
Astor, David, 117, 118
Athenaeum, 158
Attlee, Clement, 36, 37, 57, 59, 73, 118
Aubrey, John, xi, 35, 145
Auden, W. H., 37
Authors Club, 135
Autumnal Face (Muggeridge), 130

Bad Companions, The (Richardson), 156
Bagehot, Walter, 42; collected works, 164
Balliol College, Oxford, 50, 55, 61, 62, 74, 142
Balogh, Thomas (Lord), 40, 74
Balston, Tom, 142
Barber, Anthony, 82, 111
Bardwell, Hilary (Amis), (Lady Kilmarnock), 4, 6
Baring, Maurice, 67
Barnes, Susan, 34
'Baron Corvo', 142
Bartlett, Vernon, 114
Baxter, Beverley, 25

Beaverbrook, Lady (Lady Dunn), 9, 15
Beaverbrook, Lady (Gladys Drury), 9
Beaverbrook, Lord, xii, xiii, **9–19**, 25, 27, 45–7, 49 and n., 85, 86, 90, 94, 104, 105, 133, 179, 182
Beckett, Samuel, 56
Beeching, Lord, 103
Beefsteak Club, 84, 95, 198, 204
Beerbohm, Sir Max, 95
Bell, Kenneth, 142
Bell, Ronald, 51
Belloc, Hilaire, 71
Benn, Anthony Wedgwood, 31, 40, 47, 83
Berkeley, Humphry, 103
Bernard, Jeffrey, 155–6
Berry, Michael (Lord Hartwell), 203–4
Berry, Lady Pamela (Lady Hartwell), 203–5
Bessell, Peter, 17
Betjeman, Sir John, 51, 93–4
Bevan, Aneurin, 27, 44, 45, 47, 74, 75, 79, 83, 98, 103, 115, 118, 121
Bevin, Ernest, 57
Binfield, Mrs Ena May, marriage to Tom Driberg, 27–8
Bing, Geoffrey, 36
Blake, George, 77
Blake, Robert, 51
Blakiston, A. F., 187
Blond, Anthony, 150
Bloomsbury group, 37, 120, 125, 143
Blunt, Anthony, 55, 125, 179
Body Politic, The (Gilmour), 50, 52
Bonar Law, Andrew, 9, 15
Bonham-Carter, Mark, 76, 78
Bonham-Carter, Lady Violet, 76
Boodle's Club, 204
Booker, Christopher, 67, 69, 139
Books and Bookmen, 196
Bootham School, 175
Bowra, Sir Maurice, 49, 91, 143
Boyle, Sir Edward (Lord), 110, 201
Boyson, Dr Rhodes, 164
Bradford Grammar School, 55
Bradwell, Lord, *see* Driberg, Tom

Index

Brailsford, H. N., 39
Brandt, Willy, 58
Brief Lives (Aubrey), xi, 145
Brien, Alan, 51
Bright, John, 180
Brinham, George, 23
Bristol University, 185
Brittenden, Arthur, 14, 18, 90
Brogan, Denis, 51
Brooks's Club, 78, 95
Brother Cain (Raven), 150
Brown, George (Lord George-Brown), 49, 109, 119–20
Brown, Tina, 197
Buckley, Denys (Lord Justice), 142
Bullock, Alan (Lord), 179
Burgess, Guy, 28, 125 and n.
Butler, R. A. (Lord), 72, 85, 97, 118, 169, 186
Butler, Samuel, Life by Muggeridge, 132
Byers, Lord, 171

Calcutta Statesman, 132
Callaghan, James, 29, 44, 57, 59, 72, 83, 109, 172
Callas, Maria, 62
Cambridge Review, 149
Cameron, Norman, 177
Campbell, Lady Jean, 16
Carew, Tim, 86
Carrington, Lord, 50, 51, 53, 83
Cartland, Ronald, 91
Castle, Barbara, 40, 47, 48, 79, 81, 83, 120
Catholic Herald, 194
Chamberlain, Joseph, 111
Chamberlain, Neville, biography by Iain Macleod, 100
Channon, 'Chips', 42
Charm of Politics, The (Crossman), 39
Charterhouse, 61, 91, 95, 147
Chesterton, G. K., 71
Christ Church, Oxford, 25, 164, 180, 193
Christiansen, Arthur, 25, 27
Churchill, Randolph, 51, 101, 104, 107, 155
Churchill, Sir Winston, xi, xii, 10, 27, 100, 133, 139, 165, 182, 186, 197
City of London School, 3
Clark, Douglas, 19
Cobbett, William, 71, 178
Cobden, Richard, 180–1
Cockburn, Claud, 69, 71
Colony Room, Dean Street, 24, 153, 155
Communist Party, 26 and n., 55, 153, 177
Comyn, James (Mr Justice), 74
Conan Doyle, Sir Arthur, 7, 145
Connolly, Cyril, 4, 142, 197
Conquest, Robert, 7

Conrad, Joseph, 32
Consider the Lilies (Auberon Waugh), 194
Cooper, Doris, 65
Cooper, Duff, 197
Cooper, Gladys, 65
Cosgrave, Patrick, 195n
Countryman, The, 116
Cowling, Maurice, 204
Craigie, Jill, 49
Creighton, Harry, 53
Cripps, Sir Stafford, 118
Crosland, Anthony, xii, 10, 11, **29–34**, 42, 48, 55, 72, 181
Crosland, Eve, 181
Crosland, Hilary (Sarson), 34
Crosland, Susan (Susan Barnes), 34
Crossman, Anne (McDougall), 35, 36, 42
Crossman, Charles Stafford (Mr Justice), 35–7
Crossman, Lady, 35–7
Crossman, Richard, xii, **35–43**, 47, 48, 78, 79, 81, 108, 113, 139, 177, 180, 203
Crossman, Zita, 38, 42
Crowley, Aleister, 26
Cudlipp, Hugh (Lord), 103, 133, 139, 194
Cummings, A. J., 114
Cummings, Michael, 138
Curran, Charles, 195n.
Curzon, Lord, 11

Daily Express, 9, 16, 17, 23–6, 49n., 70, 85–6, 93–6, 118, 170
Daily Herald, 47, 48, 179
Daily Mail, 122, 138, 196
Daily Mirror, 39, 118
Daily Telegraph, 133, 134, 140, 145, 194, 203, 204
Daily Worker, 45
Dalton, Hugh, 29, 57, 118
Dance to the Music of Time, A (Powell), 140, 142, 144, 145, 197
Davenport, John, 202
Dawkins, R. M., 153
De Gaulle, President Charles, 82
Delmer, Sefton, 114
Denning, Mr Justice (Lord), 158
Diaries of a Cabinet Minister, The (Crossman), 38n., 42
Dicey, A. V., 157
Disraeli, Benjamin, 46
Donaldson, Frances, 151
Donaldson, Jack (Lord), 57
Donnelly, Desmond, 75
Douglas-Home, Sir Alec, 18, 52, 98, 104, 106, 107, 169
Douglas-Home, Charles, 196
Douglas-Home, William, 168

Index   217

Downside, 191
Drayneflete Revealed (Lancaster), xi–xii, 94
Driberg, Jack, 20
Driberg, Jim, 20
Driberg, John James Street, 20
Driberg, Tom (Lord Bradwell), xiii, **20–8**, 154, 177; 'William Hickey' column, 23, 25–6; Beaverbrook, 28
Duggan, Hubert, 142
Dulwich College, 124
Dunn, Sir James, 9
Dunn, Lady, *see* Beaverbrook, Lady

East Lynne (Mrs Henry Wood), 11, 13
Eden, Anthony, 58
Edinburgh University, 168
Edward VIII (Donaldson), 151
Elizabeth II, Queen, 165
El Vino's, xiii, 62, 65, 81, 155
Emery, Fred, 167
English Constitution, The (Bagehot), 42
English History, 1918–45 (Taylor), 182
Ernst, Lily, 47
Essays and Speeches (Jenkins, ed. Lester), 76n.
Establishment, The, essays (ed. Thomas), 150
Ethics (Moore), 124
Eton, 50, 142, 202
Europe and the French Revolution (Sorel), 177
Evans, Harold, 197
Evans, Sidney, 142
Evans, Trevor, 27
Evening Standard, 9, 46, 47, 53, 70, 85, 88, 95, 133–4, 143, 145, 196

Fabian Society, 7, 74, 83, 128, 130, 157, 160
Fairlie, Henry, 7, 47, 51, 122, 195n., 204
Fantoni, Barry, 69
Feathers of Death, The (Raven), 150
Fenton, James, 173
Fettes, 97
Fisher, H. A. L., 38
Fisher, Nigel, 101, 102 and n.
Fitzwilliam House, Cambridge, 162
Five out of Six (Violet Powell), 144
Fleming, Anne, 205
Fleming, Peter, 51
Foot, (Sir) Dingle, 45, 46
Foot, Hugh (Lord Caradon), 45
Foot, Isaac, 45
Foot, John (Lord Foot), 45
Foot, Michael, xii, **44–9**, 73, 83, 99, 166, 167, 179; and Beaverbrook, 10, 11, 45–7, 119 and n.
Foot, Paul, 67, 199
Forrest, William, 114

Forster, E. M., 125
Foster, Sir John, 43
Fox, Charles James, 46, 83, 115
Foxglove Saga, The (Auberon Waugh), 194
Francis, Dick, 154
Fraser, Moyra, 205
Free Speech, television programme, 48, 180
Freeman, John, 27, 79, 121
Freud, Clement, 171
From Patronage to Proficiency in the Civil Service (Robson), 158
From a View to a Death (Powell), 145
Fulford, Roger, 25
Future of Socialism, The (Crosland), 29, 32, 33

Gaitskell, Dora, 49
Gaitskell, Hugh, 49, 75; on Crossman, 35
Galbraith, V. H., 179
Gale, George, 5, 51, 170, 195, 204
Gardiner, A. G., xi
Garrick Club, xiii, 7, 54, 95, 205
Gay Hussar restaurant, 28, 48
George Watson's College, Edinburgh, 168
Gielgud, Sir John, 62, 130
Gigli, Beniamino, 62
Giles, Carl, 86
Gillard, Michael, 70
Gilmour, Lady Caroline, 50
Gilmour, Sir Ian, Bart, xii, xiii, **50–4**, 103, 166
Gilmour, Sir John, Bart, 50
Gladstone, W. E., 76, 178
Glasgow Herald, 203
Glasgow University, 85
Glyn, Elinor, 11, 12
God's Apology (Ingrams), 70–1
Goldsmith, Sir James, 70
Gonville and Caius College, Cambridge, 97, 203
Gordon, John, 85
Goschen, Lord, 76
Government and the Governed (Crossman), 37
Gowrie, Lord, 197
Graham, Billy, 139
Granville-West, Lord, 75
Great Contemporaries (Churchill), xi
Greene, Graham, 197
Greene, Sir Hugh, 109, 114
Griffiths, James, 126–7, 186
Grigg, John, 195n.
Grigg, P. J., 133
Grimond, Grizelda, 197
Grimond, Jo, 169, 171
Guardian, The, 60, 66, 70, 167
Guilty Men, 46
Gunter, Ray, 170

218   Index

Habsburg Monarchy 1815–1918, The (Taylor), 178, 179
Hailsham, Lord, 50, 77, 85, 101, 118
  see also Hogg, Quintin
Haley, Sir William, 137
Hamilton, Iain, 5, 51–3
Hardy, Thomas, 5, 189
Harp and the Oak, The (Massingham), 116
Harris, Sir Austin, 93
Harris, John (Lord Harris of Greenwich), 78
Harris, Wilson, 50
Hartington, Marquess of (eighth Duke of Devonshire), 76
Hartley, Anthony, 51
Hastings, Hubert de Cronin, 93
Hazlitt, William, 43, 46, 48
Healey, Denis, xii, 44, **55–9**, 72, 74, 171
Healey, Edna, 57
Healy, Tim, 13
Heath, Edward, 53, 74, 83, 97, 106–8, 111, 164, 166
Heavens Above, Peter Sellers film, 130
Hess, Myra, 63
Hibbert Journal, 189
Highgate School, 29
Hitchens, Christopher, 71
Hogg, Quintin, 50, 77; see also Hailsham, Lord
Hoggart, Simon, 167
Hollis, Christopher, 51
Holmes, David, 171
Home, Lord, see Douglas-Home, Sir Alec
Homes Sweet Homes (Lancaster), 93
Hooson, Emlyn, 171
Hope-Wallace, Charles, 60
Hope-Wallace, Jacqueline, 60, 61
Hope-Wallace, Mabel (Chaplin), 60
Hope-Wallace, Philip, xiii, **60–6**, 200, 204
Hopkirk, Peter, 15
Howard, Anthony, 69, 139, 196
Howard, Elizabeth Jane, 4, 6, 7
Howard, Peter, 46
Howe, Sir Geoffrey, 162, 164, 166
Howell, David, 103
Hunter, Ian, 132, 137
Harcourt, Lord, 158, 169
Hutchinson, George, 53, 71
Hutt, Allen, 45
Huxley, Aldous, 91, 151

I Like it Here (Amis), 4
I Took off My Tie (Massingham), 116
Illingworth, Leslie, 138
In the News, television programme, 48, 180
In Place of Strife, Wilson-Castle proposals for trade union reform, 81
In a Valley of This Restless Mind (Muggeridge), 136, 137
Inglis, Brian, 51, 52
Ingrams, Leonard St Clair, 67
Ingrams, Mary, 69
Ingrams, Richard, xiii, 24, **67–71**, 139, 198, 199
Ingrams, Victoria (Reid), 67
Inside Right (Gilmour), 50

James, Clive, 70, 137
James, William, 136
Jardine, Douglas, 37
Jay, Douglas, 37, 40
Jay, Peggy, 40–1
Jay, Peter, 41
Jenkin, Patrick, 162, 197
Jenkins, Arthur, 73–5
Jenkins, Hattie (Harris), 73–4
Jenkins, Jennifer, 74, 78
Jenkins, Peter, 41
Jenkins, Roy, xii, 34, 54, **72–8**, 109, 164, 170, 173
Jennings, Elizabeth, 5
Jennings, Sir Ivor, 159–60
John Aubrey and his Friends (Powell), 145
Johnson, Marigold, 82, 84
Johnson, Paul, xiii, 39, 51, 66, **79–84**, 139, 204
Johnson, Samuel, xi
Johnson, William Aloysius, 79
Johnson Smith, Geoffrey, 170
Jones, Jack, 40
Junor, Alexander, 85
Junor, Sir John, xii, 11, 70, **85–90**, 100, 158
Justice and Administrative Law (Robson), 157, 160

Karolyi, Michael, 179
Kavanagh, Pat, 191
Kee, Robert, 150
Kennedy, President John F., 102
Keynes, J. M. (Lord), 81, 124, 125, 189
Kilmarnock, Lord, 6
King, Cecil, 48–9, 194
King's College, Cambridge, 147, 150
Kingsmill, Hugh, 71, 134–5
Koch de Gooreynd (Worsthorne), Colonel A., 200
Koss, Stephen, 76

Lambert, Constant, 144
Lambton, Lord, 204
Lancaster, Karen (Harris), 93, 96
Lancaster, Sir Osbert, xi, 25, **91–6**
Lancing, 22, 25, 191
Larkin, Philip, 3, 5
Laski, Harold, 57, 81, 160

Index 219

Lawson, Nigel, 53, 194, 195, 204
Lawson, Vanessa, 204
Le Corbusier, 93
Lee, Jennie (Lady Lee), 39, 165
Leighton Park School, 45
Lejeune, Anthony, 62
Lever, Harold (Lord), 40, 205
Levin, Bernard, 51, 122, 195n.
Lewy, Casimir, 127
Like it Was: The Diaries of Malcolm Muggeridge (ed. Bright-Holmes), 138n.
Lilliput magazine, 154
Lincoln College, Oxford, 91
Listener, The, 149, 189
Little Learning, A (Evelyn Waugh), 137
Little Nut-brown Man, A (Vines), 18
Lives of the Poets (Johnson), xi
Llanelli County (Grammar) School, 183, 184
Lloyd George, David, 9, 179, 181, 182
London Government Act, 1963, 159
London Opinion magazine, 154
London School of Economics, xii, xiii, 159–61
Longford, Lord, 197; *see also* Pakenham, Frank
Lorna Doone (Blackmore), 11, 12
Lost World, The (Conan Doyle), 145
Lovat, Lord, 197
Lowrie, Henry, 16
Lucky Jim (Amis), xii, 4–6
Ludlow, 'Lobby', 15
Lunn, Sir Henry, 134

McCaffrey, Sir Tom, 167
MacDonald, Ramsay, 131, 159
McEwen, Robin, 170
McEwen, Rory, 170
McLachlan, Donald, 203, 204
Maclaren-Ross, J., 63
Maclean, Donald, 125
Macleod, Annabel (Ross), 97
Macleod, Evelyn (Baroness Macleod of Borve), 98
Macleod, Iain, xii, xiii, 52, 53, 77, 89, **97–111**
Macleod, Norman, 97
Macmillan, Harold, 10, 90, 180
Macpherson, Hugh, 195n.
Magdalen College, Oxford, 79, 178, 180, 203
Mallalieu, J. P. W., 12
Manchester Evening News, 132
Manchester Guardian, 60, 64, 116, 130–32, 134, 178
Mansbridge, Norman, 138–9
Margach, James, 117
Margaret, Princess, 165, 170
Marks, Derek, 90
Marnham, Patrick, 24, 199
Marriott, Sir John, 177

Marshall, Alfred, 189
Marten, Henry, 142
Martin, Kingsley, 38, 39, 45, 79, 108, 130, 139; and Crossman, 39
Massingham, H. J., 116
Massingham, Hugh, xi, xiii, 47, **112–23**
Massingham, H. W., 112–13, 116
Maude, Angus, 166
Maudling, Reginald, 98, 107, 108
May, Peter, 147
Melly, George, 202
Men and Power (Beaverbrook), 179
Men Only magazine, 154
Mikardo, Ian, 118
Millard, Christopher, 142
Miller, Jonathan, 79, 130
Mind, 124
Mirror group, 49, 194
Mr. Balfour's Poodle (Jenkins), 76
Mitchell, Christopher, 81
Mitchell, David, 81
Montgomery, Lord, 133
Moore, Daniel, 124
Moore, Dorothy, 126, 127
Moore, G. E., xii, xiii, **124–7**
Moore, Henrietta (Sturge), 124
Moore, T. Sturge, 124, 127
Morgan, Charles, 63
Morgan, John and Mary, 4
Morrell, Lady Ottoline, 143
Morris, Sir Parker, 74
Morrison, Charles, 53
Morrison, Herbert, 59, 118
Morton, J. B. ('Beachcomber'), 71
Mount, Ferdinand, 195n.
Mountbatten, Lord, 77
'Movement', the, 5
Muggeridge, H. T., 128, 130, 134
Muggeridge, Katharine (Kitty) (Dobbs), 128, 131, 133–6, 178
Muggeridge, Malcolm, xii, 10, 54, 64, 70, 71, 123, **128–39**, 144, 145
Murdoch, Iris, 55, 155
My Bones Will Keep (Richardson), 153

Namier, Sir Lewis, 179, 180
Nation, The, 113
National Union of Journalists, 195
New College, Oxford, 37, 38, 153
New Statesman, xii, xiii, 31, 38–40, 45, 48, 51, 63n, 69, 71, 79, 81, 83, 139, 156, 173, 179, 196
News Chronicle, 189
Nicholson, Geoffrey and Mavis, 4
Nicolson, Harold, 42, 50–51, 65, 133
Nilsson, Birgit, 62

Index

Noel-Baker, Philip, 57
Norman, Lady, 200–202
Norman, Montagu (Lord), 200, 201
Norton, Jean, 9
Nott, John, 166
Nutting, Anthony, 19

Oakeshott, Michael, 51, 160, 203
O'Brien, Conor Cruise, 51
Obscene Publications Act, 1959, 72, 164
Obscenity and the Law (St John-Stevas), 164
Observer, The, xi, xiii, 70, 112, 113, 114n, 117–19, 121n., 122n., 132, 154, 179, 189
On Drink (Amis), 7
Oriel College, Oxford, 175
Origins of the Second World War (Taylor), 179, 180
Orwell, George, 123, 130, 142
Osborne, John, 5
Oundle, 153
Owen, David, 73, 173
Owen, Frank, 46

Pakenham, Frank, 179 *see also* Longford, Lord
Panorama television programme, 139
Pardoe, John, 171
Parnell, Charles Stewart, 13
Paterson, Peter, 195n.
Paul, Leslie, 5
Peace News, 205
Pearson, Hesketh, 71, 135
Peterhouse, Cambridge, 5, 203
Philby, Kim, 125
Philosophical Studies (Moore), 124
Picture Palace (Muggeridge), 132
Pillar to Post (Lancaster), 93
Pillman, C. H., 187
Pitman, Robert, 11–12, 45, 90, 94
Pitt, William, the Younger, 83
Plato Today (Crossman), 37
Point Counter Point (Huxley), 151
Political Quarterly, 157
Pope-Hennessy, James, 23
Popper, Karl, 37
Powell, Anthony, xi, 4, 136, **140–7**, 197
Powell, Enoch, 52, 98, 107, 116, 166
Powell, John, 144
Powell, Maud Mary (Wells-Dymoke), 140
Powell, Lieutenant-Colonel Philip, 140
Powell, Tristram, 144
Powell, Lady Violet, 143–5
Praga, Anthony, 11
Pratt's Club, 95
Preston, Peter, 69
Prince of Wales School, Nairobi, 168
Principia Ethica (Moore), 124, 125

Prior, James, 147
Private Eye, xiii, 24, 32, 67, 69–71, 195, 196
Profumo Affair, 119, 194
Punch, 136, 138, 145
Pym, Francis, 166

Quennell, Peter, 197

Ransome, Arthur, 130
Ratcliffe College, 162
Raven, Simon, xiii, **147–52**
Raven, Susan (Kilner), 151
Raymond, John, 204
Rayner, John, 94
Réalités, 79
Rees-Mogg, Sir William, 82, 125, 151, 196
Reform Club, 151
Religion and the Rise of Capitalism (Tawney), 202
Reynolds News, 26, 27
Rhondda, Lady, 63, 64
Rice-Davies, Mandy, 194
Richardson, Maurice, xiii, 133, **153–6**
Richardson, William, 26
Ripka, Hubert, 179
Robbins, Lord, 7
Roberts, Brian, 204
Robson, William, xii, 157–61
Rock Pool, The (Connolly), 4
Rodgers, William, 73
Rogers, David, 103
Roosevelt, President Franklin D., 102
Rose, Kenneth, 194
Rovere, Richard, 51
Roxburgh, J. F., 25, 202
Rushton, William, 69
Russell, Bertrand, 48, 125, 127, 131, 136

St James's Club, 95
St John-Stevas, Norman, xii, 53, **162–7**, edition of collected workes of Bagehot, 114
St John's College, Oxford, 3, 4
Samuel, Dr Jeffrey, 189, 190
Sandys, Duncan, 118
Saturday Evening Post, 133, 139
Scarlet Letter, The (Hawthorne), 11
Scott, C. P., 130, 132
Scott, George, 5
Scott, J. D., 5
Scott, Norman, 171, 198
Scott, Ted, 130, 132
Scott-James, Anne (Lady Lancaster), 96
Selhurst Grammar School, Croydon, 128
Selwyn College, Cambridge, 128
Shaw, George Bernard, 81, 157, 160, 178
Sher-Gil, Amrita, 132

Sherwood, Lord, 28
Shrewsbury School, 67
Sinclair, Sir Archibald, 85
Sir Charles Dilke: a Victorian Tragedy (Jenkins), 76
Sitwell, Edith, 25
Slater, Walker concern, 53
Slesser, Sir Henry, 160
Snow, C. P., 5, 147
Soames, Lord, 165
Socialist Commentary, xii
Socrates (Crossman), 37
Some Main Problems of Philosophy (Moore), 124
Sorel, Albert, 177
Spectator, The, xii, xiii, 5, 19, 31, 38, 50–3, 98, 104–110, 122, 138, 150, 151, 156, 162, 194–6
Spender, Stephen, 197
Statesman and Nation Publishing Company, 39, 83
Steel, David, xiii, **168–74**
Steel, Rev. Dr. David, 168
Steel, Judy, 173
Steel, Sheila (Martin), 168
Stevas, Juno, 162
Stewart, J. I. M., ('Michael Innes'), 177
Stonyhurst, 79
Stowe, 202
Strachey, John, 85
Strand Magazine, 154
Strong Man Needed, A (Richardson), 153
Struggle for Mastery in Europe 1848–1918, The (Taylor), 179
Suliotis, Elena, 62
Summerskill, Dr Edith, 118, 189
Sunday Express, xii, 9, 11–13, 17, 45, 46, 119 and n., 70, 85–90, 100, 104, 158, 179, 194
Sunday Mirror, 194
Sunday Pictorial, 133
Sunday Telegraph, 119 and n., 196, 200, 203–5
Sunday Times, 117, 138, 151; magazine, 26n.
Sutherland, Dame Lucy, 180
Swift, Jonathan, 46, 112, 115, 133
Symons, A. J. A., 142
Szamuely, Tibor, 7

Take a Girl Like You (Amis), 4
Taplin, Walter, 51
Taunton School, 193
Taverne, Dick, 170
Tawney, R. H., 81, 159, 202
Taylor, A. J. P., xi, 10, 11, 25, 89, 90, 130, **175–182**; *Beaverbrook*, 10, 28
Taylor, Percy, 175, 177
That Uncertain Feeling (Amis), 4
Thatcher, Margaret, 51, 53, 77, 79, 83, 111, 166
Thirties, The (Muggeridge), 137, 178

This Week television programme, 79
Thomas, Dylan, 63, 181
Thomas, Hugh, 150
Thompson, J. W. M., 105, 204
Thorpe, Jeremy, 171, 172, 198
Three Flats, play by Muggeridge, 130
Three Weeks (Glyn), 11
Time magazine, 26
Time and Place (George Scott), 5
Time and Tide, 63
Times, The, 36, 63, 82, 125, 167, 195–6, 200, 203
To the Finland Station (Wilson), 203
Tonight television programme, 170
Towneley, Simon (Worsthorne), 200–201
Trelford, Donald, 70
Trevor-Roper, Hugh (Lord Dacre of Glanton), 51, 180
Tribune, 45, 46, 48, 71, 76
Trinity College, Cambridge, 124
Trinity College, Oxford, 29, 33
Trollope, Anthony, 151
Troublemakers, The (Taylor), 179

University College, Cardiff, 74
University College, Oxford, 67
University College, Swansea, xii, 4, 5
Unofficial Rose, An (Murdoch), 151
Urton, Sir William, 98

Vallance, Aylmer, 79
Varieties of Religious Experience (William James), 136
Venusberg (Powell), 145
Vidler, Canon Alec, 128, 134
Vines, Colin, 18
Voigt, F. A., 114

Wadham College, Oxford, 45
Wadsworth, A. P., 178
Wain, John, 5
Wakefield, W. W., 187
Walker, Peter, 33, 53
Walters, Dennis, 51
War Pensions Tribunal, 157–8
Ward, Simon and Alexandra, 199
Watkins, Alan, 195n.
Watkins, Catherine (Thomas), 183, 184
Watkins, D. J., xi, **183–90**
Watkins, John, 183, 184
Watkins, Violet (Harris), 187–8
Watson, Arthur, 138
Watt, David, 104, 195n.
Watts, G. F., 91
Waugh, Arthur, 191

Index

Waugh, Auberon, xiii, 36, 71, 147, **190–99**
Waugh, Evelyn, 4, 25, 27, 46–7, 135, 137, 145, 149, 181, 191, 194, 195, 197, 201, 204–5
Waugh, Laura (Herbert), 191, 196
Waugh, Lady Teresa, 193, 198
Way We Live Now, The (Trollope), 151
Webb, Beatrice, 81, 83, 130, 157, 160, 161
Webb, Sidney, 81, 157, 160, 161
Wedgwood, Dame Veronica, 61, 66
Welch, Colin, 71, 203
Wells, John, 69
West, Richard, 71, 198
Westminster School, 116, 202
What Became of Jane Austen? (Amis), 6n., 7n.
What the Papers Say television programme, 62, 205
What's Become of Waring? (Powell), 145
Wheatcroft, Geoffrey, 71, 199
Wheeler, Charles, 136
White, Sam, 88
Whitelaw, William, 53
White's Club, 54, 71, 104, 107
Whitehorn, Katharine, 51
Wigg, George (Lord), 119
'William Hickey' column, *Daily Express*, 23, 25–6; *Colonnade*, selection, 26

William of Wykeham, 35
Williams, Shirley, 73
Wills, David, 53
Wilson, Colin, 5
Wilson, Edmund, 202–3
Wilson, Sir Harold, 18, 41, 42, 44, 47, 58, 72, 78, 79, 81, 83, 85, 109, 119, 121, 159
Winchester College, 35, 37, 38
Winter in Moscow (Muggeridge), 132
Wintour, Charles, 70
Within the Family Circle (Violet Powell), 144
Wodehouse, P. G., 138, 197
Wood, Mrs Henry, 12
Woodward, E. L. (Sir Llewellyn), 178
Woolf, Leonard, 157
Woolton, Lord, 118
Wordsworth, Christopher, 132
Workers' Educational Association (W.E.A.), 38
Worsthorne (Koch de Gooreynd), Colonel A., 200
Worsthorne, Claude, 205
Worsthorne, Peregrine, xiii, **200–205**
Worsthorne, Simon (Towneley), 200–201
Wyatt, Woodrow, 75

Yorke, Henry (Henry Green), 142, 143